What kind of boss do you have?

Type One: THE DRIVE LEADER

A classic tyrant, he must have total control. He manages by intimidation, forcing his subordinates to prove their loyalty instead of their worth.

Type Two: THE DEFAULT LEADER

She employs the sink-or-swim method of management—subordinates get little or no guidance or feedback. If they don't perform, they're fired.

Type Three: THE DRAW LEADER

He brings out the best in his subordinates and praises their achievements. He's always eager to make innovations—even when they aren't needed.

Type Four: THE DEVELOP LEADER

She encourages her subordinates to develop competence and self-esteem and to take risks. They can learn a lot from her, and benefit by working closely with her.

Your boss probably displays a combination of these qualities. Once you've evaluated him, you'll be on your way to a better working relationship.

HOW TO MANAGE YOUR BOSS

Christopher Hegarty

BALLANTINE BOOKS • NEW YORK

Originally published in hardcover by Rawson, Wade Publishers Inc.
 Published in the United States by Ballantine Books, a division of Random House, Inc., New York, and simultaneously in Canada by Random House of Canada Limited, Toronto.

ISBN 0-345-31817-X

This edition published by arrangement with Whatever Publishing, Inc.

Printed in Canada

First Ballantine Books Edition: February 1985

Dedicated to my first and most significant mentors,

CATHERINE & MICHAEL HEGARTY

Special acknowledgments
in addition to those mentioned in this book:

Bill Boshears, Roberto Assagioli, L. S. Barksdale, Dawne Bernhardt, Nathaniel Branden, Armond Campana, Frank Ciccarelli, Lloyd Conant, Steve Gaudreau, Ellis Gold, Marion Hegarty, Eric Hoffer, Sam Moses, George Nasse, Chandler Peterson, John Phillips, Morris Pickus, Robert Stanton Rose, Judy Skutch, Bob Sprinkel, Jamie Weinstein, as well as Jane Brodie-Goldberg and Elliot Friedland.

Work is love made visible.

When you work with love
you bind yourself to yourself,
and to one another,
and to God.

—KAHLIL GIBRAN

Contents

Foreword

In 1980 I began teaching Management and Organizational Behavior in the University of Connecticut's M.B.A. program at Stamford. My students were primarily in-career managers who were pursuing their M.B.A. degree at night. They were keen, inquisitive and aggressive learners who actively sought to better understand and improve human relationships and interpersonal communication in business. Their goal was to pursue and achieve excellence as managers in industry.

Of all the topics I taught in my courses the subject of "how to manage your boss" generated the greatest enthusiasm and interest. For this reason I began to conduct research on the topic. I conducted computer-assisted searches of every available database and compiled a list of every book, article, and research report written on the topic of upward influence.

Of all the books ever written on the topic, Chris Hegarty's is by far the finest, most practical and most thoroughly enjoyable. Not only have I recommended this book to friends, colleagues, and clients, but I use Chris' book as a handout in my own seminars on "How to Manage Your Boss."

This is a "how-to" book that produces results. Many of my students and seminar participants have attested to the power, simplicity, and effectiveness of these techniques. My work as an international management consultant has also provided feedback that these tools are not necessarily culture-bound to North America. While the application of any American management theory abroad should be done with caution, these boss-management strategies seem to have a universal effectiveness.

I know that since the hard-cover edition of *How to Manage Your Boss* has sold out, there have been hundreds of backordered requests for the book. I am pleased to see that it is now available again and I recommend it highly to persons committed to excellence in managing their bosses, their subordinates, and themselves.

Dr. Bob Mezoff
Graduate Business Faculty
University of Connecticut
(Stamford Campus)

1

Why Work Doesn't Always Work

MANAGING UPWARDS is a legitimate and important aspect of career advancement. Yet many highly talented people think that ability alone is sufficient for success; they either don't try or don't know how to supplement their ability with strong allegiances. As professors John Gabarro and John Kotter of Harvard Business School point out in an article for the *Harvard Business Review:* "Some managers who actively and effectively supervise subordinates, products, markets and technologies, nevertheless assume an almost passively reactive stance vis-à-vis their bosses. Such a stance very often hurts these managers and their companies."

Your ability to establish a mutually valuable relationship with your boss is, and will continue to be, a major factor in determining your success or failure at work. In this book are practical, proven, potent methods to help you understand your boss better and be understood better by your boss. They will help you identify and overcome problems between you; help you increase your power by creating a smooth, effective working relationship; help you take charge of your work and gain greater prosperity and purpose.

No matter where you stand on the organizational ladder, you may have the power to transform your relationship with your boss. As in a marriage, the interplay between the two of you is dynamic and complex; the responsibility for making it work falls to both parties. To a large extent, you have *taught* your boss how to treat you. And, even if you have felt victimized by your boss's personality or methods, you may be able to change the way he or she treats you so that you will both benefit.

Many books claim you can best achieve success by controlling, manipulating, scheming, and deceiving. The world, according to these books, is made up of victims and victimizers, and getting ahead requires intimidation, power plays, schemes, and aggressive self-assertion. Such books could be best used for lighting your fireplace. You will see no such ideas in *How To Manage Your Boss*. Indeed, as the title suggests, our purpose is to *manage* bosses, not dominate or deceive them. Tactics that perpetuate an us-against-them or a get-them-before-they-get-you attitude create more problems than they solve. They may bring power, but usually at the expense of other people and other values. They may bring short-term success, but in the long run they come up empty, because they produce adversary relationships. In the 1980s, few ventures will succeed without trust and genuine cooperation among all the employees (much more on this later).

The methods in this book will bring practical, tangible rewards to anyone who uses them properly. They also will create an atmosphere of mutual respect and support. You will increase your sphere of influence and visibility while helping your boss achieve his goals and the organization's objectives. You will fulfill your own career objectives while becoming a more valuable employee.

The strategies and techniques detailed in these pages are based on four key fundamental premises:

1. It is as much the responsibility of the managed as it is the manager to create and maintain effective working relationships.
2. The best way to improve your relationship with your boss is to see what *you* can do, not what you can get your boss to do.
3. At a separate level, you are your own boss (you are where you are because of choices you have made; you will go where you go because of choices you have yet to make).
4. We each have a need to be contributive and purposeful in our work.

Two Directions Groups Move In

Essentially, working groups can move in either of two directions: the Three R's: resistance-resentment-revenge; or the Three C's: clarity-cooperation-commitment. In the Three-R cycle, ineffective communication causes tremendous resistance. People begin to resent what others ask of them; ultimately, they try to get even. The Three C's begin with people being one hundred percent responsible for bringing clarity to what they say and saying what they mean. As a result people begin to cooperate, and out of that comes a commitment to excellence, both for themselves and the group as a whole.

RRR	CCC
RESISTANCE	CLARITY
RESENTMENT	COOPERATION
REVENGE	COMMITMENT

People who work in groups characterized by the Three C's are cooperative and competitive simultaneously. They know how to contribute with their best efforts to collective goals, and at the same time achieve for themselves maximum satisfaction, autonomy, and self-esteem. In such a group, individuals discover the unique human joy that can be found only in productive contributive work. This book will examine simple, powerful ideas that will enable you to create the Three C's. At the same time, we will identify many of the outmoded values and methods that create the vicious cycle of resistance-resentment-revenge which, unfortunately, dominates many working relationships today.

As a management consultant and seminar leader, I speak to about a quarter of a million people each year—employees of small and large businesses, educational institutions, hospitals, government agencies, as well as high-ranking executives of giant organizations. The problems most frequently shared by all groups focus on the boss-subordinate relationship.

If you were to travel with me around the business world, you would hear managers complain of subordinates who cannot be trusted, are lazy and irresponsible, uncaring and incompetent, insolent and defiant, and who spend more time trying to get out of work than it would have taken them to do the job well. You would hear jokes like: "I underestimated my staff . . . but not nearly enough."

From subordinates you would hear of bosses who are neither trusted nor respected, who are rigid, authoritarian, overpaid, overrated, self-serving, power-hungry, and drive their subordinates crazy. You would hear jokes like: "My boss is trying . . . *very* trying."

In my judgment, negative generalizations about bosses and subordinates are counterproductive, especially when they are conveyed—as they often are—by people who occupy both roles at the same time. I frequently hear managers complain about their bosses, and then I hear their subordinates echo the same grievances about them. Bosses and subordinates alike have accepted as truth a set of false concepts about one another.

My work experience convinces me that most bosses are decent people, devoted to getting their jobs done as effectively and as legitimately as possible. Most of them are neither cruel nor indifferent. They are human beings, with strengths and weaknesses, flaws and foibles, needs and desires, likes and dislikes; on that level, they are just like everyone else. But they also have problems and concerns that their subordinates may not share, yet would do well to try to understand.

As for subordinates, many are so deeply enmeshed in the cycle of resistance-resentment-revenge that they *do* produce as little as possible; some are even overtly destructive. But my experience also convinces me that most subordinates want to perform with excellence. They want these essential things from their employers: to be paid adequately and recognized for what they achieve; to be accepted as unique individuals; and to be appreciated as human beings, not just machines that perform a function. If I were allowed one sentence with which to convince bosses of the inherent value of their subordinates, it would be: *Most people most often will live up to the level to which they are trusted; and they will live down to the level to which they are distrusted.*

Why, then, have bosses and subordinates become adversaries in their own minds? The problem, I believe, has nothing to do with the inherent worth of either group. The fault lies in their state of awareness. We have been misled by beliefs and values that were built on assumptions that are no longer accurate, and perhaps never were.

Predominant beliefs have a way of proving themselves. Erroneous assumptions lead to specific patterns of behavior, which then produce results that seem to prove the original assumption. It is a neat, and often vicious, circle. For example, in research projects, schoolteachers have been told that new students have high IQ's. They treat the class according to their expectations, which are now higher than before. The students perform better than they might have, whatever their original IQ's. Similarly, college students have been told before a semester that their new professor is a prince, and their subsequent evaluations are better than those of another class that is told the same teacher is going to make them miserable.

You have probably seen a version of this in your own organization. If a manager has a basic belief that workers are lazy, untrustworthy imbeciles, he will treat them as such. Then he will get what he expects. Out of unconscious resentment, the workers will work at half speed and make mistakes. The boss will then be able to say: "See, I told you they were lazy imbeciles." He will have bent reality to fit his beliefs.

Similarly, when workers believe that bosses are ruthless and self-serving, they behave as if that were true. The boss, perhaps in self-defense, will become defensive and authoritarian. Then the resentful workers will point to the boss and say: "I told you he can't be trusted."

Self-fulfilling prophecies, like avalanches, gain momentum, grow bigger and more devastating, and often leave a pile of rubble in their wake. Erroneous assumptions appear to be proven and validated over and over again because they create predictable action out of themselves. The past tenaciously fights for survival; we cling to our values and ideas, and do all we can to prove them true—even when they work against us, and even when we would like things to be different.

In roughly this manner, bosses and subordinates can and do bring out the worst in each other. Because of their fears and misconceptions, managers often adopt methods of motivating and rewarding subordinates that are counterproductive—they undermine cooperation, loyalty, and effectiveness. Subordinates respond in such a way as to jeopardize the boss, the organization, and themselves. Then the assumptions are reinforced, and the cycle of resistance-resentment-revenge begins anew.

Outmoded and incorrect ideas can be uprooted and replaced with productive ones, by raising the awareness of both boss and subordinate. The strategies and methods in this book are designed to do just that. Before we go any further, let's step aside and look at the current state of work from a broader perspective.

The Legacy

In many ways, today's managers function according to patterns and styles that may have been more appropriate in the past. The world of work and the people in it have changed radically in a short period of time. Less than two hundred years ago, three quarters of the American population worked on farms; now, less than 6 percent work in agriculture. Even at the turn of the century, when the Industrial Revolution was well under way, most businesses were small, usually family-owned enterprises that employed relatively few people. John Pierpont Morgan complained that his organization was so big he did not know everyone in his employ by first name. By today's standards, Morgan's empire seems a quaint operation.

As work shifted from field to factory and office, the activities of many little enterprises became absorbed under the umbrellas of single, multi-unit companies. The production and distribution of goods, and the flow of people and funds, was increasingly determined by a new category of professional—the manager. Today, even relatively small organizations have a hierarchy of managers, each of whom attempts to coordinate groups of diverse workers and activities.

As the world shifted from agriculture and commerce to industry, uneducated and unsophisticated workers left the farms to work for other people. It was a pioneering and adventurous era during which new resources and technologies opened up an undreamed-of world of prosperity. The bosses pursued profit with a single-minded, quasi-religious tenacity; profit was an end that seemed to justify any means required to achieve it.

As today, the bosses came in as many different stripes and colors as their workers. There were some viciously ruthless ones, but most were decent people with honorable intentions. Yet however much they varied in personality, their style of management was autocratic. They were taskmasters; they ran the show, usually with an iron fist. They tended to view the average employee as lacking ambition, lazy, selfish, unconcerned with the welfare of the organization, repelled by responsibility. To get subordinates to produce, bosses cajoled, commanded, persuaded, punished, rewarded, and threatened. The incentives they used were almost exclusively money and security, often illusory. To make sure their workers blundered and plundered less than the bosses believed they otherwise would, tasks were rigidly controlled and overseen with eagle eyes.

Even as humane concern for the plight of workers grew, and the more deplorable abuses of industrialization were rooted out, managerial methods remained largely unchanged. When, at the turn of the century, increased mechanization and bureaucratization gave rise to so-called scientific management, techniques such as time-and-motion study were developed for the sake of efficiency. These techniques eventually amplified the discord between the managers and the managed. Jobs were broken down into their smallest and easiest functions, a process that culminated in the assembly line and highly specialized task assignments. While economy and productivity were the stated reasons for these innovations, much of it can also be attributed to an underlying management view of workers as being incapable of handling complex tasks and difficult decisions.

The bosses' image of workers became self-fulfilling. If, through the misuse of rigorously defined job descriptions, you place people in pigeonholes, they will act like pigeons eventually. By not realizing that people have much more to offer, bosses deprived themselves of the tremendous potential of those whom they managed. "You can command a man to turn a nut on an assembly line," writes Richard Cornuelle in his book *De-Managing America* (Random House, 1975), "but you cannot command him to be creative or concerned or resourceful."

The sense of superiority and disrespect conveyed by autocratic bosses is still with us, and it remains self-defeating. They gain neither the respect and dedication they demand, nor the productivity they desire. In discussing the dynamics of the boss-subordinate relationship, John A. Leach and William A. Murray of the University of Chicago Human Resources Center indicate in an article for Management Review (October, 1979) that managers might be putting the cart before the horse. Apparently, most bosses believe "that authority and rank demand respect, and that subordinates must first earn the respect of the authority figure. Actually, the process is materially reversed. . . . The employee begins to respect the boss at that point in the relationship when the subordinate senses respect emanating from the boss." The most effective way is for both boss and subordinate to accept total responsibility for creating and maintaining a productive working relationship.

The Backlash

As a result of improper procedures, even well-meaning managers can set in motion the cycle of resistance-resentment-revenge. Not knowing of any creative way to cope with exploitation—both real and imagined—employees act so as to sabotage the boss's goals. Whether intentionally or unconsciously, subordinates get revenge by doing the opposite of what the boss wants. Resistance can take many forms: gossip, turnovers, absenteeism, time wasting, carelessness, ripping off petty cash, high-level embezzlement, or simply not giving one's best effort. At times, the exasperation can lead to blatant backlash: belligerence, defiance, mutiny.

When subordinates feel unappreciated, bored, trapped, or demeaned, their natural response is to act exactly how the boss feared they would. The very expectation that determined the boss's approach creates its own reality. Workers learn to just get by. It becomes acceptable, even desirable, to get away with doing as little as possible and taking all you can. Instead of excellence, mediocrity becomes the ideal. Indeed, in many plants and offices, it is considered hokey to be a good worker. In some groups a hard worker is looked on with disdain; the trend becomes ludicrous when new members are expelled from unions because they work too hard.

Large-scale resentment creates the need to act constructively for one's own protection. The labor movement was born in self-defense. As it grew, the lines were drawn ever more tightly; it became us-against-them. The old cold war got hot, as each side developed powerful weapons to use against the other. With each breakdown in communication, as is almost always the case, each side felt that it was the loser, and as a result the Three R's spiraled and the battle grew more fierce.

Each side fought for pride and economic gains. Employers made profits, managers obtained perks and powers, workers got pensions and better working conditions and contracts so secure that some employees cannot be fired even for incompetence. But despite their gains all sides can end up losing in the long run, if they can't work together productively.

The enemy is neither the boss nor the workers, but the faulty state of awareness (the false beliefs and values) that creates the Three R's; adversary relationships work against both sides.

When bosses and subordinates operate in an atmosphere of mistrust and competition, the result is often disaster both for the individuals and the organization.

An adversary atmosphere creates joyless work days, boredom, dead-end jobs, oversupervision, underemployment, and the sacrifice of individuality and self-esteem. The excessive pressure caused by poor working relationships is a major factor in the extraordinary costs—both human and financial—of stress-related disorders. American industry spends $700 million a year recruiting executives to replace those felled by heart disease, and another $15 billion on alcohol-related problems. And who can calculate the bottom-line impact of inefficiency, low morale, turnovers, absenteeism, insubordination, and just plain goofing off that result from the breakdown of cooperation between bosses and those who report to them? According to the New York consulting firm of Theodore Barry and Associates, American workers today waste about 50 percent of their time on the job—at an estimated cost of $350 billion a year in productivity. That makes us all losers.

Between 1950 and 1968, the annual rate of increase in U.S. productivity was 2.5 to 3 percent each year; since 1968, however, the average annual increase has been only 1.4 percent, and in 1978, it was 0.8 percent. This lowered rate of productivity has been called "one of the most significant economic problems of recent years" by the President's Council of Economic Advisors. It is a major reason for our huge national trade deficit and the decline of the dollar. Further, the growing gap between productivity and wage increases is among the most overlooked causes of inflation. There are many reasons for the decline in productivity. But an important factor is that people are not turned on by, or tuned into, their jobs.

The adversary atmosphere and the cycle of the Three R's have snowballed into a national crisis: management can't relate to employees, and employees can't relate to management; unions can't relate either to management or their own members; and no one can relate to the government. As a result, the most successful economic machine in the history of the world now resembles a high-tension line that has fallen to the ground, its wires scattered in all directions shooting off aimless sparks. The situation can be changed, and the place to begin is in the awareness of each individual manager and subordinate. The issue isn't, Can we solve our productivity problems? We can!

The issue is, Will we? The ideas we are about to discuss can help a great deal.

The New Breed

Whether or not the basic assumptions bosses hold about subordinates were *ever* valid is unimportant. What is important is that they do not hold true for modern workers. Back in the thirties and forties, research by industrial psychologists began to challenge those old premises. The famous Hawthorne studies, for example, found that paying attention to employees, and demonstrating an interest in them as individuals, increased productivity more than technical changes designed to increase operational efficiency.

The human relations school of management began to assert that the authoritarian style of management failed to acknowledge certain innate human needs. We started to realize that everyone is motivated by opportunities for self-expression; that people like to be given responsibility; and that most people have no difficulty reconciling their own needs with organizational goals, as long as there's a good chance that those needs will be fulfilled.

While the threat of poverty and insecurity remains immediate, bosses may be able to get people to sacrifice and work hard, even at demeaning jobs, through coercive management practices. But with affluence—and the sophistication that usually accompanies it—something more than material incentive is needed. Once a person's basic survival needs are met, higher needs—less urgent, perhaps, but just as strong—begin to take precedence. The joy of achievement, the thrill of a job well done, the pride of having made a valid contribution, the self-respect of being appreciated and trusted—all these become significant motivating forces when material needs are not in doubt.

American management is just beginning to learn this lesson. As F. Scott Fitzgerald wrote a half century ago: "The idea that to make a man work you've got to hold gold in front of his eyes is a growth, not an axiom. We've done that for so long that we've forgotten there is any other way."

Even recently, the old incentives worked pretty much across the board. To people who had lived through the anxiety of the Great Depression, decent pay and a modicum of security were perhaps the most important things in life. The thought of being unable to provide for one's family was terrifying. This, combined with the spirit of optimism and the new postwar economic possibilities, kept Americans working hard throughout the fifties. Everyone was out to make it; hard work was the ticket to the house in the suburbs.

We created the most affluent society in the history of the world. But at a price. Self-esteem came to be linked with outer achievement and the trappings of success. It became more and more difficult to balance making a living and making a life, for we bought the notion that the more we acquired the happier we would be. Once we accepted progress and prosperity as the keys to happiness, the next inference was easy to make: If you have a three-bedroom home, one car, and two televisions, and you feel reasonably secure and happy, then you will be twice as happy and twice as secure with a six-bedroom home, two cars, and four televisions.

We failed to realize that there is a big difference between having an adequate standard of living and having superfluous acquisitions, especially if the extra affluence is acquired at the expense of more important values. We have confused standard of living with standard of *consumption.* If a family's needs are more than adequately met, and they strive for more and more in the belief that fulfillment will follow as automatically as relief from hunger follows eating, they will end up disappointed and disillusioned. The possessions end up possessing the possessor. Many people are afraid to take a vacation for fear their possessions will be stolen. As we competed for larger slices of what seemed to be a limitless pie, the real psychological and emotional rewards of work were overlooked. Adversary relationships were perpetuated.

In a climate of competition for material necessities, bosses can make people work by holding money before their eyes. The authoritarian management techniques would seem to work, and the old assumptions would seem to be true. However, money is only one reason people work hard. In the last twenty years, Americans have gradually shifted their priorities. Their deeper needs have come to the surface. Quality of life became an issue as we realized that affluence had not brought real fulfillment. And the old assumptions are being challenged still.

As the social climate changed, so did the people. At the turn of the century, when the large modern organization was taking shape, the average employee was a male with an eighth-grade education. Today, he is sophisticated, traveled, and middle class, with an average of one year in college. In fact there is almost a fifty-fifty chance that he might not be a he at all. She might be a single woman with the sole responsibility for support of her child, or a married woman with no children. Only 14 percent of all employees now come from a family in which the husband alone is employed. As recently as 1950, that was true of 70 percent.

In a thirty-year study of 57,000 job applicants, industrial research psychologist Clifford Jurgensen studied the factors that mattered most to people about a prospective job. In the last ten years, he found, a startling change had occurred. Before 1970, security was the number one priority; career advancement was second; after that came "type of work," the company, the pay, and other factors, none of which were terribly surprising. The surprise came in the last ten years. While most of the top ten factors remained unchanged, the top slot changed hands. "Type of work" was now number one.

Interestingly, the subjects themselves did not realize the magnitude of the change. They thought they were each unique in putting type of work above every other consideration; they assumed that other people would rank pay as top priority. Bosses are just as mistaken about the incentives that bring people to work. Dr. Jurgensen's findings indicate that people would be happy to accept an adequate salary, if they were doing satisfying work for a supervisor they could trust and who helped them find purpose and accomplishment in that work.

It may surprise some readers to discover that the apparent shift in values extends to the executive level as well. Your own boss may be one of those workers whose values and priorities are undergoing radical changes. Eighty-three percent of executives responding to a national survey claim they no longer define success solely in terms of business. They are shifting from life objectives that were once primarily work-oriented to goals that have little or nothing to do with advancing their careers. Personal, private, and family-centered objectives are beginning to take precedence. And at the office, meaningful work and stimulating challenges are what they want—often badly enough to sacrifice money and status to achieve them.

Of course, human needs fluctuate with changing circumstances. If the economy suffers dramatic decline, it's possible that our priorities will shift back to basic survival needs. With the challenges that the 1980s are bringing, no one can predict which values will head the list at the end of the decade. But it seems safe to predict that we will no longer ignore completely the higher rewards of satisfying work; we know now that work can and should be a source of fulfillment, and that love of work is linked to health and longevity. It also seems safe to predict that the individuals who best adapt to the changes ahead will be those who can create work groups where people experience the joy that can be found only in productive, constructive work.

Many managers in many organizations have been struggling to understand the new breed of worker. *Their ability to adapt to the new reality, and at the same time learn to treat people equally without treating them alike, will go a long way toward determining their success.* A highly regarded chronicler of social trends, Daniel Yankelovich, states that in the 1980s, "knowledge of how the changed American value system affects incentives and motivations to work hard may well become a key requirement for entering the ranks of top management in both the private and public sectors."

New Needs, New Values

A new set of values is sweeping the country, and it gets right to the heart of the boss-subordinate relationship. In 1977, the results of a remarkable Harris Poll were presented to members of Congress. Among other things, the poll discovered:

—72 percent of the population prefer to cooperate rather than compete.
—84 percent welcome challenges to their creative abilities.
—83 percent said the country would be better off if children were educated to find inner satisfaction rather than be a success and make a lot of money.
—79 percent think it is more important to teach people to live with basic essentials than to reach higher standards of living.

The picture that emerges from these findings if of a radically different person from the one management had in mind when it formulated its existing practices. The Harris Poll concluded: "Basically, our people are far more concerned with the quality of life and far less with the unlimited acquisition of physical goods and products. These are radical findings by any measure, for they mean that the age of materialism as we have known it is going to be radically altered."

According to available evidence, many Americans at all levels are not satisfied with their jobs. A recent survey by the Opinion Research Corporation found that nonmanagement workers are more unhappy with their jobs now than at any other time in the past twenty-five years. The study reported: ". . . hourly and clerical workers in particular have become increasingly dissatisfied in recent years with their company as a place to work, with the work they do, and the way they are treated as individuals."

The evidence also suggests that the dissatisfaction is not limited to those in routine jobs. While it is not expected that anyone will top the world record of D. H. "Nobby" Clarke—an Englishman who held 112 different paid jobs—certainly the holder of the opposite record—Polly Gadsby, who worked at the same job for 86 years—is not threatened either. People now entering the work force are expected to change careers five to seven times in their lives. An American Management Association survey revealed that 40 percent of the executives polled were not sure that their organizations would provide the opportunity for them to fulfill their objectives. By all indications, they are willing to turn their backs on the old career plan—climbing the ladder in one organization—to find what they are looking for elsewhere.

Why are people switching jobs? Not, as may have been the case in the past, for more money alone. The American Management Association study found that the most important variable in an executive's decision to change careers between the ages of thirty-five and fifty-four was "more meaningful work." Second on the list was "better fit of values and work"; and number three was "chance for greater achievement." A recurring theme in the study was a desire for greater autonomy. People apparently want to create their own job structure rather than have one imposed on them.

The propensity for job switching is also related to boss-subordinate relationships. According to John Leach and William Murray of the University of Chicago, "A person's decision to change jobs or move to another organization is often actually a search for a more effective boss. That is, the subordinate is often seeking a more satisfying relationship—a career contract, so to speak—not solely salary increases, higher status, and career advancement."

Faced with reduced productivity and higher turnover, the

old-style management stragegy would call for cracking the whip and seducing employees with promises of money and job security. These incentives alone will not work with the new breed. It's not that they are unwilling to work hard. Indeed, people *want* to work, and are eager to accept challenges, as long as they are appreciated and rewarded, and as long as the work itself provides an opportunity to satisfy the inherent human need to feel contributive, productive, and proud of one's accomplishments. A University of Michigan survey found that 71.5 percent of American workers would keep working even if they had enough money to retire early and comfortably. We have learned how important work can be in shaping our lives.

It is a time for communication and cooperation, a time to rise above the old erroneous assumptions that have stood between bosses and subordinates. The challenge to management today is to find ways to adapt to new human values, as well as to new economic realities. "If, in the face of changing work values," states Ian H. Wilson of General Electric, "employers attempt to continue the traditional patterns and habits of organizing, managing, and motivating people, they will be on a collision course with the future."

The companies that survive and thrive in the 1980s will be those that learn to treat employees as whole people, that can motivate their workers to strive for excellence, and that make available the satisfaction that comes from responsible work in an interesting and humane environment for a company with a legitimate product.

"The battleground for business in the 1980s," predicts researcher Florence Skelly, "will be human resources. That's going to be where the action is." Companies will have to compete with one another in people development, not just product development. The winners will be those that replace fear and suspicion with trust and mutual respect. I predict that managers in the future will be measured by both economic waste *and* human waste. A manager's rate of turnover will become a major factor in determining whether or not he is promoted. Perhaps the balance sheet of the eighties will have a new column: People. *"Profit development through people development" will be a clear goal for creative organizations.*

The Japanese, who outperformed the United States in almost every measurable economic criterion during the seventies, have demonstrated the value of breaking down the adversary relationship between managers and subordinates. Reportedly, Japanese bosses maximize two-way communications with workers; trust is conveyed by keeping subordinates well informed. Workers are treated seriously, their personal needs and professional opinions respected. As a result, Japanese employees take pride in their work and tend to remain loyal to their companies. Perhaps that is one reason the Japanese are expected to overtake us soon in gross national product per capita.

It has been claimed that the Japanese model is not appropriate for Americans. Japanese culture, it is said, is more suitable to the sort of conditions that characterize their companies. Americans would not be comfortable with the management's infringement on areas customarily regarded as private, or with the degree of regimentation in the Japanese company. But other analysts believe that Japanese industry made effective management decisions that actually ran *counter* to their cultural heritage. In any case, the success of Japanese companies with plants in the United States gives us reason to examine their techniques. At the Sony plant in San Diego, Japanese management practices were tailored to an American work force. Some of the extremes of Japanese paternalism were avoided, but features such as one-to-one talks between managers and workers were made a matter of policy. "Any employee has the right to talk with anyone," explains general manager Masayoshi Morimoto. "Direct exposure to top management is essential."

The result is a highly successful plant—reportedly the most productive in the Sony empire—and acceptance by the San Diego community, which had been known for its tough stance on industry. Sony workers in San Diego have twice rejected attempts to unionize. The plant, which started in 1972 with thirty workers, now employs over one thousand.

In an important and provocative book that every chief executive officer would benefit by reading, *Japan as No. 1* (Harvard University Press, 1979), Ezra Vogel points out clearly how the United States could benefit by understanding what the Japanese have done to create their extraordinary economic success.

But we need not look to a culture halfway around the world for our models. We have some shining examples of our own. At Rushton Mining in West Virginia, for example, one group of miners was singled out for an experiment. They were given unprecedented responsibilities, and were allowed to make discretionary decisions. The result of this increased trust was more than just self-respect. The group had a 75 percent decrease in absenteeism; a 75 percent decrease in safety violations; a 50 percent decrease in accidents (in the first year they had only one accident that led to lost work time, a staggering phenomenon); and a 35 percent decrease in supply and maintenance costs.

An outstanding example of what can be accomplished through the intelligent and respectful use of human resources is found in the Dana Corporation, a manufacturer of axles, engine parts, and other automotive components, headquartered in Toledo, Ohio. In a time of declining national productivity, Dana's productivity per employee has nearly tripled since 1971, and sales have quadrupled.

Analysts attribute Dana's remarkable growth to the changes in managerial policy instituted by Rene C. McPherson when he became president in 1968. Now the Dean of Stanford University Business School, McPherson believes that employees know more about their work than their superiors do, and that if they are given the chance, they will devise ways to improve procedures and cut costs. "If you have opportunities for growth and freedom in your job so that you can contribute," McPherson told the *New York Times*, ". . . then there's just no limit to what you can accomplish." I predict McPherson's entry into the field of education will have a major impact on the way organizations are run in this country.

The company's policy committee states: "We are dedicated to the belief that our people are our most important asset. We will encourage all of them to contribute and to grow to the limit of their desire and ability. We believe people respond to recognition, freedom to contribute, opportunity to grow, and to fair compensation."

To an uncommon degree, autonomy is granted to both managers and workers. Most promoting is done from within the Dana family; its more than thirty thousand employees can acquire the training needed to improve in their jobs and move up in the organization by attending "Dana University." This ten-year-old institution, staffed by former Dana executives, teaches management, accounting, cost analysis, and other skills to Dana employees who reportedly respond to the educational opportunity with enthusiasm. And with good reason: over 80 percent of them own stock in the company through an Employee Stock Ownership Plan (E.S.O.P.).

The E.S.O.P., now in use in more than four thousand companies in the United States, will be seen as the most creative way to raise capital and increase productivity in the 1980s, says Louis Kelso, originator of the plan.

* * *

Transforming relationships between people at work does not require an overhaul of human nature. Quite the contrary. It requires instead an overhaul of distorted views of what human nature is. And the place to begin is with your own awareness. When you start to expand it, you'll find that you don't have to sit around hoping for a management revolution. Whether you work in the stockroom or sit in the vice president's chair, you have the power to create a small revolution of your own.

This is a book you will want your boss to read. If you have subordinates, you will want them to read it, too. It was written to benefit both managers and those who are managed; there are strategies for managing upwards, sideways, and downwards. If you read the book from all points of view, you will better understand your boss and you will be a better manager of people—whether you are in a position of leadership now or in the future. Examine each idea carefully, and put into practice those that are appropriate for your situation.

We have the opportunity to take another giant step in human evolution. Our work environments are a good place to start—or, perhaps more accurately, continue—to mold a way of life that combines productive labor and genuine human fulfillment. You can make a significant contribution to that process by learning to manage your boss and becoming a better boss yourself.

A friend once related an experience he had at a circus; the lesson in it has been with me ever since. He noticed that an elephant was tied to a stake by a thin rope. It could have freed itself with one tug of its foot. When my friend pointed this out to an attendant, he was told that, as an infant, the elephant was tied to a concrete pillar with a heavy chain. It yanked and yanked, but couldn't pull itself free. Quickly, the elephant learned that the thing wrapped around its ankle could not be broken. It stopped trying. At that point, the chain was replaced with a thin rope.

Like the elephant, most of us stop testing things once we become accustomed to them—even if they keep us down. We fail to distinguish between perceptions that are real, and ideas we have learned in the past that may no longer be true. The erroneous assumptions held by subordinates and bosses about each other have been keeping us chained to a stake. This book challenges those assumptions, and replaces them with a set of positive assertions and practical strategies that will help you gain the power to create strong communication, cooperation, and trust. It shows you how to make work work.

2

Evaluate Yourself

"The beginning of all wisdom is to stand aside."

—C. J. HEGARTY

AT THE height of his fame, Albert Einstein was asked by a reporter: "How do you feel, knowing that so many people are trying to prove that you are not right?"

"I have no interest in being right," replied the great scientist. "I'm only concerned with discovering whether I am or not."

In the next few chapters, you will be taking a new and different look at your boss, yourself, and how the two of you function. To profit from this assessment, you should, like Einstein, be more concerned with discovering *if* you are right than with proving that you are. It is often difficult to see clearly what is closest to us, particularly when the subject is the one thing about which it is hardest to be objective—ourselves. But you can do it, and the payoff is more than worth the effort. You will become far more capable of understanding your relationship with your boss.

The first step in managing your work situation is to learn to understand yourself. For that reason, we will ask you to hold up a mirror and question yourself on some fundamental issues. The resulting self-awareness will provide a solid foundation on which to build a working relationship with your boss.

* * *

Evaluate, Don't Value-Judge

Too often we set out to prove ourselves right, not to evaluate a situation honestly. Too often we bring to our assessment a cloud of preconceived notions. Too often we see people—our boss, ourselves, whoever—the way we want them to be, the way we think they should be, or the way we fear they might be. We don't always see them the way they really are. We are blinded by our past experiences.

The price we pay for this "blindness" is incalculable. When truth is distorted for the sake of psychological comfort, it's impossible to take constructive action.

Learn to distinguish between what I call "value-judging" and evaluation. You are value-judging when you attach your own values, needs, or beliefs to an appraisal and allow past experiences and prejudices to blind you. Evaluation is what Einstein had in mind—seeing reality for what it is, even if doing so proves your original assumptions wrong. Honest evaluation is liberating and always in your best interest.

One familiar form of value-judging is based on self-defense. We make ourselves feel tall by cutting off the heads of others. When, for example, did you last willingly accept the blame when something went wrong, instead of finding someone else to blame? If we are unhappy or frustrated, we tend to use people in higher positions as scapegoats. Bosses are one of our favorite targets. It is easy to feel resentful; easy to expect more of them than we have a right to; easy to blame them for our troubles. The problem is, sometimes they deserve it and sometimes they don't. The only way to know is to engage in objective evaluation.

Here are some examples of the difference between evaluating and value-judging. Suppose you are not getting along with your boss. A statement based on value judgment would be: "My boss is a real idiot. He can't understand me and he never will." Another example: You are frustrated over a lack of communication, and you say: "My boss doesn't know how to communicate with me."

Look at the difference between those value judgments and these evaluations: "My boss and I are not getting along as well as we should. What can I do to improve the situation?" Or:

"My boss and I are not communicating effectively. What can I do to make it better?"

Though subtle, such changes in perception hold tremendous value for you. The first style—the value judgment—will lead to more problems. The second style—evaluation—will lead to solutions. Evaluation is a major step toward higher awareness and effective action.

Another category of value-judging involves self-blame instead of scapegoating. Just as destructive, it derives from the same source—low self-esteem. Some people have a need to put themselves down so that no one, least of all themselves, will expect much from them. A value judgment from such a person might take this form: "I'm such a jerk, it's no wonder my boss hates me." Or: "I'll never amount to anything. I can't even communicate with my boss." Value judgments distort the truth, and the truth is the first step toward making work really work. Look to your state of awareness (the sum total of everything you've learned and the values you hold), then you will know who you are and how to deal better with your boss.

You Choose Where You Are

The first thing we must establish is that you are where you are because of choices you have made. People who are having problems with their bosses have a tendency to feel victimized. "I can't stand my boss, but I'm locked into this position" . . . "I'd love to tell my boss where to get off, but I can't afford to lose this job" . . . "I'm trapped. My boss makes the rules and I can't do anything about it."

You always have a choice. To believe otherwise is to refuse responsibility for your life. Granted, it sometimes seems as though all the alternatives are dismal. But there *are* always alternatives, nonetheless. If you think of yourself as a choiceless victim, you will be weakened, if not paralyzed. If you are helpless in your mind, you are helpless in fact.

When I was commuting to work in San Francisco, I used to start many days on a sour note because one of the toll-takers on the Golden Gate Bridge was a nasty, arrogant man who greeted drivers with a scowl. I always tried to avoid his booth, but was not always successful; I couldn't identify him soon enough to change lanes safely. Then one day I nearly wrecked my car trying to swerve at the last second.

Because of that near-accident, I realized that I had been victimized by my own emotions—I had felt victimized by the tolltaker. But the problem was really my reaction to him. I had a choice, I now realized. I could continue to get aggravated every morning; or I could drive through the booth cheerfully and not let him bother me. I chose the latter.

Had I continued to pretend I had no choice, I would have made myself a perpetual victim. Instead, I felt a surge of power. The person who accepts full responsibility for his or her reactions to events is more free than the person who sees himself or herself as a victim. If you adopt a positive attitude, you will be more alert to opportunities to change. If you *pretend* you have no choices, you will have none. The next time you feel trapped or victimized, realize the only place to look is at yourself—you *choose* your reaction.

You work where you work for whom you work by *choice.* Realizing that you chose to be where you are does two things: (1) It creates a sense of freedom and responsibility; and (2) it allows you to evaluate creatively whether or not to make new choices.

You are choosing to be treated the way you are at work. Even the most tyrannical boss cannot mistreat someone who *chooses* not to accept it. Your failure to take steps to change the situation is a signal to your boss that he or she can continue to treat you that way. By the mere fact that you did not speak up or quit when you were mistreated, you said in effect: "It's okay to do that to me."

Sometimes your situation may appear to be out of your control. But there is one thing over which you always have control: *your reaction to your environment.* While you may not be in control of a specific event, you're always in control of how you react to it.

No one has learned this lesson more dramatically, or more movingly, than Victor Frankl, author of *Man's Search for Meaning* (Simon & Schuster, 1970). His experience should be understood by anyone who has ever felt like a helpless victim.

Frankl, a Viennese psychiatrist, was interred in a concentration camp during World War II. His family and friends had been killed, and his own life was in constant peril. Physically tortured, psychologically demoralized, he was made to stand naked one afternoon before a group of Nazi soldiers who taunted and ridiculed him. A more demeaning or defenseless situation would be impossible to find. Yet, Frankl says, it was then that he experienced true freedom for the first time. A Nazi guard demanded Frankl's gold wedding band. As he removed the ring, Frankl realized that no matter what went on outside him, he was always in charge of his reaction. He always had a choice. That new awareness, he says, made him free.

Certainly, some bosses and some job situations are either beyond your ability to change or not worth the sustained and arduous effort. There may be irreconcilable differences between you and your boss. *Your boss may be one hundred percent to blame for the conditions under which you struggle. But you are one hundred percent responsible for how you react to it, and for where you go from here.* No matter who put you where you are, it is up to you to do something about it. You can stay or leave—that is, and always will be, your choice.

Make a Life Agenda

Imagine yourself in this situation. You are aboard a plane flying from San Francisco to Atlanta. The plane is on the runway, your seat belt is fastened, and the pilot's voice rolls comfortingly from the loudspeaker: "Welcome aboard. I have a pretty good idea of where Atlanta is, so we'll head in that direction as soon as we take off."

Confident? Willing to entrust your life to such a pilot? Or are you squirming in your seat wondering if it's not too late to escape?

Most of us like to have our air routes carefully planned, with continual and precise information. Yet many of us entrust our life routes to someone with an even worse sense of direction than that pilot—ourselves. At least the pilot knew where his destination was. Do you? Do you have clearly defined life goals? Have you ever sat down and asked yourself exactly what you want out of life? If not, can you expect to make the best choices?

There is a definite relationship between clearly defined goals and success. A major university recently conducted a study of graduates, all of whom had been out of school for twenty years. Only 3 percent of the graduates had ever established their life goals systematically and followed through by monitoring the goals and changing them when appropriate. Another 10 percent had given some consideration to their goals, but had not committed them to writing. The other 87 percent never had defined exactly what they wanted out of life. Which group do you think was the most successful? By every measure—personal, professional, and social—the 3 percent who had explicit goals.

In this era of vast and violent change, it is more important than ever to reevaluate continually the priorities you have selected. Don't confuse freedom *of* choice with freedom *from* choice. Make a life agenda, and update it as you and your circumstances change. Doing so will help you to reach success, and to find meaning and purpose, regardless of your successes and failures.

Take a blank piece of paper, and write at the top: MY BELIEFS. Spell out all the things that are important to you in all areas of life—family, business, personal development, recreation, civic affairs, finances, etc. Don't be concerned at this point with which items are more important than others.

After you have compiled this list, take a second sheet of paper and head it: BELIEFS BY PRIORITY. Look over your list. Which of the items is most important? Which comes next? Continue to list your priorities in descending order.

Making these lists will raise your awareness of yourself and put into perspective the relative importance of each area of your life. The next step is to see how well your behavior matches your beliefs. On a third piece of paper, write down: MY BEHAVIOR. We are going to see how much of your time and energy are actually devoted to the things you consider most important.

Most people are surprised to discover that they devote the majority of their time and energy to low-priority items. Many men, for example, claim that their families are of highest importance to them. Yet upon examination, they find that they spend less *quality time* with their wives and children than they do with their friends or co-workers. Others find that they strongly value social contribution, but devote very little time to it compared with other, less important items. Still others find that they devote a great deal of time to civic activities that serve the good of the community, while virtually ignoring the emotional needs of their spouse and children.

Making a valid comparison between your intentions and what you actually turn your attention to should take at least thirty days. Carefully and accurately monitor the amount of time you spend on each activity. Keep a running record. Unless you are a rare exception, you will find that you spend less than 15 percent of your time on top-priority items. Becoming aware of the discrepancy is the first step toward aligning your attention with your intention. In life what you SEIZE is what you get—SEIZE A LOT.

What does this have to do with your boss? On the surface, perhaps very little. But if you are to manage your boss so as to achieve your goals, you must first have a clear sense of what you want from your work. And to understand that, you must first know what you want from life. Making a living cannot be separated from making a life.

Is It the Right Job?

If you are to understand your boss as much as possible, you should first learn to distinguish between him and the job itself. Many of the problems people attribute to their bosses have little to do with the boss's management style, his personality, his demands, or anything else about him. The problems may be built into the kind of career you have chosen, the company you work for, or the nature of your particular assignment.

The key to biological survival is the ability to adapt to the occupied niche. The same can be said of work. How well do you fit your job niche? Or perhaps it would be better to ask: How well does your job fit you? Are you miscast in your work role?

Take some time to think seriously about what you want to give and get from your work. Write down a description of an ideal job. Then write a description of an ideal day at work. Be realistic. Now look over your descriptions and compare them to your actual job and a typical day at work. How well does the reality hold up to the ideal? Is it possible to approximate the ideal in your present position?

Earlier, you wrote a list of the things that are most important to you. What values do they reveal? Does your present job conflict with your values in any way?

What are your primary skills and talents? What situations do you function well in? Which activities bring out the best in you?

Does your job provide the opportunity for you to best utilize your skills and talents?

Are you a loner forced to work with other people? Or are you a sociable person stuck in a corner by yourself? If you do work with other people, are they the type you like to have around?

Do you like specific short-range assignments, or do you prefer to be given a general direction and long-term goals? Do you like regular supervision, or freedom to operate in your own way under general guidelines? Do you like having a clear vision of the "big picture," or are you satisfied with knowing your own area of responsibility? Do you like working with abstractions such as concepts and ideas, or with concrete items such as financial statements and machines? Do you prefer a tight organizational routine or a loose structure? Do you prefer explicit rules and regulations or broad, goal-oriented policies? How does your job measure up in these ways?

Do you have your sights set on moving up in your field? If so, have you assessed clearly your present position as a launching pad? What are your company's prospects? Are you in the right industry?

The best of bosses cannot make up for an inappropriate job. Be sure, therefore, that your evaluation of your boss is not in fact an evaluation of your job.

Keep in mind that working for an ideal boss in the wrong job is not paradise. In the long run, you are often better off choosing the right job with the wrong boss than the opposite, assuming the boss is at least tolerable and there will be a way for you to move up and away from him quickly. Bear in mind also that it is possible to obtain satisfaction from your work even with the wrong boss, as long as he or she doesn't prevent you from doing your job well.

What should you look for in a job? Consider once again Victor Frankl's concentration camp experience. He and others like him were able to find meaning and purpose by helping each other survive. The lesson he learned is worth sharing and applying: Don't look for happiness; if you do, you probably won't find it. Pursue instead meaning and purpose; if you find them, happiness may ensue.

Should You Quit?

This is not a choice to be taken lightly, or to be made impulsively. Hold off on the decision until you have fully evaluated (not value-judged) both your relationship with your boss and the ingredients of your job, and until you have tried the suggestions in this book and evaluated the results. If, at that time, you determine that you are in a dead-end situation, weigh the advantages of quitting with a solid appraisal of your career goals, your family responsibilities, and the job market. The choice may not be easy, but it is your choice, and that realization alone will expand your awareness and heighten your self-esteem.

Even if you have an unsolvable conflict with your boss, you may decide to stick it out. Perhaps you don't want to handle the loss of income at this time. Perhaps you can benefit from more experience or some new contacts before looking for a new job. Perhaps you want to wait and see if things change—upper management may reorganize the company, the industry may shift gears, or your boss may leave. Accept the fact that you have *chosen* to stay, and you will not be miserable like the person who spends his days moaning in self-pity, believing he has no choice in the matter.

If you further realize that day in and day out, no matter how bad things get, you still control the way you respond to events, you may, like Victor Frankl, experience a sense of inner freedom. You will have your integrity and your dignity, and you can still gain a sense of accomplishment from doing your work with excellence in spite of the obstacles. Should you choose to stay—for retirement benefits, geographical reasons, or whatever—reinforce and support yourself for the choice you make. Since whatever you do is your choice, enjoy it and create a positive perspective.

But what about getting out? Certainly that is a viable option, yet sometimes even people who have nothing concrete to hold them back hesitate to make the move. If social constraints are keeping you back, it may be time to reevaluate.

Until recently it was assumed that success meant choosing one's career early in life, joining a company, and climbing the ladder in that firm until retirement. Moving from one profession, one career, or one company to another was considered a sign of instability, even failure. According to Eugene Jennings, professor of management at Michigan State University, changing jobs "used to be abnormal, pathological, bordering on mental disturbance because of the disruption of a person's life."

That is no longer true. A growing number of people believe that job security is not worth day after day of misery. No longer is it considered a sign of merit to do something you don't like until it's time to collect your gold watch. Changing jobs, or even careers, in the name of self-fulfillment is fast becoming socially acceptable, and in some cases admirable. Indeed, a 1978 study by the National College Board indicated that as many as 40 million people were at that time in the midst of career transition. It is estimated that the average American changes jobs once every three to four years.

In many cases, of course, staying where you are is the wise and pragmatic thing to do. You may be gaining valuable experience and connections; or other attractive jobs may be scarce. Family responsibilities may also cause you to choose to play it safe. But some people have such strong security needs, and the onus of unemployment weighs so heavily on their minds, that they would endure anything to keep their jobs—even a demeaning environment or a troublesome boss.

It reminds me of the woman who was deathly afraid of losing her job in a museum. One day she shattered a statue. The boss did not fire her; instead he said he would deduct one third of her wages each week until the sculpture was paid for.

"How much did it cost?" asked the employee.

"Ten thousand dollars," replied the boss.

"That's great!" the woman declared. "That means I have a steady job."

The option to change is available, and it might be the best choice to make. Although chronic or perpetual job switching will brand you as a bad risk, most employers are not as wary of moderate job changing as they once were. It is often seen as a sign of versatility.

If you are getting older, you may feel locked in because of your age. Many people think that once they turn fifty, no one will want them. They may also feel stuck because of their company's pension or retirement plan. Those are legitimate concerns, but there is some good news. For one thing, there is increasing support for making retirement funds transferable to the new company after a person switches jobs. Second, more and more employers are beginning to realize that older people have much to offer. A study by Banker's Life and Casualty Company found that the productivity and reliability of workers over sixty-five was equal to, and sometimes better than, that of younger workers. People over sixty-five, it turns out, are absent less often than younger people; their mental abilities are equal or superior; their health interferes with their work no more often; and their health benefit claims are no more costly. Many people past age fifty have "started over." You can too.

It is never too late to change. If ever you hear yourself saying, "I never had a chance," or, "That's the way I am; I can't change now," you are in effect saying, "I'm a slave to my environment." The section on *How To Hire a Boss* in Chapter Five will show you how to present yourself to a prospective employer.

Work for Yourself?

If you are highly self-directed, consider the possibility that you should not be working under *any* other person. If you have had a history of boss problems, that might well be the reason. Some people are better cut out for self-employment, or for independent positions, such as sales; but they delude themselves into thinking they can't make it except in a job where they are managed by someone else. They might earn more money and be happier on their own.

The risks in self-employment are substantial, but minor compared to the risks of being miscast in a work role. Think of the risks and the headaches of continuing in a managed position that goes against your very nature. Which sets of risks can you best afford? For those who are psychologically equipped for it (and not everyone is), the challenge of self-employment can be quite rewarding. And it eliminates all your boss problems . . . except one, yourself! But that is a condition you always face—no matter whom you work for, you are and always will be your own boss.

This is not to say that there is anything lacking in a person who works for someone else. Most people *should* be employed by other people, since the true entrepreneur is rare. The point is that many readers of this book will simply never be comfortable working for anyone but themselves, but they stick it out because of fear, or because they have not fully considered the alternatives, or because they don't understand how to strike out on their own.

ARE YOU A SELF-STARTER?		
I do things my own way. Nobody needs to tell me to get going.	If someone gets me started, I keep going all right.	Easy does it. I don't put myself out until I have to.
HOW DO YOU FEEL ABOUT OTHER PEOPLE?		
I like people. I can get along with just about anybody.	I have plenty of friends. I don't need anyone else.	Most people bug me.
CAN YOU LEAD OTHERS?		
I can get most people to go along without much difficulty.	I can get people to do things if I drive them.	I let someone else get things moving.
CAN YOU TAKE RESPONSIBILITY?		
I like to take charge of and see things through.	I'll take over if I have to, but I'd rather let someone else be responsible.	There's always some eager beaver around wanting to show off. I say let him.
HOW GOOD AN ORGANIZER ARE YOU?		
I like to have a plan before I start. I'm usually the one to get things lined up.	I do all right unless things get too goofed up. Then I cop out.	I just take things as they come.

HOW GOOD A WORKER ARE YOU?		
I can keep going as long as necessary. I don't mind working hard.	I'll work hard for a while, but when I ve had enough, that's it!	I can't see that hard work gets you anywhere.
CAN YOU MAKE DECISIONS?		
I can make up my mind in a hurry if necessary, and my decision is usually okay.	I can if I have plenty of time. If I have to make up my mind fast, I usually regret it.	I don't like to be the one who decides things. I'd probably blow it.
CAN PEOPLE TRUST WHAT YOU SAY?		
They sure can. I don't say things I don't mean.	I try to be on the level, but sometimes I just say what's easiest.	What's the sweat if the other fellow doesn't know the difference?
CAN YOU STICK WITH IT?		
If I make up my mind to do something, I don't let anything stop me.	I usually finish what I start.	If a job doesn't go right, I turn off. Why beat your brains out?
HOW GOOD IS YOUR HEALTH?		
I never run down.	I have enough energy for most things I want to do.	I run out of juice sooner than most of my friends seem to.

Are you the type to run your own business? Here is a checklist, created by the U.S. Small Business Administration, that will help you determine whether you have the personality of a business proprietor. After each question, place a check mark on the line at the point closest to your answer. The check mark need not be placed directly over one of the suggested answers; your rating may lie in between.

If most of your checks are on the left, you might want to think seriously about going into business for yourself. Here's a formula to consider.

Pamela Whitney is a successful entrepreneur. She has founded several international businesses and has trained numerous people to reach their goals. This is her system.

First, know that success *is* attainable. Believe that whatever you make up your mind to do, you *can* do. Learn everything you can about the field you choose.

Second, choose a goal and direction that will fulfill you, one that you will enjoy. Plan out your course of action by writing down what you need to do in order to achieve your final goal. Then begin accomplishing one thing at a time, in an organized way. Determination with high intention will help you to handle areas that seem to be difficult or unfamiliar to you.

Third, always feel free to ask for assistance and advice from those who have already accomplished what you seek to do. Be willing to learn from those who already have expertise in the area you are working toward. Remember, whatever you focus on with high intention, you can create! And success will be yours if you take one step at a time and allow the process of achieving your goal to unfold in an organized way.

Finally, if things go wrong, remember it's only temporary. Step back, reexamine your approach, and begin again. Persist and you will not be denied.

Take a Good Look at Yourself

You have asked yourself how you feel about your life and how you feel about your work. One more area needs to be assessed before you can be objective about your boss: How do you feel about yourself?

A large percentage of problems between bosses and subordinates stem from insecurities on either side or both sides. One common problem is created by the need to be liked. Thousands of people who gripe about the way their boss treats them would discover—if they looked really closely at their feelings—that they are really asking to be loved. Their egos crave acceptance, often unconditional acceptance. To some, that means having the boss treat them as a pal or a buddy. To others, it translates as a pseudo-parent relationship. You must distinguish between having a good working relationship with your boss, and being liked or loved. Remember that trust is more important than affection, and that the latter is not necessary in a professional relationship.

I once had a very successful boss-subordinate relationship with someone I did not like. He was creative and competent, but he tended to be abrasive and domineering. I avoided personal contact with him. Whereas I had a friendly relationship with others on my staff, I rarely ever had lunch with him. I stayed away from him before and after meetings, but *during* the meetings, when everyone's mind was on business, he was great to have around.

Despite my reaction to his personality, I trusted and respected him as a professional. We had a working relationship that led to profits and satisfaction for both of us, even though we felt no kinship for one another.

A good relationship between boss and subordinate requires trust, honesty, mutual support, and respect. It does not have to be friendly or intimate. The measure is not whether you invite each other to your homes. In fact, a lot of good working relationships deteriorate as soon as they turn into friendships, when the dynamics of personal involvement get muddled with the dynamics of work. It takes people of exceptional self-esteem to manage both sets of roles and expectations successfully.

The sales rep and I didn't see much of each other, since he was out selling most of the time. Thus, I could ignore the personal traits that so disturbed me. If he had worked in the next office eight hours a day, I doubt if he would have lasted a week. When personal idiosyncrasies are intolerable and there is no hope of adjusting to them, quitting—or relocating—might be the only way out.

But in most cases, even those that require close, regular contact, it is not necessary that you like each other. It is only necessary that you don't *dis*like each other. The important thing is to be sure that your need to be liked doesn't lead you to make excessive unconscious demands on your boss.

Because of dependency needs, we often want the boss to take

care of us. We expect perfection of him, not just professionally but personally as well. As psychologist James P. Smith of Temple University put it, we ask the boss to be "reinforcing, nice, permissive, understanding, and to think of all our needs even when we don't tell him what we need. We feel he has nothing to do but worry about us."

Remember that no one—not your boss, not even your spouse—can have all your interests at heart at all times. They might not even know what your needs are unless you clearly communicate them. And in your boss's case, he might not care what your emotional needs are. Certainly, you should be treated with respect, but you were hired to perform specific tasks. The relationship is not meant to equal that of spouse or parent or friend.

I recall a woman who spent a great deal of time complaining about her boss. After nearly a year of listening to her, I finally met the boss himself. I expected the second coming of Attila the Hun. I could tell he would be tough when necessary, but he didn't strike me as the type to be unfair or mean. Intrigued, I dug for additional information. I found that the boss was not universally beloved, but he was universally respected. No one else complained about his picking on them, of his having it in for them, or of cruel or hostile behavior.

It turned out that the woman who complained so much had had a series of similar entanglements; in fact, her whole life seemed to be one long battle with authorities. At the time of our acquaintance, she was in a big hurry to get ahead. She was anxious to prove herself in a man's world and to achieve the professional standing she felt she deserved. In her zeal, she came to expect too much from her boss, and she resented it when he did not deliver.

Many of us are caught in a classic bind. It is difficult to live with the fact that bosses have more power than we do. Because we tend to respond to their personalities instead of their positions, it's easy to believe they don't deserve superior status. In order to accept their authority, we have to rationalize. The need to elevate the boss can conflict with a psychological block against accepting authority.

Whether ego needs are manifested as an excessive need for acceptance or a need to deflate authority figures, they can be a major obstacle to effective working relationships. Become aware of any conflicting feelings you have about your boss. Recognize that it's normal and even healthy to experience such feelings. Be certain you balance them and act in a constructive fashion toward your boss.

Is Your Ego Primitive or Evolved?

Many intelligent and competent people have serious difficulties working with others because of what I call a "primitive ego." Their existence revolves around an attempt to guard the identity they project to the world. They spend a major portion of their energy defending themselves and their ideas—both to other people and to themselves. Because they have a strong, often overpowering need to prove themselves, these people often pile up notable achievements. But the primitive ego acts as a barrier to compatibility. People with highly primitive egos often leave a trail of ruptured relationships behind them and are seldom invited to rejoin a group once they have left.

By contrast, people with "evolved" egos can deal with themselves and others in a straightforward way. Acknowledging freely that they don't have the final answer to every question, they ask others for help and are open to ideas. Within their groups, they create trust, and they enhance the self-esteem of the members. They inspire compatibility because they don't need to prove themselves superior or to get the credit for every achievement. Sometimes popular, always respected, they strive for neither popularity nor agreement.

The following questionnaire will help you to evaluate how you relate to yourself and others. If you would like an assessment of your ego state, evaluate yourself as you are, not as you think you should be or would like to be.

SCORING:
Never = 0
Sometimes = 1
Often = 2
Almost Always = 3

________ 1. Is it frustrating when you cannot get people to do things your way?

________ 2. Do you often find it difficult to stay with arrangements you have made after the people involved seem less important to you?

________ 3. Do you enjoy being "center stage" (the center of attention)?

_________ 4. Do you pride yourself on being able to outfox others?

_________ 5. Are you someone who cannot be trusted?

_________ 6. Do you feel rage when being ignored or not receiving first-class treatment?

_________ 7. Do you put people down behind their backs?

_________ 8. Do you have difficulty enjoying your leisure?

_________ 9. Would you be embarrassed to be caught shopping in a store noted for low prices by someone you are trying to impress?

_________ 10. Do you drive a fancy car if it strains your budget?

_________ 11. Are you afraid to admit to others that you are sometimes scared?

_________ 12. Do you have to look your very best when seen by other people?

_________ 13. Are you seduced by praise even when you sense it may be somewhat insincere?

_________ 14. If unable to express felt anger at someone because of their rank or position, will you explode at an innocent person?

_________ 15. Do you feel uneasy when someone is receiving what you consider to be undue praise?

_________ 16. Do you find it hard to pay a sincere compliment to someone who is doing better than you at your line of work?

_________ 17. Do you often view people you meet as adversaries?

_________ 18. Do you feel superior or inferior to certain people?

_________ 19. Do you use people for your own advancement even if it damages them?

_________ 20. Do you demand to be treated fairly (even in unimportant matters)?

_________ 21. Do you mind other people talking a lot about themselves?

__________ 22. Do you talk about yourself, your contacts, your accomplishments, etc.?

__________ 23. Will you cover up something you have done poorly if you get the chance?

__________ 24. Do you enjoy knowing that someone you dislike is having problems?

__________ 25. Is it difficult for you to be gentle? Do you see it as a weakness?

__________ 26. Do you make yourself a target of other people's anger?

__________ 27. After scoring this questionnaire, will you discount the evaluation if you do poorly?

__________ 28. Do you feel people are to be taken advantage of?

__________ 29. Would you risk your life and perhaps the lives of your loved ones to prove your "courage"? E.g., pursue a car recklessly on the freeway after it cut you off, to get even?

__________ 30. Do you have a compelling need to prove yourself?

__________ 31. Are you affected by other people's opinions of you in relationship to their importance and status?

__________ 32. Do you believe that winning is the only thing, no matter what the consequences?

__________ 33. Must you win even when enjoying your leisure time (golf, tennis, etc.)?

__________ 34. Do you "validate" yourself even when your actions are not "valid"? E.g., make lots of phone calls that are unnecessary?

__________ 35. Are you attracted to people who constantly reaffirm how important you are?

__________ 36. Are you overly sensitive when hearing unflattering comments about yourself?

__________ TOTAL SCORE–To determine your ego quotient, add up the numbers.

Explanation of evaluation

(1) 0 to 25 : You have reached a highly evolved ego.
(2) 26 to 50 : You have a reasonably evolved ego.
(3) 51 to 75 : Your ego is in a primitive state.
(4) Over 75 : Your ego is in a highly primitive state.

Your total score is your "ego handicap." If your score is in categories (2), (3), or (4), you will benefit from implementing ideas to help lower your "ego handicap." In doing so, you will become more competent and creative in dealing with yourself and others. If you have done poorly and are upset by the results, recognize this *not* as something good or bad, but rather something that *is*, and that you can change.

If in management, take this section

_________ 37. Do you tend to rule people with an "iron hand," particularly when under stress?

_________ 38. Do you constantly interfere with your people under the guise of "close" supervision?

_________ 39. Does your need to be needed cause you to play guru, e.g., make all of the decisions for your people?

_________ 40. Do you find it difficult to delegate responsibility because no one can do the job as well as you?

_________ 41. Do you resent people who disagree with you openly?

_________ 42. Do you attack people who "argue" with you?

_________ 43. Do you get upset when people don't live up to your expectations?

_________ 44. Do you have to do things to perfection to be satisfied?

_________ 45. Do you have a deep need to defend and protect your actions and beliefs?

__________ 46. Do you find it awkward to admit that you have made a mistake?

__________ 47. Do you feel, as the boss, that you must have an answer for almost every problem or situation?

__________ 48. Do you "impose" your communication on others by virtue of your authority over them?

__________ 49. Do you rationalize your errors to justify your "perfection"?

__________ 50. Is it difficult for you to laugh at yourself? Your mistakes?

__________ 51. Do you often overrule your people's decisions to prove you are the "boss"?

__________ 52. Do you practice management by anxiety, keeping your people continually tense?

__________ 53. Do you practice management by saviorhood, keeping marginal people who will always be marginal?

__________ 54. Do you suffer from the disease of having to be right?

__________ TOTAL SCORE—to determine your ego quotient, add up the numbers.

(1) 0 to 15 : Highly evolved ego.
(2) 15 to 30 : Reasonably evolved ego.
(3) 30 to 40 : Primitive ego.
(4) Over 40 : Highly primitive ego.

If your score is in categories (3) or (4), recognize that it is not good or bad, but something that is, and that you can change.

Self-Esteem

Eleven years ago, a successful executive was having lunch with his friend. The friend said: "I think you have low self-esteem."

The executive laughed. "Low-esteem? Me? Listen, I earn more money than the President of the United States. I have a home in San Francisco and an apartment in New York. I'm in charge of a large number of people and I'm considered a leader in my industry. How could you believe I have low self-esteem?"

The friend replied: "You've just removed any doubt I might have had."

The executive had been equating who he was with what he had done. His friend's remarks showed him how low his self-esteem actually was. The incident changed his life. I know, because I was that executive.

How do you really feel about yourself? When you close your eyes and look at yourself, do you like what you see? Do you enjoy the time you spend with yourself? Do you accept yourself, or do you constantly put yourself down? Do you constantly have a need to build yourself up?

Many people who seem on the surface to be confident and self-assured are actually suffering from low self-esteem. Some of our greatest achievers are driven by fear of failure; they need to prove themselves constantly in order to compensate for faltering self-esteem. Many people of low self-esteem feel their worth as a person is on the line in every business and personal transaction. Your boss might be one of them. So might you.

Bosses with low self-esteem are difficult to work for; employees with low self-esteem are equally hard to manage.

There are two extreme forms of subordinates with low self-esteem: the *underwhelming* and the *belligerent*. In *extreme* form, the underwhelming subordinate refrains from taking any initiative. Often found in quiet despair, he tends to discount his own ideas. He lives in fear of others, including his boss. By creating situations that reinforce his basic sense of inadequacy, he constantly proves how worthless he is. In this way, no one—least of all himself—will expect much of him. He protects himself and strives only to survive, not to excel.

The belligerent person is much more visible. The extremely belligerent person is quick to anger, and quick to anger others. A constant source of dissension, she talks back every chance she can get. She will do anything in her power to make the boss look bad. To this combative person, everyone—boss, colleague, subordinate—is an adversary. Winning is all, for with each victory comes a medal with which she can cover up her meager self-esteem. The belligerent person is often in trouble. Or fired. Always for petty reasons, she will have you believe: "The boss couldn't stand having me around; I made him look bad by comparison." She will claim to be the victim of power politics, because she sees everything in those terms. She is at war; each day is a series of attacks and counterattacks.

In between these two extremes are more people than you can imagine. They display some of the characteristics of either the underwhelming or the belligerent subordinate. Not all timid people cower in the corner. They may just appear as quiet, unassuming types who plug away in a competent but undistinguished manner; yet underneath, they live in quiet despair. Similarly, not all belligerent subordinates are as obnoxious as the bellicose person described above, but they may be performing their sabotage in more covert ways. They may not even be aware of the degree of belligerence festering inside them.

Whether low self-esteem directs its dissatisfaction within or without, the person's self-worth is always on the line. That can seriously damage your relationship with your boss, especially if both of you have low self-esteem. Furthermore, low self-esteem makes it difficult to evaluate your situation objectively.

Suppose, for example, you are denied a promotion. Perhaps the other candidate deserved it more than you; perhaps you weren't ready for the job; perhaps you're better off without it. Your boss may have had many good reasons for making the decision he did; it may have been in the best interests of the company, and it may have been best for you.

But if your self-esteem is low, you are likely to take it personally. You might feel rejected, unloved, cheated. You might feel anger, resentment, or self-pity. Your image of yourself as an unworthy, ineffectual person might be reinforced, and you might sink even deeper in self-condemnation. Or you might take it out on your boss. The boss might become an enemy in your eyes, because you need to deflate the authority figure in order to take the onus of rejection off yourself.

In thousands of less obvious ways, low self-esteem distorts our image of ourselves and our bosses every day. For that reason, you would do well to evaluate your self-esteem honestly. Introspection and observation will give you clues, as will the "ego evaluation" you just filled out. If you scored above 50, you have low self-esteem.

Low self-esteem is one of our biggest public enemies. We learn in America, virtually from birth, that our value is dependent on our actions—each victory raises our worth and each loss deflates it. It is sad and crippling to have to look outside ourselves for both blame and credit. It creates an overcompetitive, adversary atmosphere, based on a chronic and pathological need to pile up victory after victory, status symbol after status symbol, power play after power play. We are in a constant battle to prove our worth to ourselves and to others. By linking our worth as persons with outer achievement, we flirt with disaster. The chief executive officer of a huge international corporation, for example, leaped out of his skyscraper window when his company's earnings plummeted and his practice of bribery was discovered. Less dramatic, but more tragic perhaps, is the cripplingly low self-esteem of housewives, whose accomplishments receive no accolades from society even though raising a family is at least as vital and difficult as any professional goal.

Genuine self-esteem has nothing to do with one's station in life; the person sweeping the floor of a bank actually may have higher self-esteem than the person who occupies the president's office. Self-esteem means accepting yourself as you are. It means recognizing that your worth as a human being is given to you by virtue of your very existence. You are unique, valuable, and worthwhile because you exist. Whether you win or lose the games we play has nothing to do with your intrinsic value as a human being. You are not what you do; you are more than that.

Certainly, you are *accountable* for your actions. If you do not perform well, your boss has the right to fire you. Your boss hired you not because you are unique and precious but because you are, presumably, a competent secretary or salesman, or account executive or truck driver. You are expected to perform certain actions according to certain standards. If you don't, and your boss fires you, it does not mean you are worthless. Neither your actions nor your boss's actions have anything to do with your self-worth.

Mistakes and failures result from deficiencies in awareness, not from an inherent lack of worth. Your awareness level is constantly changing, creating at every moment a dominant need or desire that motivates your actions. If you fail at some task, if you make a mistake, then take responsibility and raise your level of awareness so it won't happen again. But don't condemn yourself. It would be as wrong to do that as it would be to pat yourself on the back for every victory.

People with genuine self-esteem do not equate their sense of worth with wins or losses. They accept themselves without reservation, regardless of how they measure up to any outside criteria. *They are not swayed by other people's opinions of them; they allow no one to put them down, and at the same time have no need to build themselves up.* They are not afraid of failure, because they know that *having* a failure is not the same as *being* a failure. At the same time, they are neither afraid of, nor dependent on, success. In their internal dialogues, people with self-esteem do not make value judgments about themselves.

"The truly wise," said a Chinese sage, "love themselves, but do not take pride in themselves." The same may be said for people with high self-esteem. They are not narcissistic; they don't puff themselves up, nor do they treat themselves as objects of adoration. At the same time, they do not feel put down by other people's comments. Self-esteem, in fact, is the very opposite of egotism, vanity, or pride, which are actually signs of *low* self-esteem. The real thing does not have to be proven or constantly reinforced. It just is.

While self-esteem can be nourished or enriched by positive, contributive actions, it is really rooted in an acceptance of one's self that is independent of other people and the outside world. Two executives illustrated how the same incident can lead to vastly different responses, depending on one's basic level of self-esteem.

Many executives have asked me to help them overcome their fear of speaking before an audience. People whose decisions affect millions of lives actually shudder at the thought of giving a speech. Two of those people, each of whom had had terrifying experiences in public speaking, reacted entirely differently when faced with the prospect of a repeat performance.

One was plagued with the fear of making a fool of himself. He could barely eat for a week; he came down with headaches and indigestion. He argued with his wife over trifles and berated his employees. He became hostile to his boss, who had asked him to give the presentation. "You're a failure," he badgered himself. "You can't even make a simple speech."

The other executive viewed his previous experience from a different perspective. He was disappointed in his attempt, but he was not destroyed. He was concerned about his next appearance, but he was not overly anxious. He was able to make fun of himself. He knew that his self-esteem didn't depend on his success or failure as a speaker. His inner dialogue didn't consist of self-pity or self-condemnation. Instead, he thought, "I've got a block against speaking in public. What can I do about it?" He came to me for assistance, not magic formulas or sympathy, unlike the other man, whose sense of worth hinged on winning every contest.

Which of the two is more likely to find satisfaction in work? Which one will have a better relationship with his boss? Which one will do a better job with his second speech?

The person with self-esteem increased his awareness by reading books about public speaking; he observed skilled speakers and asked them questions, he used tape-recorded drills to improve his ability, he rehearsed before people he trusted and listened to their feedback objectively. We spent six hours together doing videotape training. Although he's no Bob Hope, Billy Graham, or Winston Churchill, he doesn't need to be. As an executive who occasionally has to speak before a group, he learned to do a perfectly competent job.

Achievements alone will never bring genuine self-esteem. Accept yourself for who and what you are, and make whatever changes are in your best interest. Affirm that having a failure is not being one. Separate your worth from your work with this affrimation: "My work is what I do—a person is what I am."

Are You Doing Your Best?

Joe Bradley said his boss was constantly on his back. She was never satisfied with what he did and was always pointing out his mistakes. As the company was located near my home, I was able to investigate. It turned out that the boss was holding to a classic management fallacy of pointing out failures, never successes. Her techniques included oversupervision and dressing people down in front of their peers.

But while the boss's awareness needed expanding, so did Joe's. He was not working up to his capacity. For whatever reasons, he was shirking his duties by being careless and making mistakes he was smart enough to avoid. Joe created many opportunities for his boss to criticize him and mistakenly felt that the responsibility rested totally with her.

We come back to one of our basic premises: *It is as much the responsibility of the managed as it is the responsibility of the manager to create and maintain an effective working relationship.* Your first responsibility is to do the job you are being paid to do. In fact, if you really want to make work work for you, you will do *more* than you are being paid to do. *A major key in obtaining job satisfaction is to give more than you get.*

However, many people have learned to do the opposite, particularly when the boss does not provide positive feedback.

Joe's boss reinforced his negative traits, and he reinforced hers. Resentful, he did less than the boss expected. Joe looked to the boss to take the first step in improving the situation. "She's the one with the power, isn't she?" said Joe. Joe should have been evaluating how he could have improved the situation instead of criticizing the boss. Take the first step yourself. You, too, have power. Focus on how you can help solve the problem. If you do less than your best, everyone—you, your boss, and the organization lose. Do more, and everyone will win.

It is in your own best interest to be as valuable as possible. The more value you give, the more valuable you become. Some of the benefits to you are:

1. Your boss's boss expects him to be productive, creative, and competent. If your boss gets results, it reflects not just on him but on his subordinates as well. Your chances of promotion and success will be a lot better if you make your boss look good. If you can't respect your boss as a person, at least respect the responsibility of the position.
2. You will acquire greater respect and esteem from your colleagues, which will serve you well in the future.
3. Whether they express it adequately or not, most bosses recognize a job well done. In the future, he may give you greater trust and autonomy.
4. If your boss is truly impossible, doing your job well gives him less ammunition and fewer excuses to demonstrate his worst qualities. Why make yourself a target?
5. If personality problems or politics ever stand in your way, you will be able to point to your results—which you should carefuly document.
6. You will reduce the level of stress and tension in your department.
7. Most important, you will have the satisfaction that comes from knowing you are making a valid contribution.

Ask yourself how much you could increase your productivity if you were devoted totally to being as effective as you can be. Ask yourself what would happen to your organization if everyone in it were totally devoted to being as valuable as *they* could be. Isn't it true that most people already know how to do their jobs a lot better than they are presently doing them? What's holding them back?

Let's look at a creative, solution-oriented way to view work. First, recognize that we are all doing the best we can based on our level of awareness. As we expand our awareness and learn to deal with each other in a more creative, productive, cooperative way, we can make work work for everyone. Organizations can prosper, and individuals can find satisfaction and economic rewards. By ending the myths that create an adversary relationship, everyone will benefit.

Before we look at the person you report to, look at your own responsibilities. What are the value judgments you have made about your boss, and how might you change your perspective? How would your boss feel about each of those judgments? Remember, if you are dissatisfied about something at work, there is a good chance he or she is also dissatisfied. What can you do to take the first step toward creating an allegiance where there may now be antagonism?

Identify in clear language three ways you can and will be more valuable to the person you report to. (Caution: Many people resist doing this because of the Three-R cycle. It's okay to feel resistance, but don't let it stop you from making your list and acting on it.)

The Right Boss

Is there a "right boss" for you? The answer depends on a variety of factors: the nature of your work, the stage of your career, the nature of the organization, your goals, your personality, and many others. One type of boss may be right under one set of circumstances, while a different type would be best under another. One type of management approach might be perfect for you now, while another would be better in the future. It is to your advantage to learn how to manage *all* bosses; the strategies that follow will give you the skills and flexibility to do just that.

Nevertheless, there is value in identifying the type of situation that would be most appropriate for you. Remember, an uncomfortable situation may well hold more value than a comfortable one. These questions will help you pinpoint what you are looking for. Take some time to answer them carefully in writing before going on to the next chapter.

1. What do you want to accomplish during your working lifetime?
2. Are you willing and able to put up with an incompatible personality matchup if the job and environment are right for you?
3. Do you want a personal relationship with your boss, or do you prefer a strictly professional relationship?
4. Do you like close, day-to-day supervision, or do you prefer to manage yourself?
5. Do you like feedback at short intervals, or annual or semiannual evaluation meetings?
6. Do you value a boss who will act as a coach or mentor?
7. Do you want your boss to play an active role in advancing your career?
8. Do you feel comfortable with clear rules and regulations, or do you prefer a loose structure?
9. Are you willing to do things your boss's way even if you think you know a better one?
10. Is it important to you to be able to let the boss know how he or she can improve his or her performance?
11. Is it important to you that you like your boss and that he or she like you?
12. Do you need recognition for each achievement, or are you willing to share the credit or go unacknowledged?
13. If your pay and future advancement are not as good as you like, would a good working relationship with your boss compensate?
14. Can you handle criticism without feeling rejected?
15. Ultimately, who is responsible for your work—you or your boss?

The End Result

By carefully evaluating your strengths and weaknesses, likes and dislikes, you will be able to make better decisions about your present job. You will also be better equipped to make decisions about your future.

3

Understanding Your Boss

Two men meet midway between two cities. "How will I find the people in yonder city?" inquires one of the men. "How did you find them where you came from?" replies the other.

"They were despicable. Evil. They were out to get me."

"Then you will find them exactly the same in the city you are approaching."

In that ancient parable is a warning about the way you might be approaching your boss. Do you see him for what he really is? Or are you approaching him with preconceived notions, false premises, and value judgments? What are your expectations of your boss, and do they match the reality of the person and the circumstances?

No one can ever *really* understand another person, or be truly understood by another person. But, by understanding that we are each unique and different, we can communicate effectively.

"My boss doesn't understand me," is a complaint I hear quite frequently. Sometimes it's a valid statement, because many bosses do not understand, or even attempt to understand, their subordinates. However, the best and quickest way to get your boss to understand you is first to understand your boss.

This requires the practice of *empathy*, which means situating yourself so that you can attempt to see reality from your boss's point of view. Remember, you can no more see things perfectly from your boss's point of view than he can see them from yours. But, just as a competent man can help a woman give birth, you can—through the practice of empathy—approach your boss's experience closely enough to help him, influence him, and manage him so that you both reap big dividends.

An accurate evaluation, without value judgments, can help you determine the best approach for improving your relationship with your boss. Misunderstanding—and, even worse, underestimating—the boss can cause you to use the wrong strategies. I recall a bright, energetic woman who complained that her boss ignored all her terrific ideas. "He must think I'm stupid," she raged. "Either that or he wants all the credit for himself!" The angry woman never took the trouble to understand the financial and political pressures that caused her boss to reject ideas that seemed, from the employee's perspective, brilliant.

I remember another person, Harry, who concluded that his supervisor disliked him and thought him inconsequential. "She ignores me," said Harry. "I see her talking to other people, but never me." When I had the opportunity to inquire, I learned that his interpretation of the situation was way off.

"Tell me about Harry," I said to his boss. "Is he a good worker?"

"Harry is the best," she replied. "He's the only person in my department I don't have to watch over and correct all the time. Good old Harry—I trust him implicitly."

In both instances, it should be noted, the boss was inadvertently transmitting false messages. In the first case, the boss could have anticipated his subordinate's feelings and explained some of the constraints that caused him to reject ideas. He could have complimented her for the ideas he considered noteworthy, even if they were, at the time, unfeasible. He could have guided his creative employee toward more appropriate ideas.

In the second case, of course, the boss should have made clear to Harry her trust and confidence in him. She should have let him know that his good work was appreciated, perhaps by giving him some sort of reward or added responsibility. Excellence deserves attention as much as incompetence, even if the latter seems to need it more.

But despite those obstacles, the subordinates owed it to themselves and to their bosses to take the initiative. They could have gone out of their way to understand the boss. Both interpreted the situation wrongly, placing it in a negative light when it was just as plausible, and more accurate, to assume something positive. Value judgments are never as useful as facts.

No doubt you, as a subordinate, want to be treated as an individual with your own unique set of goals and values, likes and dislikes, strengths and weaknesses. If you have people working under you, you are probably aware of the need to treat each of them with that kind of understanding. You take pains to get to know them. Yet you may not be willing to grant the same courtesy to your boss.

Managers are people. Most of them are not villains, nor are they knights in shining armor. Their personalities vary as much as those of their subordinates. They too have frailties, weaknesses, and foibles, even if they have learned never to admit them. They also have strengths. Deal with your boss according to who he or she is—not who you want him or her to be and not who you imagine him or her to be.

Remember what was said earlier about self-fulfilling prophecies. In a very real sense, much of your relationship with your boss is determined by the way you perceive him. Change your perception and, in effect, you change your boss.

You can start creating mutual understanding by practicing sentence completion, a good way to get in touch with your own feelings. The best way to do this is to speak your answers into a tape recorder, and then play back your responses. If that's not possible, write down the answers.

1. My boss and I get along best when . . .
2. The thing I like best about my boss is . . .
3. The thing I like next best about my boss is . . .
4. The thing I like least about my boss is . . .
5. If I were my boss I would . . .
6. My boss could get more out of me by . . .
7. The reason I don't go all out for my boss is . . .
8. The thing I resent most about working for someone else is . . .
9. The thing about my boss that most upsets me is . . .
10. The changes I would make if I were boss are . . .
11. When I'm a boss I will never . . .
12. When I'm a boss I will always . . .
13. The thing I don't understand about my boss is . . .
14. The thing that irritates me about my boss is . . .
15. I wish my boss would . . .

16. All bosses are . . .
17. The ideal boss is . . .

What Do Bosses Do?

In that your boss is a human being with all the variation and imperfection the word "human" implies, he is just like you and everyone else. In that he is your boss, he is different.

On a professional level, your boss faces responsibilities and pressures that you should be aware of in order to understand better the person to whom you report. While you both share the same overall goals for the success of the company, your boss's concerns and priorities may be very different from yours by virtue of the fact that he has to be aware of the "big picture."

His sphere of influence and responsibility is, by definition, broader than yours. He has to be alert to the subtle and far-ranging ramifications of every event and each decision. He has to consider the long-range picture along with short-range results. He has to think about many more people and many more intertwining events than you do. He is, undoubtedly, under a lot more pressure.

You may be in charge of the accounts payable department at a bank. Your boss may be responsible for *all* accounting operations, and in addition for training employees, dealing with special customers, answering to top management at the branch and to executives at headquarters. He is concerned with the relationship of accounting to other departments. His mind is on federal regulations, bank policies, customer relations, as well as the ins and outs of your department and a number of others. All these factors compete for his time and attention.

You should become aware, to the extent possible, of the conflicting and competing demands that your boss has to deal with. As this story illustrates, it is important to get a sense of your boss's priorities. Don Sluyter was in charge of customer complaints at a manufacturing plant. His immediate boss was also responsible for sales, service, merchandising, and purchasing. Sluyter was having trouble getting the service department to process repairs faster; the service head claimed to be following the boss's established procedures. Sluyter wisely called a meeting and asked the boss to spell out his priorities. He then discovered that reducing service time from sixty to thirty days would require a capital investment of nearly a million dollars and so much overtime it would cause trouble with the union and wipe out any profit that might be gained from the reduced service time.

Bosses usually have bosses. The person above your boss on the ladder may have a big influence on you, for he has a big impact on your boss's decisions as well as his emotions. If, for example, you think your boss is being unreasonable, consider the very real possibility that *his* boss is being unreasonable, and that you are only the recipient of a policy your boss can do little about. If your boss seems irritable, it may have nothing to do with you. You may only be a convenient scapegoat for his anger; the real target may be his boss, whom he cannot take it out on without dire consequences. Your own problems should make you sympathetic to the ones your boss may be having with his superiors.

Does your boss seem reluctant to launch a new project that you are eager to get off the ground? I hear that complaint all the time. Before you start retyping your résumé, consider the differences between the boss's political situation and your own. If the project doesn't succeed, you will have learned from the experience. Your boss, on the other hand, may lose his job. Or, if he is sole owner of the company, his shirt.

Consider the case of Jane Rachel. Her boss was president of a large company, which was one of many in a huge conglomerate. At her boss's request, Jane initiated and supervised a major cost-cutting research project. The study determined that building a plant in Mexico would lower costs significantly and increase profits. Jane was anxious to get the project off the ground. It would be, she knew, a feather in her cap. She sold her boss on the move to Mexico, and he promised to bring it up to the executive committee of the parent firm.

Her boss made the presentation. When he returned to the company's offices, he announced that the move to Mexico wouldn't be made. No one, least of all Jane, knew why. Later, at a cocktail party, the president told me what had happened. He had defended the move to the parent company, but the chief executive officer, after listening to the plan, had said: "Okay, you can go ahead and build the plant . . . as long as you're willing to bet your job on it."

Bosses may make more money, but they also take bigger risks.

My father used to tell me something that I've always remembered, and have always found accurate: "It doesn't take much of anything to *go* into business, but it takes an awful lot to *stay* in business." If you think your boss is stingy with raises, or penny-pinching when it comes to expenditures, you owe it to your boss, and yourself, to acquire some understanding of the company's financial picture. It just might be that a few dollars saved in each department could make the difference between profit and loss. Your boss's job, or his entire company if he owns it himself, may hinge on his showing black ink at the end of the year.

In addition to matters of capital, your boss has to be thinking about the future of the company, or of his department. He might have to be aware of social trends, economic indices, the activities of competitors, the changing demands of customers and suppliers, advertising techniques, the psychological and financial needs of his employees, the pressures of stockholders, and, increasingly, government regulations. Sometimes your needs may have to be compromised because of any or all of those variables. Your boss may not be as callous as you think—he has to make difficult and unpopular decisions.

Be aware of the general condition of your company, the industry you are in, and the overall economic picture. For example, in 1970, half of the investment firms in the United States went bankrupt or merged; 60 to 70 percent of the personnel in the industry moved on to other fields. Most executives in the investment field were living with the very real possibility that they would not make it to the end of the year. Personal fortunes and high salaries were at stake. In that volatile environment, an employee must approach his boss differently from the way he would if he were in a booming business. Your concerns would seem especially trivial at such a time, even if they are vital to you.

Learn as much as you can about the things your boss has to think about daily. Sit in on meetings as often as you can, even if it means making up for lost work time later. Read trade journals that can teach you what the industry is all about, even if doing so seems out of the range of your immediate needs. Find out what magazines and newsletters your boss subscribes to and read recent issues. Attend conventions and trade association meetings, at your own expense if necessary. Talk to your boss's peers, and his or her assistant. By picking up as much inside information as you can, you will not only be able to make a favorable impression on your boss—who will almost certainly admire your initiative—but you will make great strides in developing your competence as well as gaining empathy for the boss.

If possible, put yourself in your boss's place. Andrea Hornbrook is a secretary at a small company in California that sells hot tubs. She noticed that her boss and his salesmen occasionally exhibited their products at county fairs. With the approach of a fair, things at the office got hectic. The boss grew nervous, irritable, worried. Because Andrea was in the most vulnerable position in the office, working closely with the boss, she bore the brunt of it. She took it personally, until she noticed the connection with the fairs. So, she volunteered to help out at the next fair on her own time. She didn't contribute that much to the success of the exhibit, but when it was over, she understood why her boss was hassled by each approaching fair: eighteen-hour days, hundreds of sales presentations, big expenditures, and fierce competition.

Your manager is, in part, a trained professional with a functional knowledge of his field—marketing, engineering, economics, manufacturing, whatever. But he is also an artist, or at least he should be, for he has to work with a multitude of raw materials, both abstract and concrete, and fuse them into a working system of schedules, goals, controls, services, data, paperwork, programs, policies, and plans, most of which involve that most unpredictable of items—human beings.

Your boss has to organize. He is responsible, most likely, for the division of labor within your department or organization. He has to organize a system of communications, a definition of responsibilities, and a delegation of authority that is both clear-cut and adaptable enough to meet unexpected demands.

Your boss has to coordinate all the people involved in your operation. In many cases, that means a large number of persons with overlapping and conflicting needs, demands, and priorities. He has to be sure that the channels of communication allow for a free flow of ideas and information. The various specialists involved in creating the product, performing the service, have to be integrated in a smooth, cost-effective way.

Your boss, in order to motivate the people who work for him, must identify their needs, skills, and talents. He has to provide a structure within which people can be both satisfied and productive. He has to know how to reward, select, train, counsel, and evaluate his employees. And he needs to deal with the effects of poor motivation—grievances, absenteeism, turnovers, and conflicts. He has to do all this within budgetary constraints, and in accord with company policies.

Your boss has to plan. He needs either to establish goals or to interpret the goals set by those above him. He needs to communicate these policies to his staff and establish timetables and programs to achieve them.

Your boss must be prepared to abandon a course of action, shift gears, hire new people, make new rules, change priorities, establish new policies, devise new systems, set new standards—all based on constant feedback from a variety of people above him, next to him, and below him. Add the fact that he has bosses and customers and subordinates and stockholders and maybe even government regulators pressuring him continuously, and it's easy to see that bosses pay a tremendous price for success.

Obtaining an objective picture of what your boss's work is like will help you understand why he does the things he does and put you in a better position to be of value of him. That's the key ingredient in your working relationship.

Quirks and Foibles

Frank Kaufman had been a liquor salesman most of his life. Now retired, he moved to California and worked in sales part time for a nearby winery. One day, he was in the office of the president, who was giving Kaufman some sales tips. Kaufman reached for a piece of paper on which to take notes. He had taken a piece of expensive, gold-embossed stationery that the president used only for special correspondence to customers and suppliers. The boss asked Kaufman never to waste the stationery.

Kaufman was so put off by what he perceived as petty stinginess that he quit. "I can't work for cheapskates," he later told me. "I've had enough of them."

The stationery was one of the boss's peculiarities. It had taken him many years to turn the winery into a profitable venture. During the lean times, when he could barely afford stationery, he acquired thrifty habits that he still maintained. His employees had learned to live with the boss's idiosyncrasies, but Kaufman couldn't handle them. He closed the door on an arrangement that had already proven to be lucrative.

Earlier, we spoke of the need to know what your boss does. It is equally important to know who he is. Before we go on to the traits that make one boss different from another, let's first discuss some of the characteristics that they tend to have in common.

Many bosses feel they have to present a certain image to the world. They try to appear to be made of steel, competent and emotionally detached, cool in a crisis, objective, rational, and above the concerns that plague most people. The truth is that your boss is as human as anyone else. He or she has emotions and feelings, petty whims and personality quirks, and quite human needs.

One of those needs, in many cases, is to appear the very image of the textbook manager. He might like to portray each decision as a rational one, based on sound judgment and flawless knowledge. To a degree, that is accurate. But only to a degree. The best managers are those who skillfully combine solid rational thinking with intuition. The exceptional ones work from the gut level, playing their hunches with such uncanny skill that you would think they were wizards. Several years ago, *New Realities Magazine* (P.O. Box 26289, San Francisco, Calif. 94126) did a series of articles about major business leaders who relied on intuition to make decisions that seemed contrary to sound business judgment. The leaders often would not tell their employers or board members how much they relied on their intuition. Because of continuing interest in the subject, *New Realities* is currently working on an update on this very important subject.

In that a good business leader works as much with intuition as he does with logic, he is just like a good scientist or artist. But for a variety of reasons, intuition is often looked on with cynicism, and so the intuitive boss will try to appear logical and rational. He will back up his decisions with facts and figures, and he will explain them in a perfectly logical way. In many cases, though, the decisive insight or crucial choice came from the gut. Don't try to understand your boss in purely logical terms.

Similarly, bosses want people to think that they are in complete control at all times. You will seldom see the boss flustered, confused, or unsure of himself. That's not because he is never flustered, confused, or unsure of himself, but because he doesn't show it in the presence of his subordinates. It can be lonely at the top. Bosses are often cut off from emotional support; they have few peers with whom they can let their hair down.

Bosses always want to know what's going on. They feel as if everyone expects them to have all the answers. When they don't have all the answers, they'll sometimes act as if they do. The truth is, bosses are often enmeshed in such complex situations that they don't know many of the factors involved. Their range of concern is far too broad to be well informed on every count. That is one of the reasons you are there. Bosses look to subordinates for information. They know less than you think they do about some things, but more than you think they do about others. No boss has *all* the final answers.

That is especially true about you and your job, by the way. Particularly in large organizations, bosses are not always clear on what you are doing; they often have a mistaken notion of your assignment, your instructions, and your actual day-to-day responsibilities. And they are often unaware of the problems and complications your work involves. When evaluation time comes around, you might be sorry you didn't educate your boss earlier.

You should, in fact, find ways to educate your boss on all matters about which his information is limited. Keep in mind that, because of his isolated position, the boss is often cut off from the best sources of information—parties, water-cooler gossip, conversations overheard on the elevator, the grapevine, etc. Keep the boss up to date and do it subtly.

Most bosses thrive on control and predictability; uncertainty makes them feel less powerful. But life in the modern world is marked by accelerating change and unpredictability. Even the most powerful people are often not in control of the events that influence them. Because they have far less certainty than they would like, bosses try to keep events and people within their range of direct influence—such as their subordinates—as predictable as possible.

Try not to surprise your boss. Learn to break news by minimizing the shock value. If you plan anything new, give him time to adjust gradually. Whenever possible, protect him from surprises from outside; if you know a problem is cropping up, let your boss know as early as possible, so that he can be well prepared.

Another need some bosses have is for power. Power can be defined as the ability to influence and direct people and events. Dr. Mark Silber, an internationally renowned consultant and seminar leader who has conducted programs on management effectiveness in more than a dozen countries, points out that power is not based exclusively on organizational authority. "It is a skill," says Silber, "an art that can be acquired and cultivated for both ethical and effective use."

Silber explains that there are two components to power in the organizational world: "the potency to project one's wills, wishes, and wants; and positioning oneself to influence the destiny of the decisions."

When appropriately channeled, power can work to everyone's advantage. Problems arise when a person is too immature to direct power toward the fulfillment of anything other than self-centered interests.

Many effective bosses have a strong need for power. The difference is the way it is directed. "Good managers," writes noted psychologist David C. McClelland, "are not motivated by a need for personal aggrandizement, or by a need to get along with subordinates, but rather by a need to influence others' behavior for the good of the whole organization."

Your job is to recognize the boss's need for power and help him or her channel it in a way that is to your and the company's advantage.

The boss with strong power needs has to feel in charge of everything: shaping, focusing, and directing others. As an aware subordinate, you should assist in that process. Help to see that projects carry the boss's stamp and that his own personality is expressed in them. Let other people know that the boss is creating and organizing; let the boss know that he is successfully fashioning the work and motivating the people. In that way, he will get job satisfaction, and ultimately give his people more freedom.

If you have strong power needs of your own, you and your boss might conflict. The best thing you can do is hold your own power needs in check until you are in a position to use power effectively. One of the best ways to learn how to use power is to serve someone who also has high power needs. Play a supportive role to a powerful boss and be aware of the things that work well for him and for yourself. Someday, you might be in charge of subordinates like yourself who have high power needs. Play on your boss's team as a way of preparing yourself to run your own show later on.

Personality Traits

Many people believe that the average American executive is self-assured and emotionally secure. Many average American executives think so too. Not so. In fact, one major reason for the low level of trust and cooperation in organizations is the low level of self-esteem among executives.

Because showing emotion hasn't been acceptable in the business world, executives try to convey an impervious image—Clint Eastwood in pinstripes. But the increase in alcoholism, drug abuse, depression, and other disorders related to stress bears witness to the potentially fragile emotions of the executive psyche. A boss may appear to be steel-nerved, yet he or she may be suppressing emotions that are manifested in other ways.

It is crucial for subordinates to realize that bosses are not invincible; they relate to the world through feelings, just as everyone else does. Try to respect their needs, just as you would like to have your own needs respected.

An unaware subordinate might inadvertently hurt the boss's feelings by, say, going over the boss's head with an idea or a grievance, pointing out one of the boss's mistakes in front of other people, or making the boss feel as if he or she were a has-been, not needed by the bright young star who might one day pass the boss by. Treat your boss's feelings with care, and try to understand them.

The Need to Be Liked

The boss who manages for popularity usually has employees who feel ambivalent about their work, who are unsure of where they stand or even what they are supposed to do. David McClelland found that such a boss "tends to have subordinates who feel that they have very little personal responsibility, that organizational procedures are not clear and that they have little pride in their work group."

The chances of being a successful manager when your primary need is to be liked are very slim indeed. No matter what people may say to the contrary, trust and respect are far more important than popularity. You cannot lead merely by being liked.

Tony Blaire started a real estate complex with three other executives. He and Frank O'Keefe had sales backgrounds, and so they shared the responsibilities of sales management. Tony was the tough one. He was demanding, and as a result not very popular; but he was listened to. Frank, on the other hand, was well liked, but his people were not getting results. Tony couldn't figure out why. Then one night at a national sales conference, he noticed, as he headed for bed after a late meeting, that his partner was playing cards with some of his new representatives. Next day, they were not as alert as they should have been. That afternoon the new reps were on the golf course with Frank while Tony worked with another group.

Frank O'Keefe is among Tony's dearest friends. But Tony would never consider another business venture with Frank if it meant that Frank had to manage people. He needed to be liked too much, and as a result failed in a series of management jobs.

If your boss has a strong need to be liked, show her that respect and results are more important than being popular. You might say something like: "I know you have to make a difficult and possibly unpopular decision. But it's in the best interest of the group, and it will get the job done." You might even volunteer to announce the decision for her. Compare decisions that work and decisions that don't work to demonstrate that the boss who vacillates because of fear of being disliked always ends up hurting the very people he or she is trying to help. Show her the problems created by her need for popularity, and show her that the group functions better when she is willing to risk being disliked or misunderstood if necessary: "You're a considerate person, and we all appreciate everything you do for us. But I just want you to know there are some instances when I think we would all benefit if you could be stronger and clearer."

The Need to Be Disliked

There are people who look in the mirror every morning and say: "You're the meanest! You'll show them who's boss around here." They are abrasive. They cut people down. Like drill sergeants, they make people toe the line, partly because they believe that otherwise subordinates would be lazy and irresponsible, but mainly because they need to prove constantly how mean they are. The more their people cower and tremble in their presence, the more they feel like they're in charge.

I have seen new bosses come into a company and immediately start firing people. "I'm the boss," their actions convey, "and if you don't shape up, I'll have your head." About the worst display of this I have seen was the boss whose first act in a new job—before he even met the people he was going to manage—was to have a maintenance man remove the doors to everyone's offices.

The need to be disliked can be as crippling as the need to be liked. Each in its own way is a colossal handicap; each can anger subordinates and keep productivity down. Certainly, bosses have to be tough; they need to be able to make unpopular decisions when necessary. But there is a big difference between being *willing* to risk being disliked and *needing* to be disliked. The former is imperative for success; the latter is destructive. There is also a big difference between being clear, tough, and decisive, and being ruthless.

Bosses who need to be disliked do not end up with strong, competent people, but with timid subordinates whom they have to beat and whip in order to get anything done—if the subordinates stick around, that is. And the bosses love every crack of the whip. They need to keep all the responsibility for what goes on, and the way they treat their people ensures that they will have every excuse to keep that responsibility. Their subordinates become so afraid they repress all initiative. They are only too happy to let all the weight fall on someone else's shoulders while they stay out of the boss's range. Then the boss will point to their behavior and say: "They're a bunch of weak-kneed cowards and incompetents. I have to take charge of everything and threaten them to get a decent day's work out of them." As a result, of course, the boss is hated and feared, and the cycle of resistance-resentment-revenge is perpetuated.

The tactics may work for a while. The boss may make spectacular progress when he first takes over. But it won't be long before the sabotage begins. In the long run, he will have no allies; in fact, he will have no staff, except the timid ones who stick around. And when the boss leaves, or is out sick, no one will be ready to step into his shoes.

The best way to deal with a boss with a strong need to be disliked is to ignore his rages and to catch him doing something good. The first time the boss does something likable, thank him; let him know that it helps you get the job done. Constant reinforcement, properly administered, can gradually take the chip off his shoulder. However, bosses with a *deep* inner need to be disliked are among the most difficult to deal with. If, over time, catching him doing something good doesn't work, you might be better off leaving than remaining in an atmosphere of continual anxiety. Remember, as a subordinate you are not there to act as a psychiatrist, nor are you there to be a target for your boss's inner rage. His *real* target is something within the boss himself.

The Need to Be Needed

Many bosses need to feel valuable. They need to be needed. They also need employees who are self-sufficient, capable of being left alone to do the job.

Be alert to the need to be needed because it is widespread. Let your boss have ths satisfaction of proving he can handle certain things as well as or better than anyone else in the department. He may have put some of his hard-earned skills on the back shelf when he became an executive. Many a manager is placed in that position because of excellence in some technical area—engineering, research, sales, or whatever—that may have little to do with the skills needed by a manager. That phenomenon came to be known as the Peter Principle, which states that people rise to the level of their own incompetence. I don't buy it. The Peter Principle is often used to explain away problems between bosses and subordinates. It can be used as an excuse to avoid responsibility. I propose to replace it with the Hegarty Leadership Heresy: "People rise to the level of the boss's and their own level of ignorance." The problem is one of awareness. It often begins when one person promotes another without knowing how to assess whether that person is suited and/or trained for the new job. Handled correctly, letting your boss feel needed will win for you greater autonomy. Mishandled, it will lead to greater interference in your work.

Does your boss get upset if he doesn't hear from you several times a day? Does he need a constant flood of memos? Does he call the office every day when on vacation? Does he delegate only trivial tasks? Does he take over whenever there's a crisis? If so, he probably has a strong need to be needed. The number of crises is often the giveaway. Show me a boss who excels at putting out fires and I'll show you a pyromaniac.

Some bosses have an insatiable need to be needed. They need to feel important even more than they need to succeed. These people create havoc wherever they go, and their subordinates never learn to cultivate leadership talents. Until I learned what management is all about, I was that type of boss. I had twenty-three sales managers throughout the country, and I wouldn't let them do anything without clearing it with me. I wanted to know who they were calling on, what they were saying, and everything else they did. Whenever possible, I got myself involved in the action.

Sometimes I would create a crisis so that I could fly in like Superman and save the day. Once I got a call from my New York executive who told me he had set up an important meeting with some Wall Street people for the following Wednesday at 8:30 A.M. "I'll go with you," I said.

I made that commitment in full knowledge that the night before I would be in Los Angeles at a sales conference. I flew all night on the "red-eye special" to New York. Bleary-eyed and groggy, I arrived at dawn, checked into an airport hotel for a quick shower and a change of clothes, and dashed to Wall Street just in time to make a grand entrance.

Things worked out well enough at that meeting; but in retrospect I am sure my subordinate would have handled it just fine without me—if I'd let him and if I'd prepared him properly. Further, the experience would have helped him handle meetings I couldn't attend. Indeed, although the company succeeded, I often wonder how much better it, and the people in it, would have fared had I allowed my subordinates to grow and learn instead of acting on my need to be needed.

If your boss needs to be needed, take away as many responsibilities as you can, and prove to him he is a good manager for allowing you to do it. Every time circumstances prevent him from doing something all by himself, let him know how well things went, how much you learned from being allowed to do it yourself, and that you'll look forward to doing it again. Show him the difference between directing a symphony orchestra and trying to be a one-man band. Show him the folly of trying to be the best worker in the group when he is being paid to lead and motivate others. Show him how to measure himself and others by results only.

If your boss does something like I did when I flew to New York to run the meeting myself, schedule a second meeting almost as important as the first. Thank him for coming all the way from Los Angeles just for the meeting and then say: "Now you're going to see how well *I* can do. We have another meeting today." It is a bold move, but you must be bold with a boss like that. Soften the blow by saying: "I learned a lot working with you and watching you run meetings. I can handle it myself now. Let me earn more of your trust by running this meeting."

For your boss's sake, expand his awareness. The need to be needed can lead to mental and physical illness. "One of the symptoms of approaching nervous breakdown," wrote the philosopher Bertrand Russell, "is the belief that one's work is terribly important. If I were a medical man, I should prescribe a holiday to any patient who considered his work important."

What Makes Your Boss Unique?

A wise subordinate will look for anything relevant about his or her boss that will help in the process of gaining empathy. Where did your boss grow up? Where did he go to school? What did he major in at college? Was he in the service? Was he an athlete at school? Is he married? Does his wife have a career outside the home? Do they have children? How old are they?

Such information can teach you a lot about the person you work for. Wouldn't it change your perception of your boss if you found out he was an immigrant's son who had to support his parents while going to school at night? Wouldn't it change your image if you discovered he lost his only son in Vietnam? Wouldn't it alter your awareness to find out your boss grew up with a silver spoon, went to the best schools, and got his position because of his father's connections?

What clubs does the boss belong to? What are his outside interests, hobbies, charities? What does he do for recreation? Where does he take his vacations? What books does he read? What music does he listen to? What shows does he see? Does he spend a lot of time with his family?

What is his personal life like? Is he under outside pressure? Is he having problems with his kids? Understand as much as possible; but don't pry or spy, just be alert and aware. The more you know, the better you will understand how to deal with your boss in a way that both of you will value.

It is well known that executives take their problems to the office as much as they take their business home. Becoming aware of the boss's private concerns can help you understand him better, particularly if he suddenly breaks from his usual patterns. Suppose he began losing his temper over trifles. If you discovered that his teenaged son had been arrested for possession of cocaine, you would certainly change your evaluation of the boss's reversal. By changing your awareness, you would change the way you respond to him.

What has your boss's business life been like? How long has he been with the company? What did he do prior to joining the firm? Did he have jobs unrelated to the present one? Has he been on a straight career track, or has he done a variety of things? Was his career marked by ups and downs? Has he always worked for large companies, or did he once run his own business?

What is your boss's standing within the organization? Is he on the way up, in line for bigger responsibilities? Is he aggressively seeking promotion? If so, he will want you to play a certain role. It might be worth your while to sacrifice some of your own independence, perhaps some of the credit, in order to advance yourself.

Is the boss on the slide? Is he under fire from above? Is upper management losing faith in him? If so, your strategy will be different. You won't want to go down with a sinking ship, but you don't have to be disloyal either.

Perhaps the boss is going neither up nor down. Maybe he is living out his contract, looking forward either to a new job or retirement. If so, you have to be supportive, but you also have to make yourself known to powerful people outside your immediate department. You may want to use your boss as a coach; people in that position are frequently willing to delegate responsibility, to teach, and to let you take risks that they would not permit if their career advancement was on the line.

Find out, in addition, what particular pressures your boss faces. What are his deadlines, his conflicts? Who is on his back? Who is competing with him? Who are his allies, his foes? Even if you don't care to get involved yourself, you will understand your boss better if you learn as much as you can about the politics of the company. Who is in and who is out? What are the opposing camps and where does your boss sit? Is anyone after his job? Is he after someone else's?

How does your boss react to stress? Does he drink heavily at lunch every time he has a tough morning? Does he blow his stack when things go wrong, or does he keep it inside? When under pressure, does he bury himself in his work, staying all night and coming in on weekends, or does he escape by scheduling a trip to the branch office in Hawaii? Does he play it safe under pressure, or take bold steps to resolve the crisis? Does he take tranquilizers or smoke excessively? Does he become obsessive, worrying over trivia, or repeating himself at meetings? Does he miss appointments? Does he think everyone is out to get him? Does he brood?

Knowing how your boss responds to stress does several things for you. First, you will be able to recognize the signs of severe stress, and as a result know when to approach him and when to leave him alone. Second, you can help alleviate the strain by taking on some of the burdens, or diverting troublesome people. Third, you will have a clearer idea of when his behavior is actually directed at you and when he is misdirecting his anxiety. Fourth, you can eventually learn what upsets and annoys him, and defuse problems before they arise.

Analyze your boss's work style. Become aware of the dozens of little quirks that make your boss unique. Keep your eyes open and look for patterns in your boss's behavior. Here are some examples of things to look for:

Is your boss a morning or an afternoon person? Some people gather energy as the day progresses, while others start off with a bang and come to a gradual halt by five o'clock. Others again are a mixed bag, perhaps starting off strongly, slumping by late morning and reviving after lunch, only to slide to a dull finish. There are, of course, endless variations that are influenced by the characteristics of the particular business. If you work in a restaurant that does a heavy lunchtime business, for example, your boss's energy and disposition will probably change as noon approaches. If you work in a TV studio and your boss begins each day with a production meeting, his energy level might vary according to what happened in the meeting.

The point is this. Become alert to your boss's personal rhythm, and determine the best times to deal with her. When is she most amenable to suggestions? When is it best to drop bad news on her? If, for example, your boss is a morning person, you might suggest having breakfast together when you have something important to discuss. Catch her at her best, before she gets bogged down with work or starts to feel the pressure.

Naturally, there are weekly, monthly, and annual rhythms just as there are daily ones. These depend more on circumstance than personal metabolism. Look for patterns and use them to advantage. Many bosses come under great pressure at certain times of year. In some companies, for example, tax time is a horror; it may not be the best time to ask for a raise, or to present a study that requires careful reading.

Amy Rector was an editor at a large publishing house. Enthusiastic about a manuscript, she wanted to purchase the rights, but couldn't without consulting the editor-in-chief. She paid no attention to timing. It was December, and the executives were up to their necks with the Christmas season. Amy pressured the editor-in-chief into reading the manuscript. To appease her, he gave it a cursory reading, but turned it down. Not satisfied, Amy protested, became a pest, lost respect, and lost the manuscript to another publisher. Had she waited two weeks, she might have lost the manuscript anyway, but she would have kept her boss's respect.

Frequently, bosses have to file reports at regular intervals. Suppose, for example, your boss has a report due on the first of each month. If you watch closely, you will see how he is affected by that obligation. He might become increasingly tense beginning on the twentieth of each month, and reach a peak just before the deadline. If so, you might want to stay away from his desk from the twentieth on, postponing matters that require the boss's attention.

See how he responds in the aftermath of the deadline. Does he recover quickly? If so, he may be ripe for a new idea or an unusual request on the second or third of every month. On the other hand, he may take a long time to unwind from the pressure, or he might take a full week to wipe his desk clean of work that piled up while he was working on the report. In that case, save your important discussions until after the eighth of the month. These are only some examples of the importance of your boss's rhythms. Be alert to nonwork influences too. What is he doing this weekend? Is he taking a packed briefcase home? Is he driving his kids to college? The boss's actions on Monday morning are often based on how he spent the weekend. Do you try to catch him first thing on Monday, or do you wait until Wednesday?

An acquaintance of mine, Robert Bitonte, wanted to launch a big project that, if successful, would have given him greater visibility and just the right ammunition for the raise he planned to ask for. It was July, and Bitonte, being sensitive about how best to work with his boss, decided to wait until September to propose the project. Why? His boss had three children who spent most of the year in another city with their mother from whom the boss was divorced. He loved his kids, and he looked forward to their infrequent visits. That summer, Bitonte knew, the boss would be taking long weekends and leaving the office early. While he would be in a pleasant, receptive mood, he would not be able to provide the concerted effort and careful thought needed to make the project a success.

Bitonte was wise to wait. In another instance, however, summer vacation might have been the perfect time to inaugurate a project, especially if he wanted to take charge himself. With his kids around, the boss would probably have been more amenable to delegating responsibility.

Does your boss like to see things in writing or talk about them? Is he a visual person or a verbal person? If he likes to talk, practice your delivery, and determine the best place to do your talking. Then see to it that you are not interrupted. If he prefers to read reports before discussing, be sure you prepare thorough, well-documented reports. Do your homework, having someone edit it for you, if necessary. Is he visually oriented? Prepare a flip chart or slide presentation.

Does your boss prefer to put his attention on only one thing at a time, or is he the type who likes to have several things going at once? Knowing this can help you adapt to his style.

Are some situations easier for him to handle than others? Do some things drive him up the wall? My observation of Richard Nixon, for example, was that he was the type of chief executive who could deal effectively with large-scale international issues. When it came to strategic matters involving the Soviet Union and China, he was decisive and authoritative. But when he had to deal with problems that related to Nixon, the person, such as criticism by the press, or Watergate, he caved in.

What does your boss hate doing? What are his vulnerabilities? Does he turn purple when he has to deal with a union? Does he chafe at the prospect of a trip to headquarters in Cincinnati? Does he have fits when he has to speak at a conference? How can you adapt to, and perhaps alleviate, some of those irritants?

What are your boss's strengths and weaknesses? Is he, for example, big on substance but short on style? Or is he the essence of charisma but lacking in knowledge and expertise? Is he great with numbers and things but uneasy with people? Is he great when things are going smoothly but useless in a crisis? Or is he only turned on when his back is to the wall? Is he great with abstract ideas but weak on details? Or is he the administrative type, flawless with rules, procedures, and systems but unable to grasp the "big picture"?

In whatever way you can, understand and adapt to your boss's approach. Complement his strengths, compensate for his weaknesses. Deal with him in a way that creates a feeling of harmony without sacrificing your individual goals and needs.

Your evaluation and examination will dramatically increase your ability to manage your boss. With the exception of understanding yourself, nothing is more important. When the boss's actions are a mystery, there is the tendency to make assumptions about what is going on—that he is out to get you, perhaps, or that you are doing something wrong. Neither may be true. Demystifying the boss gives you an objective way of assessing the situation and adjusting to the reality. It takes away the sense of powerlessness that comes from trying to deal with the unknown.

Even if you can't change your boss, the insight will help you manage yourself in relation to your boss. You will emerge from your evaluation with a more accurate and empathetic view. If you had a tendency to think of the boss as invincible and omnipotent, he will no doubt become more of a mortal once you understand him better. If you thought he was unfair or incompetent, you will probably discover that he is more equitable and more proficient than you imagined. In other words, your boss will probably emerge as a rounded human being—a decent, well-intentioned person, trying to get things done as well as he can under difficult conditions, and responding to personal and professional pressures in his own unique way. His shortcomings are more than likely the products of erroneous thinking and learned responses, a question of awareness rather than innate character. Change his awareness and you change his needs; when his needs change his actions will change.

If, for example, he appears not to trust anyone, distrust is probably something he learned early in his career. He may have been "taught" that people are lazy and deceitful. As long as he accepts these acquired prejudices, he will need to mistrust and manipulate. He may never have learned how to communicate trust. Even anger and ruthlessness are learned responses—he was probably taught by his own bosses that managers are supposed to behave that way.

In most cases, your evaluation of your boss will enable you to adopt strategies to raise his awareness. While doing so, your job is to adapt as well as you can to his whims and idiosyncrasies without sacrificing your integrity or your goals. Accept his faults, if you can, and respect his virtues. Evaluate—do not value-judge.

Never become complacent about your understanding of your boss. Never take it for granted that you know as much about him as you should. Once you shut down your antennae, you are in big trouble. Be observant at all times. And if you ever find it hard on a given occasion to decide exactly how to evaluate your boss's actions, lean in a positive direction. Always give him the benefit of the doubt. You run far less risk by giving him more credit than he deserves than by giving him less. *To underestimate your boss could be catastrophic, and is never in your best interests.*

In the great majority of situations, acquiring a deep understanding of your boss will help you establish a better working relationship. But some differences between people are beyond the power of understanding. You may adjust but not happily. Indeed, your investigation may convince you that you have no future working with your boss. If, for example, you are a minority group member, and you find out that your boss is a bigoted person who hired you only because of government regulations, you might be better off elsewhere. If you absolutely can't stand muzak and your boss insists on piping it into your office, you might have to choose between quitting and a nervous breakdown. If your boss demands frequent overtime and you have kids waiting at home to be fed, your conflict may be impossible to reconcile.

Most differences, however, can be worked out—and even managed to advantage—if you are resourceful and if you understand yourself and your boss. David Terrell wanted very much to excel in his new position. His boss was convinced that the only way to succeed was to see clients in the evenings, and for a long time his successful employees had done it that way. David, however, had strong family values; it meant a great deal to him to spend as much time as possible at home. For a long while, he struggled with an inner conflict. When he was out at night, he felt he should be at home; when he stayed home, he wondered if he shouldn't be seeing clients.

Finally, David sat down and discussed it with his family. They agreed to get up one hour earlier, and to make each breakfast a special family event to replace some of their evenings. David agreed never to make an appointment on a Tuesday or Friday evening, reserving those for the family. Then he went to his boss and convinced him to go along with a plan to build up his daytime business, under the contingency that, if David's work declined, he would return to his previous pattern. He now went out in the evening only when necessary and it no longer caused him conflict.

He broke all sales records at the company.

There are hundreds of examples of differences in outlook, style, or personality that are beyond hope of reasonable adjustment. And there are just as many combinations that are custom-made. But the great majority of matchups between boss and subordinate are made neither in heaven nor hell. They are simply pairs of human beings—complex and imperfect—thrown together for the purpose of accomplishing certain goals. Your challenge is to understand all you can about your boss, assess your range of alternatives, and make intelligent choices that will enable you to manage the relationship to your mutual advantage. Again, do not pry or spy, but be alert to understanding as much as you can. Get what you want by helping your boss get what he wants.

4

Denominations of Leadership

"The goal of most leaders is to cause people to feel reverence for the leader. The goal of the exceptional leader is to cause people to feel reverence for themselves."

—C. J. HEGARTY

EXCEPTIONAL LEADERS create a permanent impact on the lives of the people they lead. Early in my business career, I worked for Warren Gregory, who was the most exceptional manager in a large firm with over 160 offices. It seemed that he could make no mistakes, that he had been blessed with a genius for handling people. I later discovered that he had not been born with a gift for management; he had paid a price to acquire his skills. In fact, his first attempt at management, after a distinguished sales career, had failed.

After less than a year in his first management position, he stepped down voluntarily and returned to sales. He devoted his free time to learning what it took to be a good manager. Eighteen months later, Gregory asked for and received a second opportunity. This time he set a new record for sales managers, and quickly moved up to become the most respected vice president of sales in the firm's history.

The story illustrates a powerful and hopeful truth: While some of the requirements of a good leader are innate, most of them must be learned. Anyone can become a better boss. Most of those who are inadequate do not have bad intentions, nor do they have hopeless personality deficiencies. They simply lack know-how, they have learned improper managerial habits, and they are operating under false assumptions about human beings and work.

Whether a person is a new boss or has spent many years in management positions, whether he has been a success or a failure, he can increase his leadership effectiveness significantly. There are a number of powerful and practical ideas that will help any manager move rapidly toward becoming an exceptional leader. An excellent how-to book is *Excellence in Leadership* by Frank Goble (Caroline House, 1978).

In this chapter, we describe four styles of operation that contrast sharply in both form and effectiveness. We also discuss some of the most common leadership weaknesses, and contrast them with the specific strengths that make for excellence. This chapter is important to the would-be manager of bosses for two reasons: First, you will understand your own boss better and therefore set accurate targets for improving your relationship. Second, you will become a better boss yourself; the more effectively you manage your own subordinates, the more leverage you will have with your boss.

Warren Gregory—who went from failure to success after learning how to manage—felt in retrospect that there was one major difference in how he approached his job the second time around. He expected his people to do well. He had discovered a very valuable truth: *The manager gets what the manager has a right to expect.* A manager who knows how to select, train, develop, and communicate with subordinates has earned the right to expect people to do well. His warranted high expectations represent the single most potent force in leading a troup to success. Managers without these crucial skills, but with high expectations, will get better results than if they did not have those expectations. But the person who has both the expectations and the skills makes a perfect mentor—he or she is able to develop the autonomy, competence, and self-esteem of subordinates.

The leaders described in this chapter differ from one another in skill and in what they expect of their subordinates. See if you can recognize some of your boss's traits, keeping in mind that few bosses will fit neatly into any single category. Most will display some combination of the qualities described.

TYPE ONE: The Drive Leader

Mr. Nails barges into the office of his subordinates. He pounds on a desk. "Sales were down last week," he bellows. "What the hell have you guys been doing? Don't I have one competent person on my staff? How many people do I have to fire before I get some results around here? You, Smith, I see you leaving early much too often. You're here to work, fella, and don't you forget it! Jackson's the only one around here who looks like he's working. The rest of you think you're at a country club. Well, from now on we're going to work a half-day schedule and I'll tell you which twelve hours you'll work. If you don't buckle down, you'll all be pounding the pavement!"

Nails leaves the room to a mixed reaction. Some of his people cower; they are scared and hop to the telephone immediately. But they are so nervous they risk offending their clients. Others, probably Smith included, snicker defiantly: "Screw you, Nails!" Others wait until Nails is out of earshot, then entertain their colleagues with vicious imitations of the boss. The frightened ones beg them to cut it out before they all get into trouble. Jackson, the hard worker, has mixed feelings. He is glad the boss singled him out, but he feels the others consider him a traitor, and he feels guilty because he knows that some of the others actually get better results than he does.

That business is in trouble, and the declining sales figures are only the tip of the iceberg. The cause is Mr. Nails, although he would be the last to admit it—perhaps even the last to know it.

Nails is a "drive" leader. He may be an honorable person, but on the job he acts like a classic tyrant. A one-man band, the drive leader likes to have total control. He lets it be known that he is boss. He leads by punishing mistakes, and is always looking for mistakes. He demands respect, but succeeds only in creating animosity.

There are many drive leaders in America, unfortunately. Most of them would be more at home in a Marine uniform than a business suit—and more useful as well. They're not all as outwardly belligerent as Mr. Nails. They may be people who believe that their way of doing things is the only way to get the job done. There are blatant drive leaders and others who are more subdued.

Subordinates of drive leaders don't try to excel; instead, they learn to survive. If they don't quit in fact, they quit in spirit. They learn to stay out of trouble and protect themselves.

I was once asked to do consulting work for a small company whose productivity was going down. In order to observe their operations objectively, I worked inside for a day as a laborer, which enabled me to observe all ten employees of a particular department. One young man, Josef, stood head and shoulders above the rest. His colleagues goofed around for half an hour before getting to work, and took frequent breaks throughout the day. Josef accomplished at least one third more than the others.

Unfortunately for both Josef and his boss, the boss was unaware of how to measure people by their results. Josef's boss was a drive leader, and drive leaders tend to be impressed by superficial displays of loyalty and devotion. They tend to make unusual, and often unnecessary, demands just to "separate the men from the boys." One of their favorites is to demand that people stay late and give up their days off. Nails was doing that when he praised Jackson, not on the basis of results but on the appearance of hard work. You may be surprised at how many employees are thought to be devoted workers when they are actually putting on a show, or staying overtime to correct errors they should not have made in the first place.

Josef's boss demanded overtime, even though he didn't pay for it. The other employees learned to deal with him in the classic manner—they pretended dedication, but got revenge by goofing off when they should have been working. Josef had more integrity. He also had a family with whom he liked to spend his evenings. He tried to reason with his boss: "If I stay until six thirty or seven, I get home too late to be with my kids. So, I come in early and I work hard so I can leave at quitting time."

But Josef's boss didn't know how to handle allowing him to leave before the others. As a result, he lost his best worker.

Drive leaders are themselves driven, usually by low self-esteem and a strong fear of failure. They believe that success comes from sweat and strain. They demand hard work of themselves and others. They often treat their own bosses with deference. They believe in loyalty and are often more impressed by outward displays of busyness than by results. If a drive leader were forced to acknowledge that a hardworking employee did not necessarily get results, he would find his entire approach to management in jeopardy. He would be forced to consider whether he too might be less competent than he thought.

Equating the appearance of work with effectiveness can reach ludicrous proportions, as with the printer who smeared his face with ink every day and always quickened his pace when the boss was around. The boss noticed the printer's apparent devotion and promoted him to shop foreman. But the other employees were aware of the ploy, and began to sabotage the printer's efforts. Ultimately, he was fired.

Many employees of drive leaders learn to work at the appearance of work, not work itself. The result is good for no one.

Here is another example of a drive leader. A woman in the marketing department of a copying machine company enters her boss's office with an urgent message: "I just discovered that our major competitor is introducing a special ninety-day campaign, featuring a substantial price reduction and an extension of their service contract. It'll put us at a big disadvantage. Their machine will cost nine hundred dollars less than ours and they're allowing an extra three hundred in service. That's a big difference, and they're about to launch a major ad campaign in all the newspapers."

The boss responds: "I'll be in your office in an hour with instructions for a new ad campaign. Tell all the sales people that I want them to get out there and call on their customers. They should tell them we're a better company, and good companies aren't built on ninety-day campaigns. Tell them to emphasize the quality of our machines and service. If they don't believe in our machines, they shouldn't be working here. We'll show them, even if we have to work all night to do it."

There you have a typical drive leader's response to a problem. You can see the belief that hard work is the answer, you can see the drill-sergeant mentality. You can also see that he took complete responsibility for the solution. Drive leaders, because of their erroneous approach to management, feel that they alone own the problems and they must be the ones to solve them. Theirs is the final and usually the only word. They think they must be able to do each subordinate's job better than the person doing it. Because they have learned never to say, "I don't know," or, "I made a mistake," they always come up with answers and then impose them on others. If things don't work out they will seldom take the blame.

Drive leaders are very uncomfortable delegating responsibility. The result is an imbalanced workload, in which the leader is overworked and the subordinates underchallenged. He issues commands, not responsibility. He treats people as expeditors who follow orders, and help put out fires by filling up buckets, while he points the way. Drive leaders typically hold onto outmoded ideas long after they are proven invalid. To change would be to acknowledge a mistake, and that is unthinkable to a drive leader. They suffer from the disease of having to be right.

Drive leaders frequently distort and pervert the true role of a boss. They get caught up in trivia, sometimes wasting time on such absurdities as the color of the carpet at the regional office. For example, the owner of an art gallery went through five assistants his first year. He would hire bright, intelligent people, and then turn them into little more than decoration. He insisted on being called in on any potential sale; he even typed his own letters.

Workers who are not given responsibility commensurate with their potential either quit or resign themselves to frustration. But how much of themselves will they invest in getting the job done? They bury their initiative, suppress their creativity, lose their motivation.

The typical drive leader believes people do what the leader *inspects*, not what he *expects*. He is unaware that the best approach is to let people inspect their own work and admit when they make mistakes. He trusts very few people and respects even fewer. He oversupervises, wasting his energy and that of the group. He whips and drives and exhorts—the only way, he believes, to get people to work. He manages through punishment, and the thought of acknowledging good work never occurs to him. "That's her job, isn't it? That's what she's paid for." Why compliment her for doing it? Instead, he looks for mistakes to punish, and he destroys self-esteem in the process.

Certainly there are times when punishment is called for. If an executive shows up for an important meeting inappropriately dressed, punish him. If a police captain finds a patrolman drinking on the job, he should punish him. But when a boss *focuses* on leading through punishment, using it as his only managerial tool, then trouble is bound to happen. A good manager knows how to correct a mistake without punishing the person who made it. He isolates the behavior from the individual, thus correcting it without threatening the subordinate's self-esteem. He will rarely criticize an employee in public.

If an employee repeats a particular mistake often, a wise manager will first ask himself some serious questions: How was the person trained? Why was he selected? Was he properly oriented to policies and priorities? Is he fully aware of our procedures and expectations?

But the drive leader does none of those things because he can't admit he might not know what to do. He is the kind of person who would keep a pencil handy while reading the Bible so he can make corrections as he reads.

Don't surrender to a drive leader. Remember the words of management expert Mark Silber: "Loyalty is not conformity." You can remain loyal to your boss and your organization while doing your job the way you think is most effective. But handle the boss with care. Never wait too long before finding out the limits. Evaluate him objectively, so you know whether he can be managed or whether you should look for a new boss. If your boss is tough and demanding, but fair, working for him can be productive and profitable. If he is ruthless and demeaning, what possible reason could there be to share his misery?

While the drive leader is upset by errors, he is even more threatened by disagreement. His meetings are one-way affairs in which he imposes his will. He does not allow suggestions; he dictates what is to be done and how to do it. Negotiation is prohibited: "Those who want to do it my way say, 'Aye.' Those who don't want to do it my way say, 'I quit.' " He creates clones who think just as he does. If he lays down a plan, and you suggest that step three can be eliminated, you're asking for trouble, although you may find step three eliminated, at the boss's bidding, somewhere down the road.

The subordinates of the drive leader get the message. The boss is threatened by disagreement? Okay, from now on I'll keep my mouth shut. I'll agree to do it his way, even if I know it can be done better; or I'll do it the right way, and not tell anyone.

The drive leader demands agreement, and he usually gets it. But he does not get what he should be after—acceptance and assistance. In fact, he often gets the opposite. People look for the first opportunity for sabotage.

I know an administrative assistant whose boss regularly asks her to stay after hours, who is berated for showing up five minutes late, and who is never allowed to extend her lunch break for a dental appointment or Christmas shopping or whatever. She learned that it is possible to put on a show of dedication for a drive leader—you just do what he says. If, however, she were evaluated for results instead of superficial appearances, she would prove to be inadequate. She is there when the boss wants her there. But is she really there? Does she extend herself? Will she take initiative? No. She engages in petty sabotage instead.

She makes personal long-distance calls on the company phone. She uses the mailroom for all her correspondence. She gossips about the boss. She is not quite as courteous as she could be. She likes doing little things to prove her boss wrong. Once a call came in for her boss while he was out. The caller sounded urgent: "I've got to make a big decision. We need to make an investment before the fiscal year ends. Could you rush me all the information on your offerings?"

The assistant is intelligent enough to know what she should have done: Send the package by express mail immediately, and call the client the next day to see if it arrived. Instead, she waited until the end of the day and sent it regular first class. The package did not arrive on time, and the man went to another company with his investment. She was never caught by the boss.

We come back to one of our basic maxims, one the drive leader does not buy: People live up to the level to which they are trusted, and down to the level to which they are mistrusted. Drive leaders trust no one. They do not really give the job to the employees, yet they expect them to get it done.

I am not advocating that work be a love-in. Bosses must be tough, clear, decisive, up front, and willing to risk being disliked and/or misunderstood. Few will succeed without those qualities. But some drive leaders are not just tough; they are ruthless. Learn to distinguish between a tough leader and a ruthless one. A tough leader will make unpopular decisions when he has to, he will make demands on people when he has to, but he won't disregard human factors. He'll let you know where you stand, he'll delegate authority along with responsibility, and establish clear, unambiguous priorities. Not so the ruthless leader. Here are two examples to illustrate the difference between a tough boss and a ruthless drive leader.

A meat-distributing company landed an important account with a state fair. Labor Day weekend was approaching, and in order to keep the account, the company had to meet the needs of the fair adequately. That meant working day and night before and during the holiday weekend. The ruthless drive leader stood before the group and informed them of what he expected. He left no room for argument. "If you want to keep your jobs, you'll be here," he said. "If you can't hack it, find another job."

A tough leader would have called the staff together at the earliest possible time and said something like this: "You all know that Labor Day is coming up. In order to meet our commitments, we're going to have to work like hell the week before and right through the weekend. I know it will be tough on you, and I expect you to do your best. To make up for the extra time, I'd like you each to arrange with your supervisors to have an extra five days off sometime in the next few months."

Here is the second example. The president of a large conglomerate had been with the company for over thirty years. He felt that one of the firm's new policies was a mistake and should be changed. The chairman of the board and chief executive officer was so threatened by the disagreement that he threw the whole company into shock. He called an emergency board meeting and forced the board to take sides. Of course, he had arranged it so that he had all the power. He had, in effect, said, "It's him or me." Since the board was not prepared to overhaul its leadership, it took the chairman's side. His vote won, the chairman then fired the dissenting president, who was, tragically, less than two years from retirement.

That is ruthless. A tough person would have gone to his opponent and said: "Look, you've been a good executive for over thirty years; you've contributed a lot, and now you're close to retirement. I have all the votes in my control. Obviously, the decision is going to go my way. Can we work it out between us, or do I have to fire you?"

Within a year, the chairman became a victim of his own ruthlessness. He went on a campaign to change the company's rules so he could stay in power after he reached retirement age. He was so offensive that the board fired him before he would have been required by company policy to retire.

A subordinate who doesn't care to take responsibility, who wants to be directed, to whom work is not an important personal expression—that person might find it appropriate to work for a drive leader on a long-term basis. If you are working for a drive leader en route to a higher-level job, it can be an extraordinary boost to your self-esteem to be able to handle working for him. If you can handle an overly critical, overly suspicious boss who is always looking for mistakes, it might expand your skills and abilities, and equip you to understand drive leaders you might work for later on, or who might work for you.

The person who can best survive with a drive leader is someone with high self-esteem, who realizes that he or she is not the real target of the boss's wrath. Someone who can separate his work, and the treatment of others, from his value as a person will not feel personally diminished or destroyed by the drive leader, even though he may not enjoy the treatment he receives. If you work for a ruthless boss, remember: "My work is what I do; a person is what I am. I am not the target of anyone's putdown."

How should you deal with a drive leader? You have to demonstrate—through actions, not words—that you're willing and able to take on part of the responsibility for getting things done. You may have to demonstrate that over and over again, but in most cases it will make a dramatic difference to how your boss handles you.

You must be prepared to stand up to a drive leader or lose your self-respect. But remember that saving face means even more to him than to most of us, so learn to negotiate without attacking him. Never correct him in front of others; negotiate only in private, and *never* when there is a crisis. If possible, enter your discussions armed with a lot of evidence to support your case. With a drive leader, those who fare best are those who are more interested in getting what they want than in getting revenge or having a day in court. If you value your freedom more than fairness, you have a better chance with a drive leader. Don't get even—get ahead!

Suppose your boss calls a meeting and says, "We've just been given orders to get out sixty thousand units by the end of the month. Here's what we're going to do . . ."

You disagree. You know that if the firm follows your boss's plan, you will spend too much money and possibly send out defective products. See the boss privately after the meeting: "You are responsible for the whole division, and I spend all my time looking after quality control. I realize there may be more to this than I can understand. But before you enforce the decision you made today, please take a look at these figures. Tell me if you think we can accomplish the goal better by adding this procedure."

Let's take another example. You work in a parking lot, and your job is to drive the customers' cars down from the upper floor of the garage. You drive conservatively, because there are sharp corners on the ramps. But your boss expects you to zip the cars in and out at top speed. One busy night, he exhorts you in front of your peers and the customers: "Get moving, you jerk. We've got people waiting!"

After the rush is over, go to your boss privately. "I like my job, Mr. Harsh, and I want to do it well. I've never had an accident. I treat the customers' cars as I would my own. If I'm slow, it's because I'm careful. I can't work well when I'm criticized, so I'll make a deal with you. I'll do my best to get the cars down faster, but I won't jeopardize safety. If I'm to work for you, please evaluate what I do and whether the customers are satisfied."

Always try to get the drive leader to identify the intended results of each assignment. Ask him to identify what he is trying to accomplish. If, for example, he says: "I want those financial staements in my hands by tonight," you might respond: "Fine. Before I begin, can you tell me what it is you want to accomplish by having them done tonight?"

Notice, you do not simply say, "Why?" or, "What for?" Such a response would sound belligerent or impertinent. Since you merely want clarification, you should sound polite and nonthreatening. Most bosses will explain their purpose, if there is one. If there is none, your boss might be the type who gives orders for the sake of giving orders.

Get the drive leader to evaluate you by results, not just activity. Remember the example of Josef in the meat company? He was outperforming everyone else, but his boss didn't evaluate by results. Josef might have kept track of his own work and compared it to that of his peers. He might have kept count of the number of cartons he unloaded in a day, or the number of units he completed. Then he would have been able to point to his results when meeting with the boss.

Many drive leaders have good intentions, and if handled carefully and communicated with clearly, they can be managed successfully.

TYPE TWO: The Default Leader

Dean Klemons accepted a job as a sales representative for a large company. The day he was hired, his boss, Mr. Null, painted a rosy picture of the position. "You're sure to earn big commissions," said Mr. Null. "It's one of the best territories in the region. Just go out there and do the job; you'll be fine."

Klemons felt fortunate indeed. He had a pleasant, amiable boss, who seemed to have enough confidence in him to grant him more autonomy than he had had on his previous job. He had the promise of high income and a choice territory. Before long, however, the bubble burst. At first, Klemons thought his difficulties were due to his lack of familiarity with the product line and the customers. Later, he began to wonder if he was doing the job the way it was meant to be done, or whether he had misunderstood his assignment. There was more to it than Mr. Null had indicated.

Klemons's attempts to get clarification from Mr. Null were unsuccessful. Null was inaccessible. When Klemons finally did corral him, Null was congenial, but Klemons felt he wasn't as precise as a boss should be. On returning to the field, Klemons didn't feel buffered. If anything, the job got more difficult.

At a sales meeting a few months later, Mr. Null seemed to ignore Klemons. A week later, the pink slip came. Poor sales figures was the reason cited.

Mr. Null was a "default" leader. Such bosses often create more animosity than even ruthless drive leaders do; they command less respect, and they are often more difficult to work for. A drive leader may hang over your shoulder, but at least you know where you stand. A default leader abandons you. A drive leader gives you feedback, even if it's primarily negative. With a default leader, you operate in a vacuum, which is the worst kind of criticism. In many cases, it is better for a subordinate to be punished than ignored.

Like Mr. Null, most default leaders pursue and seduce new employees, only to abandon them once the hiring is done. They paint a terribly attractive picture of a job, but they don't define the position properly or let the candidate know what will be expected of him.

A good boss would have told Klemons the truth before he gave him the job. "Mr. Klemons," he might have said, "you are applying for a challenging position. Are you aware that the responsibility for the territory will fall one hundred percent on your shoulders? Are you aware that there are a lot of tough competitors out there? Ninety days from now, you will have to show *X* product sales, with *Y* product mix and *Z* profit. Our sales reps do very well, but it's not an easy job. To do well, you're going to have to work hard and think hard. You'll have to keep on your toes and make things happen. Do you think you can handle it?"

Many things a default leader does on the day of firing should have been done on the day of hiring; then there would be a lot less firing. By giving a full disclosure of all aspects of the job, both negative and positive, the leader can take a major step toward creating the Three-C cycle. By painting a falsely rosy picture, the Three-R's will follow.

If the drive leader is guilty of keeping all the problems to himself, the default leader is guilty of making his subordinates deal with problems alone. He's not involved. He may provide goals and objectives, but they are often vague and ambiguous. He expects people to sink or swim on their own. Do the job or get out. He doesn't train, instruct, develop, support, or encourage. Like the drive leader, he punishes, but he does so in a more insidious manner. He will ostracize a person by ignoring him, or by excluding him from meetings, making offhanded insulting remarks, taking others to lunch, denying him some perquisite, or resorting to similar gambits. The drive leader overmanages; the default leader overlooks.

For the most part, however, the default leader's favorite form of punishment is dismissal. Because employees play guessing games about how well they are doing, dismissals often come as a complete shock. You don't know you're in trouble until you get your notice. The boss offers no performance criteria, no regular evaluations.

Default leaders are uncomfortable dealing with people. They are much more at home with numbers and things—predictable entities that do not challenge their awareness. As a result, they tend to treat people the way they would things—as instruments to be used and discarded. They think people can be replaced like paper cups. With their attention on the financial beat of the organization instead of the heartbeat, they ignore human factors such as communication. In truth, both financial and human factors are equally vital. In effect, the default leader doesn't lead at all.

What *does* he do? He plays with numbers and politics. He is reminiscent of the automobile company executive who was fond of pointing out that a particular car had exactly 4,179 parts, to which an engineer once responded, "I can't think of a more useless piece of information." When it comes to people, the default leader sees his main job as hiring and firing, and he does neither well.

Mr. Null hired Klemons and sent him out like a sheep among wolves. He offered no guidance, no feedback, and he never made clear his expectations. All he did was watch the figures. When the figures showed that Klemons was not doing well,

Null dropped the ax, never asking why Klemons did not do better, nor what he, as boss, might have done to help.

Bosses should evaluate by results; but Null, like most default leaders, had a distorted concept of what that means. They wait for large quantum measurements that indicate a person is not doing the job well. They *seem* to measure results, but what they are actually doing is playing accountant, not leader. Drive leaders look for superficial displays of dedication and hard work; default leaders look for superficial indices of accomplishment. Neither is adequate, particularly if the employee is not given clear objectives. Both types of leader will hold on to inept workers and fire workers who have potential.

Klemons should not have had to wait so long for feedback. Results should have been measured in small increments on an ongoing basis, right from the start. Even in sales, where it often takes quite a while for actual results, there are ways to provide feedback from day one. What are the steps that lead to sales? How can these be evaluated? Because they don't understand human beings, default leaders don't realize that saying nothing constructive is destructive. Nor do they realize there are ways to measure competence beyond those that can be gauged on a balance sheet.

Many default leaders have come up through the ranks, having achieved status working with technical matters or finances. They often haven't learned how to communicate, guide, or inspire. How do they last? In small entrepreneurial companies they tend to be exposed quickly, because in such organizations every department is visible. But in large organizations with complex political systems, you will find in charge of others a lot of default leaders who would be better off in solitary jobs. Yet they get by—either through politics, or by working for another default leader.

Because their bosses are not people-oriented, subordinates of default leaders often find themselves in jobs that are totally wrong for them. True, the default leader will delegate, but he does so inappropriately. He gives away jobs he should keep, and he keeps tasks he should give away. And he often delegates a job to the wrong person.

In some cases a minimum of supervision is the best way to manage. If, for example, you were put in charge of a group of mature, experienced, highly competent research scientists, who were used to working with each other, you would probably be wise to stay out of their way. Your boss, too, may be undermanaging for a good reason. But that is not default leadership. Even in the case of the research scientists, a leader is important. Competent professionals need feedback, clarity, and a human connection.

While the drive leader overwhelms, the default leader underwhelms. The form of resistance-resentment-revenge will differ in each case. Drive leaders tend to receive more overt resistance. People take advantage of them, often competing with one another to see who can get away with the most. They will lampoon and harpoon the boss. Default leaders, on the other hand, create a more subtle resistance. They sap the energy, motivation, and morale of the group. Since they are given no clear objectives and no reinforcement, employees can't possibly excel.

The default leader lets people sink or swim on their own. She does not stay away from her employees because she assumes they are capable and trustworthy. She does not necessarily have faith in them. She stays away either because she is uncomfortable with people or because she just doesn't realize that true autonomy is created through clarity, cooperation, and commitment. She figures that people will do what they will do, and as long as she fires those who don't measure up, she feels she is doing her job.

It should be noted that few leaders are either one hundred percent drive or one hundred percent default. Most frequently display some characteristics of each. An example of a drive/default combination would be someone who rarely contacts subordinates, but when he does will try to beat them into shape.

Someone who needs a lot of encouragement and feedback, who needs a personal relationship with his or her boss, who takes direction well and is not self-directed, will find it very difficult to work for a default leader. People who do not work well when left on their own should not work for a default leader.

On the other hand, a person with a high power need, who drives and accomplishes, and loves to take charge, would do all right under a default leader, as long as he can keep the boss clearly and continually posted on his results. You must provide constant feedback to fill the vacuum created by the default leader.

How can you deal with a default leader? It depends largely on whether you are dealing with an ignorant default leader or an intentional one. The latter knows what she is doing and chooses to do it, either because she believes it is the best way to work with people, or because she is just biding her time before retirement and has lost all real interest in her department. With her there is less hope than with the ignorant default leader, who means well but doesn't know how to manage any other way. She might have been groomed by another default leader, or has simply never had any experience relating to people.

Warren Gregory practiced ignorant default leadership during his first try at management. While learning to be a supersalesman, he had always been left pretty much on his own. Naturally, he assumed that all he had to do as a manager was hire the right people and let them go. In between sales management assignments, he discovered that he had an erroneous impression of the boss's role. He subsequently learned to make things happen with people and was eminently successful the second time.

You can change your default boss by adopting some of the strategies outlined in the next two chapters, particularly those like the "mutual support agreement" that bring him closer to the work scene.

When dealing with default leaders, it pays always to keep in mind that many of them are just not interested in human factors. They like to deal with things like costs, statistics, budgets, research findings, technology.

Pull the default leader into what you are doing; don't let him remain aloof. Show him results, even if he doesn't ask for them. Enhance his position and support him any way you can. Teach him not to fear the human touch. Many default leaders can open up—they simply have never learned how.

Here is an indirect way to teach your boss without letting her know you are doing so. Tell a story that seems to have nothing to do with her. "I had a big problem in my department recently. One of the administrative assistants was going through a divorce. She is usually very competent, but she became erratic. She took time off, she drank more, she was distracted. I came close to firing her, but decided to talk with her first. That's when I learned about the divorce. When she realized how much it was affecting her work, she really pulled herself together. I'm glad I had that opportunity to find out what was going on beneath the surface. It would have taken three or four weeks and several thousand dollars to replace her, not to mention the time it takes to break in someone new."

If the boss is at all receptive, such lessons will influence his or her approach. Notice that the statement did not dwell on the importance of compassion for a loyal employee. Instead, it brought in concrete elements such as the amount of money saved. That's what many default bosses relate to.

If your boss issues vague directives, don't waste time and energy running in the wrong direction. Instead, have the boss clarify exactly what he or she is trying to accomplish. This will get your boss thinking about results. If you start off trying to do something you're not sure about, you are almost certain to run into problems later on. The boss may balk, but it is important to find out early in the game just what working for her will be like. Inevitably, the day will come when you *must* ask for clarification. Learn to obtain that clarity at the outset.

If you handle it well, most bosses will not get too uncomfortable. But even if she does, discomfort is not the worst thing; it is certainly preferable to your becoming frustrated. Upset the boss mildly; make her just a tad nervous. Shake her gently into a response, but don't make her feel threatened. Never be afraid of causing mild discomfort—it can lead to growth.

The same holds true for inappropriate delegation of responsibility. If you have been given an assignment you feel would be better handled by someone else, don't balk or suggest that the boss made a mistake. Ask for clarification.

A salesperson at a clothing boutique was told by her boss to fire the cashier. That was not her job, but the boss was too uncomfortable to do it herself. "Ms. Kelly," said the salesperson, "I'm not sure I know how to go about this, since I've never fired anyone before. Can you help me?"

"Just go do it," said Ms. Kelly. "Don't worry about it." Wisely, the salesperson did not give in; doing so would have established the wrong precedent. "You know, Ms. Kelly," she persisted, "it will cost us a lot of money to recruit a new cashier and break him in. Maybe you can tell me exactly what it is about John you don't like, and instead of firing him, I'll help him do his job better."

By refusing to fire the cashier and reinvolving the boss in the problem, the salesperson rightly refused to accept improper delegation. The process of questioning improper assignments will make the boss more aware of what she is doing, and less likely to do it in the future.

To manage a default leader, find creative ways to involve him in your job. Draw him to you by dealing in solutions and carefully increase the trust between you.

TYPE THREE: The Draw Leader

We now turn to the positive side of the ledger, to bosses who have skill in dealing with people. "Draw" leaders manage in such a way as to draw out the best in people. Employing intelligent and creative communication procedures, they give precise feedback so that people are always aware of how they are doing. If you deserve recognition, you'll get it from the draw leader.

This example illustrates the difference between a draw leader and the less effective bosses. Suppose a salesman has been in a slump for several months. The drive leader might berate or threaten him. The default leader will simmer in silence, look at the figures, and wonder how soon he'll have to fire him. The drive leader will do the job himself; while the default leader will do nothing. But the draw leader will let the salesman know he is aware of the slump, solicit his view of the situation, and attempt to help him solve the problem.

Then suppose the salesman breaks out of the slump with a big sale. The drive leader will give him a slap on the back and an exhortation to get out there and make up for lost time. The default leader might think, "The guy finally closed one. I guess even a blind squirrel can find an acorn once in a while." He will say nothing and wait to see the next set of figures. The draw leader, however, will provide precise feedback: "That was a terrific sale you made! It looks like you're really getting moving again. Tell me, how did you swing it? And how do you plan to continue increasing sales?"

Notice that he is not so exuberant as to lull the salesman into a false sense of security. He hasn't forgotten the slump. He gives the man the positive feedback he needs and a boost of confidence. He might even add a creative incentive, such as: "Pull off another one like that within the next two weeks, and you'll earn a weekend in Mexico for you and your wife."

Draw leaders will involve their subordinates in assessing their work, a process that is essential to a good relationship. They help them to clarify—for themselves and the boss—what it is they are trying to achieve and how they are trying to achieve it.

Draw leaders are open to innovation, whereas the drive and default leaders are not. Let's use a real example to point up the difference. Veronica Warwick worked in a gift shop. One day she noticed a competitor doing a brisk business on calendars. She learned that a large ad offering a discount coupon was responsible for the good business. Studying the ad during her lunch hour, she came up with one for her shop she thought would be even better.

Some bosses would appreciate that kind of initiative. But Veronica worked for a drive leader, who responded to her idea by saying: "That's nonsense. I don't care what other shops do. I know my business and I don't need any help."

The boss was threatened by Veronica's initiative. He owned the problem himself and had to have all the answers. What Veronica should have done was present the idea as a throwaway line: "I was having some fun at lunchtime, and I came up with this idea. It worked over at Corona Gift Shop. You probably already thought of it, but I'll leave it on your desk in case you want to take a look."

That presentation is less threatening than one with wild enthusiasm. It enables the drive leader to change the idea and make it his own. Veronica might not get visible recognition, but the boss will remember.

A default leader in the same situation would be unimpressed by enthusiasm or hunches. With him, Veronica should hold off until she has the facts and figures to support her: "I found out that Corona did thirty-five percent better on calendar sales the days they ran this ad. I designed one I think can work even better. It uses a smaller graphic, although the headline is just as big, so we can mention other items besides the calendars, and the ad will cost two thousand dollars less. We could then run it for a full week for what the other one costs for three days." That might get the default leader to act.

A draw leader will be a more receptive audience. In fact, he may intentionally inspire you. He, too, is crucially interested in the bottom line, but he will make his evaluation with other factors in mind as well. Your enthusiasm will count. He, too, will want to see numbers, but the fact that you are excited indicates that you are sufficiently motivated to make the idea work. Even if the idea is rejected, your initiative and motivation will have registered, and your suggestion will be treated with respect. If it's used, you'll get the recognition you deserve.

One of the draw leader's outstanding features is the use of creative ways to provide feedback. Some years ago, Emery Air Freight established a simple, clear feedback system right down to the production line. Everyone in the company evaluated his or her own performance every day without fear of reprisal or revenge, and everyone was also evaluated by his or her supervisor. The company claims the change meant an additional $3 million in profits in two years. They claim it saved $125,000 in operating costs in one division alone. They got those extraordinary results by making people responsible for their own work, and for the evaluation of their own performance. It was a dramatic departure from the old axiom: "People do not do what you expect, they do what you inspect." At Emery, people did better when allowed to inspect their own work. This is not to say that any one such change will permanently improve productivity.

Here's another example. A Midwestern state, concerned about the incidence of stolen cars, began issuing awards to Highway Patrol officers who recovered one. Any officer who recovered five stolen cars got a second award. The state tripled its recovery rate.

While draw leaders elicit a high level of performance from their subordinates, theirs is still not the best form of leadership. The draw leader has to look constantly at the work environment, changing the specific feedback he gives each person, so that he can keep them advancing from one level of performance to the next. He has to be on his toes, always involved in evaluating, giving feedback, and creating new ways of communicating. Draw leaders run the risk of becoming stale; recognition can be overdone, and it begins to lose its impact. Also, if the draw leader hasn't established adequate opportunities for his people to advance, the subordinates can get restless. Most important, the draw leader's involvement is always needed.

The draw leader is a good manager for most types of subordinates. Those who require a lot of feedback get it; those who are reasonably autonomous and self-directed are dealt with in a way that does not offend them. For most people, working for a draw leader is a positive experience.

Some draw leaders can overdo the feedback, or fail to finetune and change their feedback style. There comes a time with a new employee when the draw leader should back off and give less feedback less often, and in a different way. If the boss is over-eager to give feedback, he can turn off the subordinate. The role requires subtlety.

In his attempt to improve the environment, the draw leader can overdo it. He may disrupt good procedures if he gets into the habit of changing things merely for the sake of change. A good rule of thumb to follow is, when in doubt as to whether to innovate, don't do it—think it through and examine it carefully before making the change.

You can manage a draw leader best by using the same techniques on him that he uses with his subordinates. Give him good feedback. If he makes a change that works, compliment him. Don't let him live in a vacuum. If he has a tendency to overdo, just knowing that his intentions are good should solve the problem in your own mind. However, if other people are being affected adversely, let him know that he has developed the staff enough to back off a little. If he is overmanaging, you might say: "A lot of your new procedures are really working, better than any we've tried before. I notice you're changing some of them. I'd like to ask you to rethink the changes. We can still get a lot of value out of these procedures." Since the draw leader is interested mainly in results, there should be no trouble giving him that kind of feedback.

TYPE FOUR: The Develop Leader

The "develop" leader causes his people to feel reverence not for him but for themselves.

"When the best leader's work is done," said the Chinese sage Lao Tzu, "the people say, 'We did it ourselves.' "

He must have been talking about the develop leader, who encompases all the advantages of the draw leader and adds to them the ability to develop his or her subordinates' level of competence, self-esteem, and autonomy. He clearly understands the components of success in his field. He can isolate them and teach them to his subordinates.

The develop leader believes in people before they believe in themselves. He recognizes potential and develops it. He trains and develops subordinates to the point where they need him less and less. He puts people on his shoulders so they can see at once everything he's learned. The goal of most leaders is to cause people to feel reverence for them; but the develop leader causes people to feel reverence for themselves. He is a conscious mentor.

The develop leader trains people and lets them learn by taking risks. He encourages independent decision-making, realizing that properly guided people can learn from mistakes. He bows out of the picture as quickly as possible, but isn't absent like the default leader.

Certainly, every boss has bottom-line responsibilities for the entire group. He has to know what is going on, and he has to make unpopular decisions sometimes. But a manager who trains and develops skillfully will not be needed every minute of the day.

The develop leader often has a high rate of turnover, and it's upward. Indeed, helping people move up is one of his goals. Even if the subordinates don't stay long, they excel while they are with him, and they often return at a higher level. Because the develop leader creates such a high level of competence, he always has someone to step in when someone else moves up. No one is badly missed, because the leader is like a football coach with a strong bench.

The develop leader minimizes his own role, working instead on his ability to train and teach. And he trains people not only in skills but in thinking. He shows his people *how* to think, not just *what* to think. He makes people realize their value to the organization, which increases their desire to contribute. A develop leader will be tough and decisive as needed, but won't impose his will; instead, he encourages and creates disagreement. He doesn't have the disease of having to be right. He is authoritative when requried, but he knows that authority is worthless without allegiance. He gets allegiance by treating people with trust and respect. The drive leader, by contrast, *demands* allegiance, but seldom gets it.

The develop leader and the draw leader are operating from a different set of assumptions about subordinates than are the drive and default leaders. They don't just want good performance, they have the right to expect it, and that expectation is communicated—not just verbally, but with ongoing evidence of genuine trust, freedom to operate, and effective procedures for helping people reach their potential. Their words are backed up by their actions.

The develop leader is both task- and people-oriented. He balances concern for people with concern for production. He is a coordinator and integrator. If the drive leader is a one-man band, the develop leader is a symphony conductor.

Spending money on training and development does not, in itself, make someone a develop leader. Some training managers have a perverted view of what training and development mean. They emphasize learning, and they gauge their success by how many classroom hours their employees put in, or how many new subjects are offered. But learning and growth are two different things. Learning is knowing about something; growth means being able to apply what you learn to become more effective.

The develop leader is in touch with the objectives of the organization, and gauges the success of his training and development programs by how they contribute to reaching those goals. He measures results continuously, and isn't impressed by methods and systems unless they bring measurable results.

Many managers have a passion for keeping up with the latest ideas in the field. They feel compelled to try the latest concept. They embrace it for a while, and then abandon it for the next fad before it is properly evaluated. Their people learn a lot, but they grow little. Here are seven steps a good develop leader will employ in making programs valuable.

1. **Investigate and evaluate.** Many ideas are attractive on the surface, but hold little lasting value; others, like meditation or transactional analysis, are perceived at first as frivolous, but turn out to have extraordinary benefits.
2. **Appropriateness.** An idea may be perfectly good, but not right for that company at that time. For example, it might require group participation from people who are on the road a lot.
3. **Application.** It is easier to create an attitude than to change one. Therefore, make sure a new program gets off to a good start. The first days or weeks will have a strong impact on how much people will get out of it in the long run.
4. **Measurement.** Before a program is implemented, standards of measurement should be established. In addition, the participants should be allowed to evaluate it fairly and candidly without fear of reprisal.
5. **Commitment.** It often takes six or more months to gauge accurately the value of a program. If an idea seems practical, proven, and potent, it is worth a commitment of both time and money.
6. **Integrate.** It can be destructive to foist a new idea on people every few months. Train with continuity and integrate the successful components of previous programs with the new ones. Don't abandon good ideas. They deserve a long-term commitment.
7. **Review.** Every program should be evaluated regularly,

and if necessary modified or eliminated. Blind commitment is as dangerous as being promiscuous with new ideas.

Even the most exceptional leader will have blind spots. He will have areas of weakness and vulnerability—we all do. But, if you're wise enough to be working for a develop leader, take full legitimate advantage of the situation. Spend as much time with him as possible. Volunteer for any assignment that will allow you to learn more about how he thinks and how he works, even if you have to volunteer without pay. This is a good idea for anyone, but if you aspire to be a good leader yourself, learning from a develop leader is vital.

Because of his acute perception of an employee's potential, the develop leader might throw someone in over his head too soon. If your boss seems to be giving you too much responsibility, don't hesitate to ask for it to come a little slower. But keep in mind that develop leaders often know their subordinates' potential better than they do themselves. You may be more ready than you think, yet lacking in confidence. Don't be afraid to take risks with a develop leader. They create an environment of "creative discomfort," keeping people reaching and striving, but making sure the risks are low and that no harm will come from making mistakes. Remember that a leader gets what the leader has a right to expect. Mentors have a magical effect on their subordinates. The extraordinary impact that Warren Gregory has had on hundreds of people has permanently increased their competence. I, like many others, will value his contribution all my life.

Leadership Weaknesses and Strengths

While draw and develop leaders get better results than drive and default leaders, certain common strengths and weaknesses may be found in managers of *all* denominations. We have described a number of these; let's look at some more.

Leadership Weaknesses

1. Lack of training. Many bosses are technically adept, but unprepared for dealing with people. Not even business school graduates receive appropriate managerial training, since the schools train them to be task-, not people-oriented. On the other side of the coin are managers who are good with people, or who understand functions such as sales or marketing, but cannot deal with finance. There are those who can coordinate but not administrate. In other words, few managers are thoroughly prepared for all facets of their responsibilities, particularly those that relate to human factors. The competent manager must be both task- and people-oriented.

2. Lack of clear purpose. Many managers lack a clear understanding of their organization's goals. My conviction that lack of purpose is common has been reinforced in my consulting work. This scenario is typical: I was consulting with a group of top executives, including the president of a firm, all keen, alert people doing a good job. They expected a speech from me. Instead, I said, "Before I begin, I'd like you to tell me what the purpose of your company is."

They couldn't say. Scratching their heads, they finally came up with, "To make money."

"Fine," I said, writing "make money" on the blackboard. "Now, show me your books. I'd like to see your income from drugs and prostitution."

They were astonished. "You said your purpose was to make money," I explained. "Those are among the most profitable businesses in the world."

"We wouldn't be involved in drugs and prostitution."

"Oh, then there are limits to how you make money. Tell me more about that."

Three hours later, a statement of purpose had been agreed on: "Our purpose is to offer a legitimate service to our clients in such a way as to enhance their financial status and maximize their profits."

Then I said, "If I came back in ninety days, how would I know if you are fulfilling that purpose?"

Again the managers were incredulous. I explained that a purpose is incomplete without a standard of measuring how well it is being achieved.

Look carefully at the purpose of your organization. Ask ten people and you'll likely get ten different answers. Then help them create one that everyone agrees is accurate.

3. Resorting to the familiar. Managers often have a strong need to do what they did before, simply because it is familiar. They even repeat behavior that no longer gets results. I call it "validation drive"—they want to validate their importance. Some bosses yell and scream because they always have; sales managers will continue calling on customers, even though their salesmen should do it, because that is what they did before becoming managers.

"That's the way we've always done it," you will hear—an absurd attitude in a world that changes rapidly. Bosses are often afraid of rocking the boat, even when the boat ought to be capsized. Resorting to familiar action in the face of new demands puts a boss at a distinct disadvantage in a competitive marketplace. For example, there are executives who still will not hire women for management positions because they believe women don't have the drive and persistence of men. They are grossly mistaken and may be contributing to their own failure by refusing to take the risk of doing something that feels uncomfortable.

Validation drive is one reason the automobile industry is in trouble. The executives got stale. Suffering from intellectual incest, they lacked the boldness to change established approaches to their market. Failing to adapt to changing values and needs, their only innovation for years was to make cars sleeker. Sometimes the old way is the best way. But that choice should be based on results only.

4. Managing by being a savior or guru. The boss/savior tries to keep people afloat who will drown anyway. He feels personally responsible for marginal employees who might be in the wrong jobs or are simply incompetent. Because he has an emotional need to save them, he often ignores his top people, who would benefit most from his input. He spends little time with the productive few who get the most done, trying instead to lift up the ones at the bottom. In some cases, he does help. But most often he keeps them just short of failure, postponing the inevitable day when they change jobs or get fired.

The boss/guru needs to be needed. He wants to be involved in everything. He has to make both big and small decisions. Allow him to feel important without sacrificing your integrity.

5. The disease of having to be right. I once worked for a man who had more executive talent than any two people I've ever known. He was versatile, brilliant, and had many exceptional talents. But he couldn't admit to being wrong. He knelt at his own altar. At one point he hired an administrative vice president who had been a top executive at a large, established company. In his new organization, the VP had a different role to play and he could not handle it. Yet my talented boss was unaware of his own blind spots; he could not admit he hired the wrong man. To avoid admitting his error, he tried to do the other man's job for him, and took the company into bankruptcy in the process.

6. Low compatibility. Even brilliant, hardworking executives often fail because of their inability or lack of desire to create alliances with peers, superiors, and subordinates. Says Victor Lindquist, director of career services at Northeastern University: "More peoople are fired for their difficulties in getting along with others on the job than for lack of skills."

Those who succeed are both competent *and* compatible. Without competence, a boss might get by if he has a compatible and competent staff; but without compatibility, he will suffer from a lack of cooperation sooner or later.

7. Demanding agreement. Many bosses have not learned the value of causing disagreement and accepting dissenting points of view. They will hold a meeting and dictate exactly what is to be done to people who are actually better in touch with operations. If anyone suggests an alternative, the boss will be put off. What will happen the next time that employee has an idea? He'll keep it to himself, agree with the boss, and carry out the boss's plan even if he knows it won't work.

Bosses should seek acceptance and assistance, not agreement. A subordinate might have little choice but to agree with the boss, but that doesn't mean she'll accept the decision or assist the boss as best she can.

8. Confusing efficiency with effectiveness. Efficiency means doing things the quickest and easiest way; effectiveness is making sure everything you do is productive. Some managers get hung up on efficiency at the expense of effectiveness. It is important to adhere to rules and procedures, but an obsession with them can interfere with getting the job done.

There are two aspects to a manager's job—control and creativity. Compulsive control mechanisms, such as the paperwork that buries many organizations, leave no room for creativity.

Joni Krause took a job on a commission basis as an employment counselor with a large company. She was aggressive and outgoing, and established an immediate rapport with the personnel directors of leading banks. But there had been some confusion in the office about which counselor was to call on which clients. So in the name of efficiency the manager divided the clients alphabetically, assigning to each counselor a section of the alphabet. Joni Krause didn't get the banks with whom she had already established a potentially profitable relationship. The boss wouldn't alter the plan, to the detriment of Joni and the company.

Efficiency and effectiveness should be balanced. Here is a case where a creative boss did just that. Ken Nard was concerned that employees were losing work time to get their hair cut. So he installed a barber's chair in an attractive office with a nice view. He found an excellent hairstylist, who agreed to come in one day a week. Men and women were allowed to make appointments through Nard's secretary. The haircuts were paid for by the company. The boost in morale and the savings in time were the boss's benefits, and the company barbershop became a place to brainstorm and create new ideas. Everybody won: the employees got free haircuts and the company got a lot of good ideas, as well as a lot of time saved.

While efficiency and effectiveness should be balanced, if one has to be compromised, it should be efficiency.

Leadership Strengths

1. Causes disagreement. A good boss not only tolerates disagreement, he encourages it and even creates it. Because he cares about results more than protecting his ego, he continuously searches for ways to improve his and his group's performance. An effective manager, for example, might address an emergency meeting this way: "There's an emergency. The home office ordered us to double our production this week What's the best way to do it?" By contrast, a drive leader would say: "This is what the home office wants. Here is how we are going to do it."

When a situation demands immediate, authoritative decisions, the strong manager will make decisions and stand behind them. But in most cases he will first elicit the group's ideas, and have everyone defend his or her proposed solution. If his group has a sound approach, he'll give them free rein to do it their way. If he disagrees, he'll enforce his own way of doing things, but do it so the group feels no resentment.

2. Manages with continuity. Most jobs are episodic. Knowing the scattering effect of people moving from episode to episode, the competent manager creates a sense of continuity underlying these changes. Archie Moss, a regional manager, announced at a district meeting: "Our accounts receivable have gotten way out of line. Home office wants each of you to get out and collect the money that's due, and don't worry about placing new orders." Then he was gone, leaving the district representatives to rush about trying to collect on past sales. Two weeks later, in came Archie Moss on another campaign: "The Federal Trade Commission has changed its labeling requirements. We have ninety days to empty the warehouse of our existing models. Get out and sell!"

On the surface, it would appear that Moss was the type of boss who unloaded episode after episode. But underlying the episodes was a clear six-month agreement with every employee. Twice a year they sat down individually with Moss and discussed the various aspects of their job. They talked about policies, methods, priorities, procedures, objectives, and anything else related to the job. In between, Moss was available to discuss any of these issues. Each employee knew that every six months they would have the opportunity to review any matter of concern and that the policies established half a year earlier would be reexamined.

The important thing is to have no surprise contracts with subordinates. They will handle the episode part of their job if they have a sense of continuity.

3. Matches people with work. A good manager puts the *right* people in the *right* jobs for the *right* reasons, and makes choices not only on the basis of training and education but personality factors as well. Using appropriate testing procedures as well as his own judgment, he will assess the candidate's values, attitudes, and style, in addition to practical requirements for the job. For example, someone with strong social commitments might not be suited for a job that involves constant travel. Someone with a strong power drive should not work in isolation. Someone who has an affinity for numbers and details might not be suited for work involving intimate contact with people.

A good example of matching people with jobs is the case of the company that needed people to package butter. There had been a high rate of turnover because most people saw the job as boring and monotonous. At a consultant's suggestion, the manager decided to try employing handicapped people. They were glad to have the opportunity and they viewed the work as a challenge. Productivity went up by 40 percent.

4. Understands the job. A good manager sees himself primarily as a facilitator. Ineffective leaders often try to build up their own empires; they lose sight of the real role of a manager.

Effective managers bring out the best in subordinates. "He has the responsibility," writes Peter Drucker the famous writer on management, "to build the structure in which men can achieve the most, and to find the right spot in that structure for each of the [employees]."

In developing trusted, valuable employees, the strong manager will fulfill these four objectives:

—Cause the person to feel he or she is with a worthwhile organization.
—Cause him or her to feel that he or she counts.
—Cause him or her to want to contribute.
—Cause him or her to feel ever more certain of his or her abilities and talents.

5. Respects feelings. Even when it may not seem practical to do so, an exceptional boss will remember that people respond to the world on the basis of feelings. He understands that subordinates have strong emotional needs, and while he does not cater to them, he understands clearly the importance of respecting them. The competent boss recognizes that whatever level a person is on, the decisions a person makes are critical and crucial to that person. That goes for trivial concerns as well as vital ones. For example, the mail clerk who can't decide whether to send something first class or fourth might experience the same pleasure as the tycoon contemplating a big investment. The leader will listen carefully, and instead of deciding, will cause the clerk to make the decision himself; he will show him *how* to approach the problem so he'll be able to handle it himself next time.

6. Gives people autonomy. Autonomy can be granted only to the extent that the boss genuinely trusts his subordinates and conveys that trust to them. Most people in most jobs can do their work better than they are currently doing. If they are dealt with in a way that creates high levels of trust, and if there is autonomy and responsibility, they'll invest more of their ingenuity in getting the job done better. Dramatic improvements in productivity have been accomplished in exactly this fashion.

Once, when visiting a client company, I noticed three secretaries working on the same forms. Only after the form had passed to all three was it completed. I asked what they were doing. The first woman was making entries connected with insurance; the second was making entries on investments; the third was classifying the forms for filing.

I suggested to their boss that each work a form through, beginning to end, and initial it so that mistakes could be traced and good work recognized. Six months later, productivity in the small group had increased by 30 percent, and the error ratio dropped to one fifth the previous rate. They were given autonomy and trust, and they responded.

Similarly, a telephone company that originally assigned daily jobs to installers, tried putting the assignments on the board and letting the installers work out their own schedules among themselves. They doubled the number of phones installed each day. Given with care and responsibility, autonomy benefits both the workers and the organization.

7. Eliminates boredom. Some jobs can't be made interesting. But the vast majority of jobs can be dealt with in a way that will eliminate boredom and motivate people to increase productivity and reduce errors. An effective leader will be successful by using some combination of the following ideas.

(a) Encourage employees to develop objectives for their own jobs.
(b) Let them use their own means to reach their objectives.
(c) Don't allow them to work in a vacuum.
(d) Make the task easily measurable by them and the boss.
(e) Make the job as challenging as possible.
(f) Use training to raise awareness and increase the sense of achievement.
(g) Encourage lateral movement within all departments, to decrease monotony and give each person a vision of the whole.

Allow people to fashion and focus their work to suit their own needs as long as they get the job done. For example, a manager knows that his workers are getting bored at night waiting for the trucks they are to unload. Allow them to come in early in the morning instead. If you can measure results and determine that the change did not reduce productivity, you will have increased job satisfaction and eliminated an inefficient operation.

8. Seeks results, not methods. Some bosses get so hung up on devising new methods and procedures that they forget what the methods are supposed to be accomplishing. A good boss always has his attention on results. His goals are always in mind, and he never lets his methods become ends in themselves. A classic example of someone taken with methods was a hotel magnate whose procedures were so novel he was invited to lecture about them all over the world. At the height of his speaking fame, his company went into involuntary bankruptcy.

The effective boss is not the slightest bit impressed by any method or strategy unless it gets measurable, cost-effective results. He will continuously look at ways to improve what he is doing, but he will never lose sight of the requirement that any method must produce results quickly and measurably.

9. Uses positive feedback, not criticism. Significant improvements rarely follow from criticism. In most cases, criticism makes people defensive. If they change at all, it is with reluctance, and the change is short-lived. When the heat is off, they revert to their old ways.

Even with the best intentions, constructive criticism will seldom work. A good manager will provide information without criticizing, especially in public. Compliment in public and criticize in private—that is sound policy, but still better is catching people doing something good.

We have a tendency to say nothing when people do what they are asked to do, and we speak up only when they don't cooperate. We scold children for making noise, but never thank them for playing quietly. Here is an example of how to use positive feedback instead of criticism.

Ed Rubin had a subordinate who had to relate to the public, but tended to dress sloppily. Rubin wanted to fire the woman, but held back because she had potential. By frequent criticism, Rubin hoped he could change the woman's dress habits. Each time he seemed to succeed, only to have the woman revert to slovenly ways within a week.

I asked Rubin if he ever praised the employee when she dressed appropriately. He did not. When I encouraged him to do so, Rubin was irate—he saw no reason to compliment someone for doing what she is paid to do. But he agreed to try nonetheless. The next time she dressed sloppily, Rubin criticized. Then when she came in the next day properly dressed, Rubin thanked her. By strategically complimenting at regular intervals, Rubin succeeded in bringing about a permanent change.

10. Combines cooperation with competition. Groups that function in a way that causes the individuals to be competitive and cooperative simultaneously outperform other groups by a wide margin. Appealing to competitive instincts works well in certain instances, such as when the company needs to reach a short-term goal quickly. But the opposite drive—to cooperate—unfortunately is underplayed. In a Harris Poll on preferences, 72 percent of those surveyed said they "prefer to cooperate, not compete, with others."

It is commonly felt that successful people are highly competitive, and as a result, most managers look for competitive types. But a recent study by Robert L. Helmreich and Janet T. Spence at the University of Texas found that a high degree of competitiveness can actually have a negative effect on productivity. They studied a group of successful people and found that the ones who achieved the greatest success scored high on scales that measured (1) desire to work hard; (2) preference for difficult, challenging tasks; and (3) unconcern for the reactions of others. They scored markedly lower on competitiveness.

Managers should realize that if competition destroys cooperation, then the high-quality results will also be destroyed. A highly competitive subordinate might learn to care little about the group's results as long as he looks good. A strong leader will not set up comparisons between workers that cause them to see each other as adversaries.

The best way for groups to function—and the one that the develop leader uses—is for people to be highly competitive and highly cooperative simultaneously. They are able to do both without doing one at the expense of the other. Those organizations that cause employees to be competitive and cooperate simultaneously will have the greatest chance for success; organizations run in a way that divides people and causes associates to be adversaries rather than allies will be in constant peril.

This examination of the strengths and weaknesses of leaders, combined with your evaluations of you and your boss, should provide enough groundwork to build a strong, mutually beneficial strategy for managing your boss.

5

Strategies for Boss-Management

THE PROVEN strategies in this chapter will help you create the pattern of clarity-cooperation-commitment. Accept the responsibility to select, modify, and improve these methods according to your particular situation, your personality, and your boss's personal and professional idiosyncrasies.

Deal in Solutions, not Problems

I once had a bright but inexperienced associate named Dennis who would come to me only when he had a problem. I soon came to associate his name with trouble. Whenever I saw a memo with his name on it, I became upset. When my secretary told me he was on the phone, I often avoided taking the call.

The effect Dennis's behavior was having on our working relationship became clear to me when one day I bumped into him unexpectedly. Assuming he was going to lay another problem on me, I felt defensive, and noticed that he, too, was disturbed by the chance encounter. He had been avoiding me as much as I'd been avoiding him—no doubt because of the way I reacted to his barrage of problems.

We sat down and discussed our mutual dilemma, and here's how it was resolved. I said: "I'm willing to listen to any problems you have. And from now on, they are to be accompanied by a solution. State the problem and tell me how you expect to solve it. Rank each of your proposed solutions from zero to ten.

Zero means you think it has no value, ten means you think it has exceptional value. Then sign your name to it."

Dennis was visibly disturbed by this; the new arrangement seemed to him an awesome responsibility. After a short time, however, he became accustomed to it. Within weeks he began to like it and to recognize that there was virtue in it. The procedure transformed our relationship, and it caused Dennis to grow as a person and as a professional. Our association for the first time became mutually rewarding. We had reached the state of high energy—high confluence. Within a year, Dennis resigned to create his own company, which is now doing quite well. We still do joint assignments together.

Creative, competent subordinates take some of the load off the boss's shoulders. Be a subordinate who solves problems rather than creating them. Whenever possible bring your boss good news—he or she has enough bad news from other sources. If you bring problems inappropriate to the boss, you are giving nothing. One of your major responsibilities as a subordinate is to be alert for difficulties. A valuable employee will spot danger signals before they become full-fledged disasters, and should be rewarded for that ability. But spotting the smoke is only half the battle; you still have to put out the fire. Think how much more the boss would appreciate your fire-spotting if you came in with axes and hoses, not just the alarm.

Whenever possible, hold off your report until you have had a chance to investigate potential solutions. For example, instead of barging into your boss's office, as my associate Dennis once did to me, shouting: "We have a problem! That shipment of materials never arrived in Youngstown," take a minute or two to check out some facts. Then you might report in this way: "The shipment to Acme Steak in Youngstown never made it. I've put a tracer on it. And I've found out there's a flight that arrives in Youngstown at 10 A.M. tomorrow. If you can spare someone from the shipping department, we can drive a new package to the airport on time to make the plane. Another alternative is to use Ace Air Express. It's more expensive, but they'll guarantee delivery, at the door, by 9 A.M."

What a difference between those two approaches. And what a difference in how the boss perceives you, if you consistently come to him with solutions, not just problems.

If you are sincerely interested and concerned about the organization, make it known to your boss. Don't wait to be asked. Be alert to problems and volunteer to help, even if your job description doesn't call for it: "I realize that things will get hectic around here before Christmas. I want you to know I'm trying to get far enough ahead in November so my staff and I will be available to help out elsewhere if the need arises in December." Or: "I'm aware that there's a new employee in Page's department, but Page is out for the week. Would you like me to show her around?"

When it comes time to delegate responsibilities, when it comes time to promote someone, who do you think the boss will call on—the problem carrier or the solution carrier?

There is yet another advantage to giving your boss worthwhile solutions to problems that arise: you are preventing him from imposing solutions that you might find difficult to live with. However, if there is a problem your boss should be involved in, create possible solutions to it and advise him before taking action.

Catch Your Boss Doing Something Good

Beverly Euclid was head nurse in the emergency ward of a hospital. The doctor in charge was a volatile person, who threw fits whenever the slightest thing went wrong. Unfriendly and domineering, he would go into a temper tantrum if one of the nurses did not follow his orders to the letter, or if anyone on the staff made a mistake. As a result, turnover was skyrocketing, and the staff always seemed to find new reasons to stay away from the emergency ward.

Beverly thought that pointing out the effect his temper was having on the staff would cause the doctor to change his ways. She decided to confront him. She expressed her feelings as politely as she could. But the doctor replied coldly: "I'm in charge here. The staff will have to learn to live with it."

Beverly changed her tactics. She decided to apply something she learned about changing bad habits: "Catch a person doing something good and give the person immediate feedback." The next time she saw the doctor interact with the staff without criticizing or getting angry, she thanked him. "Doctor, it's enjoyable working with you when you don't get upset. The entire staff works more effectively then."

Careful not to arouse suspicion by overdoing it, Beverly continued to look for signs of appropriate behavior and to reward the doctor at such times. If a nurse made a mistake and the doctor didn't have a tantrum, she thanked him. Within months, the doctor's behavior changed substantially. He had thrown his last fit.

Like bosses, subordinates too often wait until they have something negative to report before giving the boss feedback. Catching your boss doing something good and rewarding him is a far more effective way to change his behavior than criticizing or complaining. The doctor might have lost his entire staff if Beverly hadn't taken action. Even worse, he could have jeopardized a patient's life because of his behavior. Had Beverly not spoken up, it is doubtful that her positive reinforcement alone would have done the job. Although the doctor's initial response to her comment had been discouraging, the message got through. The doctor was, in effect, put on notice. Then, when Beverly rewarded his good behavior, the reinforcement meant something.

Most cases are not as drastic as that doctor's. However, it is likely that at some point your boss's behavior might be counterproductive. Positive reinforcement alone should work, given sufficient time.

Suppose your boss has traits you would like to change, but she displays them so consistently you can't find an opportunity to reward her. There are two things you can do: Ignore the negative behavior; and reward *increments* of positive behavior.

Some bosses know that their behavior is having a negative effect, but they have a psychological need to continue. They might even get a boost out of making life difficult for their subordinates, rationalizing their behavior by thinking that shaping them up is doing them good. Sometimes they do things just to get a reaction; they enjoy seeing fear on the faces of subordinates. Don't give such a boss any indication of resentment, fear, anger, or hostility. To him, such signs are forms of reward. If you deny him the reward, the boss will likely lessen or discontinue the negative behavior.

As for the second tactic—rewarding increments of good behavior—it's difficult to imagine any boss being so consistently poor in any particular area that there is never *something* to reward. If nothing else, there are degrees of negativity. If she gives unreasonable assignments, there will be times when the assignment is slightly less unreasonable. If she tends to criticize in public, there will be times when she criticizes in private. If she never lets you make your own decisions, there will be times when she at least gives you a say, or lets you make a small decision. Those are the times to reward her.

Look for any movement in the right direction, then let her know that you like it, and that it helps you do your job better: "Thank you. That little extra time you gave me to compile these figures enabled me to do a more thorough job"; or "I appreciate the fact that you didn't tell me this in front of the others. It means I can work better with them"; or, "Thanks for asking my opinion."

It may take time and patience to change your boss's old habits, but by catching little pieces of good behavior you can turn him around. Soon he will see value in the change, as long as your actions operate to the benefit of him and the organization.

While there is tremendous value in catching the boss doing something good, don't overdo it. Insincere praise can lead to results as disastrous as criticism. Bosses are perceptive—that's one of the reasons they are bosses. Most of them have no use for phonies, yes-men, and apple polishers.

Excessive praise can have a negative result; it may make a boss feel suspicious or uncomfortable. An exceptional manager once spoke to me uneasily about a subordinate who had told him, "You're the best manager I've ever had."

I said, "That's a compliment. Why are you upset?"

"Because he's placed a tremendous burden on me," the boss said. "He thinks I can do no wrong. How can I live up to those expectations?"

Be Your Own Publicist

In a recent national study, it was determined that 86 percent of executives looking for jobs had failed to call their superiors' attention to their accomplishments. While bosses often are more aware of you than you think they are, about some things they often are less aware than they should be. It's up to you to let them know what you achieve. Always try to get the credit you deserve. But do it in a way that is not exploitative.

Visibility and recognition are vital to your success, but they must be achieved in a legitimate and subtle way. Trying too hard for recognition will backfire; broadcasting your achievements loudly will cast you in a negative light. The paradox you must work around is this: In most organizations, the people who succeed are those who earn recognition for what they do, and who do so in an understated way. A quiet awareness of your own competence, combined with a subtle, effective campaign to communicate your achievements and your value, is the best approach.

Why is publicity necessary? Because just doing your job well often isn't enough. Your competence has to be made visible. One of your boss's duties is to evaluate your performance. It is therefore incumbent upon you to help him make that evaluation accurately and positively. Keeping in mind that bosses rely on informal sources of information—memos, inferences, overheard conversations—as much as they do formal criteria, make it your business to keep your achievements in his awareness without being overbearing or vain.

Suppose, for example, you prevented the loss of an important new client when you substituted for another executive who was unprepared for a key meeting. You averted a potential disaster. But since your boss might never become aware of the event and your role in it, you must make known your achievement. Don't barge into the boss's office and tell him how great you are. Instead, write a letter to the client: "It was a pleasure to see you at the meeting, and I'm as happy as you that we were able to resolve the misunderstanding caused by the broken deadline."

How will the boss know about it? For one thing, it is not inconceivable that the client will remark on the alert, capable person who saved the day. The fact that you wrote that letter will keep your name in the client's mind. In addition, send a carbon of the letter to your boss. If appropriate, call his attention to your efforts by adding a note to the carbon: "I didn't bother you with this at the time it occurred. But in case the client discusses it with you, you'll know what happened. Can you tell me if there's anything else I might have done?"

This approach gets you legitimate, earned recognition, and it enhances the boss's self-esteem by asking him for guidance.

Put yourself in position to publicize yourself by being aware of the "big picture" in your company. Understand the needs and problems of departments other than your own. Suppose another department, also under your boss's supervision, was having problems. You might write to the department head, and send a carbon copy to the boss. This can be a powerful yet subtle way to call attention to your value. "I am aware that your division has had trouble with installations. We had the same problem and corrected it by changing the lead time for calling on clients. We now contact them thirty days earlier and it gives them ample time to prepare for the installation. It seems to be working out well. If you think it would be of any value, I'd be happy to explain the details."

What you are saying, in essence, is: "I've done something good, and I'm willing to let you benefit from my ideas." You needn't be a department head or supervisor to use this strategy.

Look beyond the boundaries of your job description. Take advantage of allegiances outside the company as well as those within. Bosses enjoy being told by outsiders that they have an exemplary subordinate. Suppose, for example, you do business with a peer in another company, and you'd like your boss to know how well you handled the project. Say to your peer, "I've enjoyed working with you, and I'd like to write a letter to your boss telling him how well you handled this project." Without being asked, the person is likely to do the same for you.

Take advantage of opportunities outside work to make yourself visible. Perhaps you are a member of the United Way. There you meet an executive who does business with your boss, or is an old school chum. Doing something special for United Way, and letting the boss's friend know whom you work for, may be all you need do to have your name brought up before your boss. Or you might volunteer to participate in company social events, or in community activities, such as the tour of your factory or the charity picnic.

Is there a company publication or a trade journal? Most of them are continuously searching for material. Why not write something for one of them? "I can't write," I hear you saying, "and besides, what have I got to say?" You'd be surprised. Don't belittle your own observations, judgment, experience, and intuition. Look at the quality of articles in those publications. Couldn't you add something valuable or interesting? It might require only a little research, and perhaps some editorial pointers. You don't have to be a professional writer to be published. The publisher, or an English teacher from a local college, can help edit your material. Why bother to write? Because having your ideas in print indicates competence and value. It raises your stature; many people have good ideas but never write them. To your boss, it shows that you are confident, knowledgeable, and enthusaistic—or else you wouldn't have bothered.

Obviously, public relations can backfire. If your actions are too contrived, you'll be seen as a "sharpshooter" trying to get acknowledged at the expense of the group. Don't devote an inordinate amount of time and energy to your own publicity, or attempt to push your way into the spotlight. Never compromise your principles in order to achieve recognition. If your boss is a staunch Rotarian, it will serve you well to belong to the local Rotary Club or to speak at one of their functions. But it would *not* serve you well to do those things if you didn't believe in Rotary, or if you didn't want to take the time away from your family to attend their meetings. Insincerity will almost always be discovered. Take every opportunity to make yourself and your achievements visible legitimately.

Demonstrate thoughtfulness. Congratulate the secretary whose daughter just got engaged; compliment someone to the person's boss every chance you can do so legitimately. Bosses value employees who have created allegiances with others. Lack of compatibility is one of the big reasons for firing someone or overlooking him or her for promotion. Hearing you mentioned favorably indicates to your boss that you are respected and trusted and ready for more responsibility.

The objective is to gain trust, confidence, and respect from your boss. One caveat should be added: In some instances, even when it is deserved, you stand to gain more from letting recognition pass you by rather than risking turning your boss off by seeking it too eagerly. Whenever in doubt, opt for *not* being recognized.

Zig Where Your Boss Zags

Your boss, like all bosses, has a combination of strengths and weaknesses. Your ability to compensate for the latter will go a long way toward gaining recognition and winning the boss's trust. You'll be seen as worthwhile, a person willing to do what is necessary to get the job done, and a complement to your boss.

Bosses are often more aware of their own weak spots than they let on. Fill in those areas with diplomacy and sensitivity. Acquire skills your boss lacks; take on obligations he or she loathes. While zigging where your boss zags may go unmentioned, it will not go unnoticed.

Suppose, for example, your boss dreads the prospects of speaking before a group, a common problem for executives. There are several ways you can compensate for this and at the same time earn deserved recognition. One obvious method is to learn to be a good speaker (which is much less difficult than most people think; with a skilled instructor and video equipment, six hours is all that's needed). Volunteer to speak at company functions, or at trade association meetings. If your boss is asked to speak, volunteer to represent him. Present your offer on his terms: you know he is busy and that he prefers not to speak.

If he takes you up on your offer, he may well begin to treat you differently. Since you now represent the boss, you must be given the knowledge and stature to do so properly. If you are not in a position to stand in for the speech-fearing boss, you can zig where he zags another way. Get him off the hook by suggesting creative alternatives: "Since you don't enjoy public speaking, let's arrange for you to answer quesions from the dais instead of making a formal speech."

Does your boss hate certain meetings? Volunteer to attend in her place, suggesting that you can fill her in on the major points discussed, and that perhaps she could drop in at the end of the meeting to express her views. Does your boss hate writing reports or articles for the prestigious publication she is expected to contribute to? Write them for her, allowing her to alter them as she sees fit. Ghost writers get little credit, except where it counts—from the person they write for. Does your boss relate badly to certain people? Keep them off her back, or take over some functions that would otherwise bring those people into contact with the boss.

Here are some examples of how subordinates have zigged where their bosses zagged:

Hugh Daniels was an accountant for a company that was trying to obtain a loan in order to purchase more modern equipment. Two banks had turned down his boss's loan request. Although Hugh's job was simply to portray accurately the company's financial picture, and although he had already done that, he decided to find out why the loans were turned down. By reading a book on business loans and chatting with the loan officer at a bank, he discovered that financial statements, while critical, were not the only thing a bank looks at when considering an application. A number of factors contributed to the banker's subjective impression of the applicant. Hugh discussed a different approach with the boss, and was given permission to work on it.

Hugh looked over his boss's prospectus and discovered some

unclear writing in the sections on the business's history and the purpose for the loan; apparently the boss didn't prepare those sections carefully, thinking they were unimportant. Hugh rewrote the prospectus and showed his boss the suggested changes, explaining why he felt they would impress the bank officials. The strategy worked. The firm obtained its much-needed loan, Hugh's stature soared, and he was elected to the board of directors of his firm.

One of my favorite examples of someone who successfully zigged where her boss zagged is Adelle Platt. She was assistant to a national sales manager who took pride in being a "people person" rather than a "numbers person." The boss was great at motivating his sales force and teaching them to relate effectively to clients; but he knew nothing about finance and cared less. On her own time and expense, Adelle took accounting courses at a local college. She came to understand the cost of doing business, and how to relate to upper management in terms her boss could not.

Adelle's new skills helped her to assist her boss in making sound decisions. Her efforts and competence soon became visible to top management, and she was promoted to Vice President of Marketing. She became her boss's boss.

Make Your Boss Your Partner

Marion Mike was in charge of the production department at a major corporation. At a seminar, she learned about the use of videotape and decided to look into it further. She pursued the idea, and acquired the necessary financial data. She now was convinced it had significant value in solving some of her training problems. The use of video could cut down her training time by 50 percent; ultimately, that could mean an increase in productivity that would redeem the cost of the video equipment within one year.

Marion had a problem, however. She had already committed so much of her annual budget that she would not be able to cover the initial cost of the equipment. Further, video technology was a new and as yet unproven concept in her field, and the boss was not known for his willingness to let employees take risks. Marion could have waited six months and worked it into her next budget. But that would have meant losing money in the long run, since the cost of the equipment was due to go up, and the old procedures would remain in operation that much longer.

Marion went to her boss. "Mr. Dundee, you asked me to give you a budget every September," she began. "The last budget I gave you was lean but adequate to get the job done. Since then I've discovered a valuable new procedure. I've run the numbers through, and it seems that an initial outlay of $30,000 will enable us to cut training time in half. The equipment can pay for itself in twelve months, and make a big difference from then on." Marion continued: "I'd like you to back me on this. Because I know it will work, I'm willing to take $15,000 out of my remaining budget, even though it will make things tight, if you'll advance me $15,000 on next year's. I think it will show big returns."

What did Marion's strategy accomplish? First, it demonstrated to her boss just how much she believed in the idea, since she was willing to put herself on the line. Second, it got her boss involved. The boss's involvement means greater support down the line, and greater cooperation from other people involved in the project. Perhaps most important, by making the boss her "partner," she gave him the opportunity to share the credit for the idea.

Are you willing to share some of the credit for your ideas in return for the freedom to get them off the ground? If so, you stand to gain in autonomy and esteem. There are many ways to make the boss your partner. Doing so is ultimately in your best interest. It might mean letting the boss share the spotlight, but that is a small price to pay if it gives you freedom and recognition.

Establish Rapport with the Boss's Assistant

One of the least appreciated but most powerful individuals in any organization is the boss's secretary/assistant. That person can be one of your greatest assets in managing your boss, as he or she is likely to know the boss well and influence him greatly. Establish a solid working relationship with the secretary/assistant.

One of the keys to successful boss-management is understanding your boss's idiosyncrasies, his likes, his dislikes, his habits. No one knows those better than his secretary/assistant.

He or she can help you raise your awareness and increase your sensitivity to your boss's way of doing things.

But be careful. Like anyone else, assistants are sensitive about being used. Be sure he or she knows you are not out to take advantage of anyone. The assistant's loyalty is to the boss, and one of his or her first jobs is to protect the boss. Establishing good working relationships doesn't mean deceiving the assistant or becoming obsequious in courting favor. You needn't send her flowers or give him tickets to the ball game. It means being courteous and polite, friendly and helpful. Remember, the secretary/assistant is often under terrific pressure, since everyone who wants the boss's time usually takes some of the assistant's.

Informally, your cooperative relationship with the secretary/assistant can teach you a great deal about your boss. "Does he prefer written reports or verbal discussions?" "Is it better to see him in the morning or afternoon?" "Does he read memos or ignore them?"

By creating rapport with the secretary/assistant, you may become aware of information you can use legitimately. "I'm dreading next week," the assistant might say. "The boss has to give a speech to key stockholders, and his kids are coming home for their vacation the day before." That news might alter your strategy for dealing with the boss that week. "I can't talk now," says the assistant. "I've got to get the boss tickets for *Madame Butterfly* and the box office closes in ten minutes." Is the boss an opera buff? The news might come in handy some day.

If you have a good relationship, the assistant can aid you in more direct ways as well. Cultivate his trust by treating him with respect. For example, you might call the boss's assistant and say: "Bill, I have a very important matter to discuss with the boss. It might mean thousands of dollars for the company. I know how busy he is, but it would be great to have his undivided attention for fifteen minutes when he's not under pressure. What do you suggest?"

If your relationship with the assistant is only ordinary, he might just squeeze you into any available slot. That would be unfortunate, because timing is often the key variable when dealing with the boss.

Go a step further, if you feel it's appropriate. Ask the assistant's opinion. "Bill, this proposal means a lot to me, and I think it will mean a payoff for the boss. I'd really value your opinion on it. Would you take the time to read it before I see the boss?''

You will likely obtain important advice by doing this. Even if his or her input in terms of content is slight, the assistant might read the report and say: ''I think you should cut it in half. Believe me, Mr. Brown hates to read long reports. I suggest leaving out the technical description on pages eight through ten—he usually skips over that kind of stuff anyway.'' Valuable information!

Or the assistant might tell you: ''I think you should put the material in the conclusion right at the beginning. He likes to know right off what the bottom line is. He's very alert to the cost of doing business. Be perfectly clear on how the cost of the project will be recovered.'' Or again: ''The boss recently wrote an article on this subject. Here's a copy for you to read. It will help you gain insight into his views.''

Then there is the matter of getting the boss's attention when you need it. Some assistants and secretaries have a lot of clout regarding whose phone calls get through to the boss and who gets to walk through the door. If you are seen as always trying to grab the boss's attention, you'll find him ''busy'' more than others will. If you are someone the assistant doesn't like hanging around his or her desk while you wait for the boss, you might find yourself dismissed with a ''Come back tomorrow,'' or, ''The boss is busy, why don't you send him a memo?''

If, on the other hand, the assistant perceives you as someone with something valuable to offer, if you are neither pushy nor obnoxious, if you are someone whose career goals he or she feels good about supporting, then you might be given more access to the boss. You might even find that the assistant persuades the boss to see you even if he or she doesn't really want to see anyone. Bosses often rely to a great extent on assistants to determine who they see.

If the assistant hands your boss a message from you with a smile instead of a scowl, or if he says, ''I think this deserves your attention,'' instead of, ''Here's another one from so-and-so,'' you might discover that your boss's response will be entirely different. She might read it instead of skimming it or tossing it into a pile with a dozen others. And when the boss does read it, her psychological mood will be partially affected by the assistant's introduction.

Indeed, your boss's image of you may in large part be dictated by the impressions he receives from the secretary/assistant. It is not uncommon for a boss to ask: "What do you think of Nocera? How do the others get along with him? Do you think he can be trusted?" In a hundred indirect ways, the boss's perceptions are influenced by his secretary and assistant.

The Responsibility-Authority Dilemma: Don't Take One Without the Other

One of the most common complaints of middle managers and one of the most stress-provoking situations imaginable is to be given the responsibility to do something, but not the authority. You might, for example, be dispatched to a branch office to handle a crisis, but when you examine the situation, you are paralyzed because your boss did not authorize you to spend the money or commit the company resources necessary to solve the problem.

Make your dilemma perfectly clear to your boss when you are given an assignment without sufficient authority to carry it out. If you accept the responsibility without getting the necessary authority, you will often find yourself stuck in the middle. Candidly and clearly insist on both authority and responsibility. You must be absolutely clear as to what you can and cannot do; let the boss know that if he wants to keep the authority himself, then he must hold on to the responsibility as well.

One way to handle this is to throw the problem back to the boss so that he can exercise his authority; in this way, you will at least be spared the onus of failure and the risk of alienating other people. For example: "You've asked me to have the maintenance department bring the exhibits to the civic auditorium this weekend, but I don't have the authority to authorize overtime pay for them. I'll do as you ask, but would you call the payroll department and get approval? I'll take it from there."

Alternatives to asking him to phone the appropriate people include: "Can I write to the head of research in your name? I'll show you a draft before I send it." Or: "Can I call the regional office now, while you're here?" Or: "Can I tell the vice president that you personally approved his request for an increase in his budget?"

Sometimes the absence of authority is all-inclusive, and that can make life difficult. For example, I was once given the responsibility to manage a sales department, but my boss still had all the salespeople report to him. It was maddening; they circumvented me all the time, even on orders I handed down directly from my boss. Finally, prepared to quit if necessary, I had a talk with him: "You've given me responsibility for the sales staff, yet they report to you. You continue to make changes that make it impossible for me to supervise them. I'd like to discuss with you whether or not you want to keep the department yourself or truly put me in charge. If you want to give me the responsibility, you must also give me the authority to hire and fire and make whatever decisions are necessary to run the department."

When he saw I was ready to quit, he reluctantly gave me the authority I needed. While I lost a few of the long-time salespeople who resented being unable to run to the big boss, a year later the productivity and profits had sharply increased.

Sometimes you can seize the authority by default. Use the strategy of "Unless I hear from you . . ." For example, Melissa Galip wrote a letter like this to her company's vice president: "Dear Mr. Green, I am aware that you want to select the carpeting for our new offices. However, if the selection is not made within ten days from the date of this letter, the offices will not open on time, and that will result in considerable financial loss to the company. If you would rather handle it yourself, we still have ten days for you to act. If I do not hear from you within that time, I will make the decision."

If she does not hear from the boss within the allotted time period, she has obtained the authority to make the decision by virtue of his silence.

Withholding authority is one way bosses have of expressing a lack of trust. The first question you must answer, therefore, is: Does he mistrust me, or does he mistrust everyone? If it is you he mistrusts, you may be the victim of some deep-rooted prejudice, or some personality conflict. Or you may not yet have earned the trust you think you deserve. Analyze the situation carefully.

If the boss is simply mistrustful by nature, it is sometimes appropriate to be up front. What you should *not* say is: "Look, I get the feeling you don't trust me." That is an attack. Try this instead: "I value my job here, and I think I can perform better if I understand exactly the way you want me to function. At times I sense a hesitancy about what I am to do. Can you help me clarify what my role is?" Then, if possible, follow by asking him to use Vital Tasks Management (see the section on *How To Be Measured by Results* below).

Inspire the boss to begin trusting you. How? By showing that you are worthy of his trust. Take the initiative. Ask for small opportunities to exercise authority, never going too far, and checking with the boss at every step. On a gradual basis, he may give you more and more authority until you are operating with a lot of freedom.

Realize that trust is a process, not a miracle. If you are given a lot of responsibility and authority and screw up on a big project, you may have to take a giant step back and start again.

Whatever the reasons for your boss's reluctance to delegate, it is up to you to change his mind. Prove to your boss that very little is impossible for the person who doesn't have to do it alone. The effort is worth making. Even if you don't succeed in changing things substantially right away, you may find your work more rewarding.

Be prepared to expand your realm *gradually;* don't try to grab too much too soon, as it might be threatening to your boss. In addition, be prepared to share—or if necessary relinquish—the credit. In the long run, keeping a low profile, while maintaining a persistent attitude, will pay off. Your first step, however, should be to get your boss to let go without fear. Again remember, a trusting relationship is a changing process, not a permanent innovation. It will fluctuate depending on how well you perform. While you may take a step back now and then, it's up to you to keep it moving upward over time.

Here is another example of someone who negotiated major concessions one step at a time. Mike Christopher was in charge of a sandblasting crew. His boss oversupervised, took charge of everything, dictated every decision from his desk, leaving Mike and his staff nothing but routine tasks. Mike constantly had to deal with problems created by the fact that the boss was out of touch with the actual conditions on the job. Mike felt he should have autonomy on a number of issues: determining who worked which jobs; ordering equipment; hiring new personnel; and others. But knowing his boss's reluctance to delegate authority, he isolated a few components and started from there.

"I can do an even better job for you," he told his boss, "if you will allow me to set some work assignments. Since I'm on the spot and familiar with each individual job, as well as weather conditions and other factors, I'm in the best position to know if we should alter our priorities. But usually I can't do so, because it's impossible to contact you on short notice. Let's try an experiment. For one month, let me handle the work allocations. That will free up your time each morning. At the end of the month, you can decide how productive it is."

Mike showed he was willing to accept authority, and that he was concerned with increasing productivity. The boss reluctantly agreed to try it. The arrangement was successful, and very soon thereafter MIke got the boss to delegate decisions on assigning equipment. Each new request was presented carefully and responsibly as an experiment that could quickly be judged by results.

As you get your boss to begin delegating authority, always remember it remains a delicate matter. Make sure both of you have the same goals and objectives. Review the results continuously so the boss begins to feel comfortable with your approach. Be sure he has the opportunity to make suggestions, and listen actively to his concerns. Don't make it a major issue when you succeed. Be sure the boss continues to enjoy some of the credit. Make it a joint idea, not yours alone.

How To Be Measured by Results

My experience as an international consultant has enabled me to see a continually recurring source of problems between bosses and subordinates: the myth that the boss and subordinate have similar views of what the subordinate is supposed to do daily in order to perform his job responsibilities with excellence.

Job evaluations in the vast majority of organizations where I have done consulting are nothing more than subjective personality appraisals; they fail to evaluate the subordinate by the cost-effectiveness of his results. I continuously see appraisals like: "He is argumentative," or: "She is moody." Seldom do I see a concrete evaluation of how well the person does the job he or she is paid to perform.

The disparity between the boss's and subordinate's views of the subordinate's job causes a severe communications problem even with people of the best intentions. The "Siamese twins" of work assignment and job evaluation should be looked at carefully from both the manager's and the subordinate's position. Recognize that most bosses don't know how to evaluate the effectiveness of their workers. Because of the extraordinary recurrence of unclear identification of the subordinate's job, I developed a process that has been used by a wide range of organizations, with positive and sometimes extraordinary results. It helps clear up the communication gap between what the manager expects the subordinate to do and what the subordinate thinks he is supposed to do.

The procedure is called "Vital Tasks Management." We will present it here the way it is presented to managers in our seminars, since you may *be* a boss as well as *have* a boss. It will have an extraordinary effect on the group you manage. If you aren't a boss or can't have your boss use Vital Tasks Management with you, we'll show you afterward how to use it with yourself.

Bear in mind that Vital Tasks Management is something many managers think they are already doing, only to be startled when they discover the discrepancies between how they think their subordinates view their jobs and how they actually view them. Whether hiring a new person or dealing with an experienced subordinate, don't *assume* his view of his job. Discover how he actually views it. Here are the seven steps in performing Vital Tasks Management.

1. **The manager looks at each person who reports to him/her, and identifies the specific, identifiable tasks that each could do to perform the job with excellence. The manager makes a list of these in clear language.** Be certain that you treat each position equally. A senior member of your staff may have several tasks in common with a newcomer with the same job title, but will almost certainly have several that are unique to his situation.
2. **The manager then has each of the persons look at his/her own specific job and identify his/her perception of the specific tasks that would cause him/her to do the job with excellence. The subordinate makes a list of these in clear language.** Have each person treat his or her job as a unique situation, so that subordinates don't create group agendas. This will add clarity to the working relationship.
3. **This is one of two crucial steps necessary to make the program work. Individually, the manager and subordinates merge the two lists. This is done through negotiation, not the imposition of the manager. The result is that each person now has his/her own vital tasks agenda.** At this point, it is crucial that negotiation is employed. Each subordinate should agree without coercion to the description of vital tasks

that will be used in the program. Patience and clear communications pay very good dividends in this stage. Don't impose your list—listen to the subordinate, and carefully create a list both of you agree on.

4. The subordinate grades his/her performance against the vital tasks agenda, and gives his/her self-evaluation to the manager regularly. This should be done weekly, if possible, and no less than once a month, even if it has to be done by mail or telephone.

The subordinate now has the responsibility of measuring his performance against each vital task that has been identified, negotiated, and clearly understood by both the boss and the subordinate. This begins a very crucial part of Vital Tasks Management. The sense of responsibility about his own job begins to become clear to the subordinate. At first he may be hesitant to grade his own performance, but when he finds he can be candid about weaknesses without danger of reprisal, he'll begin to assess, and solve, his deficiencies. The tasks agenda will heighten his awareness and clarify communications with the boss.

5. This is the other crucially important step. The manager reviews the evaluation with each person, never criticizing or offering solutions. In the areas where the person is performing poorly, the manager asks how he or she is going to improve performance. The manager listens to each person carefully, and offers suggestions only when asked. He doesn't impose solutions.

This is the most crucial of the seven steps. If handled incorrectly, it will dramatically diminish the value of the program. If handled correctly, it will begin to move the manager and the subordinate toward a clear, productive work arrangement. It is difficult for many managers to resist all the things they have learned about being a boss: imposing solutions and criticizing people as a way of shaping them up. If a worker admits weakness in one or more tasks and is reprimanded, cajoled, or demeaned, he will certainly learn to play games with the manager. In addition, if the manager, because of a need to be needed, is quick to offer solutions as to how the subordinate can meet his vital tasks, he will be telegraphing to the subordinate that he, the manager, owns the problem. The subordinate will then feel far less responsible for doing the things that he needs to do.

6. Each person then uses his/her ingenuity, and experi-

ments with different strategies to improve the tasks where his/her performance is lacking. The responsibility for doing the job is now clearly invested in the person doing the job. In most situations, the people doing the work already hold the solution to making their job performance excellent. Vital Tasks Management focuses their attention and interest on doing exactly that.

7. **The manager then does a vital tasks agenda for his/her own job, and evaluates his/her performance on a regular basis no less frequently than twice a month.** Many people who do this for themselves dramatically improve their job performance and enjoyment. It's a good way of aligning your intention and attention.

If your boss isn't open to practicing Vital Tasks Management with you, or if you're in a relatively unsupervised situation, you can create a self-administered vital tasks program for yourself that will dramatically improve your performance. Identify your vital tasks; put them down in writing. Regularly evaluate your performance against each of your performance standards.

For example, you are in charge of customer complaints, and one of the vital tasks you have established for yourself is to call back, the same day, every person who has called in a complaint. Upon evaluating your performance, you find after a month that you have only done it 35 percent of the time. Look carefully at what strategies you can change to increase your ability to call them back sooner. Continuously examine and modify your standards, and the strategies you use to meet them.

Most of the tasks you set should be measurable, at least in terms of the percentage of time you take to perform the task. Some of your vital tasks may not be measurable; leave them in your written agenda to help you keep your attention focused on them. The area to focus on most is the specific tasks that can be measured. Regardless of the nature of your work, evaluate your performance. Once a week is the longest you should go between evaluations. If you come across a problem you can't solve with your own ingenuity, then and only then should you get someone to guide you to a solution.

Using this idea, people who work alone have been able to increase their output dramatically. For example, here is a self-administered vital tasks agenda created for an independent salesperson, and designed to identify the vital tasks that contribute to top sales performance. Each task identifies and isolates one component of effective sales results. For example, task number one is a way of focusing attention on a crucial issue for salespersons: many can't distinguish between refusal and rejection because of a craving to be liked. Fearing rejection, they usually end sales calls without asking the customer to buy anything. No matter what type of work you do, you can create a vital tasks agenda; use this one as a model and modify it for your own work:

1. I ask for *specific action on every sales call*, even if there is no chance for an immediate sale.
2. I listen *to*, not against, others.
3. I probe for a deeper understanding of *each* account on *every* sales call.
4. I delegate everything I can to everyone I can!
5. I teach people to treat me as a professional.
6. I call on the *biggest prospects* in my territory.
7. I call on the *major decisionmaker* at such prospects.
8. I use *creative visual aids* on every sales call.
9. I keep *creative records* on all accounts.
10. I *organize my time* for maximum efficiency and effectiveness.
11. I devote two hours per week to *creative planning/evaluation.*
12. I keep *open communication* with my manager.
13. I operate at ever-higher levels of *self-direction.*
14. I operate from an ever-deepening *sense of calmness.*
15. I am a legitimate sales executive full time.

Evaluation: Identify what percentage of time you take to perform each task (e.g., if you call on the major decisionmaker one in four times, your score would be 25% of that particular task). Performing at 75% or more on each task will dramatically raise your effectiveness and results.

Raises and Promotions

The best way to prepare the ground for a raise or promotion is to work with Vital Tasks Management. If that's impossible, make sure you are being evaluated by results. There should be no ambiguity about what you have to do to rate a positive evaluation. Indeed, these questions should be decided when you first hire your boss, and should be reappraised regularly. In addition, you should remind your boss regularly of your goals (many bosses like to maintain the status quo as long as things are going well, and conveniently forget that you want to move up), and you should keep your boss appraised of your accomplishments.

If you think a raise is overdue, ask yourself whether that conclusion is justified. Put yourself in the boss's shoes and evaluate your performance against company policy and the company's financial condition. *Would you give yourself a raise?* If so, why? If not, why not? You must go to your boss with solid evidence to back your request. Being a loyal employee is not always sufficient to warrant a raise—you must be able to cite things you have done or are equipped to do that will increase your value to the organization.

Have you reached all the goals you have been given? What improvements have you brought about? Have you found ways to save your company or department money? Have you found ways to boost productivity? How has your contribution decreased costs or increased profits? Have you acquired new skills since taking the job? Have you acquired training in new areas? If you're in charge of other people, how have you improved their performance? What have you contributed to morale? What have you contributed by way of new ideas, programs, policies? How has your work affected the company's future positively? Can you back up each of these points with proof?

If you go to your boss with a portrait of sterling achievement, be prepared for a counterargument. He might point out ways in which you did *not* achieve goals and objectives. He might point out some of your mistakes. Perhaps he might point out costly losses. Faced with such objections, many persons cower. Realize that mistakes are part of the game and that the boss does not expect perfection. The way you respond to his criticism will make a difference in whether you get the raise or not.

Don't pass the buck; don't look for scapegoats. If factors outside your control contributed to problems, point them out realistically, without making excuses. Take responsibility for losses as well as victories. To paraphrase Mark Twain: Anyone who wants to take credit for the sunshine has to take credit for the rain. Remain positive, optimistic, and solution-oriented. Point out the steps you took to solve the problems your boss has brought up. Point out what you learned from your mistakes, and how you took innovative steps to prevent recurrences.

Point out how you managed to cut short your losses. Don't argue. Bring the boss's attention back to positive results, and get him to look for your future contributions.

Timing, of course, is critical to a raise request. Tax time might not be best, but just after a big deal has been signed might be ideal. Consider your boss's mood. Is he under pressure? Has he been on the road a great deal? Is there an important meeting coming up? You want to see him when he's in a good mood and his slate is relatively clear. Your meeting should be unpressured and unhurried. Here is where your relationship with the secretary/assistant will count.

Promotions should be handled in a similar manner, although you can't move up in most organizations until someone else moves out. *Avoid organizations where career tracks are established with rigidity and promotions are given on the basis of seniority, not talent.* Remember, the ladder narrows the higher you rise; it's up to you to outperform the requirements that determine promotion.

Sometimes, those criteria are vague. Getting your boss to be clear and up front is critical, and will give you an inside track on the promotion. Also critical is making sure you are always evaluated according to the stated criteria. Further, make it your business to understand company politics. Find out why and how promotions were given in the past. The hidden criteria are often the most important ones.

People whose self-esteem hinges on status and outer achievement see promotions as crucial to their self-worth. Many an executive, however, has been sorry he or she ever took the promotion, because the added pressure, the immense responsibility, the change in actual work routine, and the alteration of social and personal life, made him or her far less happy than before. In some cases, the added stature and the increased salary just do not compensate. A raise that puts you in a higher tax bracket may not increase your net income.

Long before you are offered a promotion, you should determine whether or not you actually want it. Tell yourself the truth and assess the next rung. Talk to the person now in the job; visit someone in a similar position. See what their days are like. Many jobs seem irresistible but can be hell in actuality, if the match between the position and the personality is ill-fitting.

The situation is particularly acute for salesmen, who are always assumed to be heading toward the sales manager's position, and also in academic circles, where professors are thought to aspire to be department chairmen. Often, too little is done to determine if the person who is next in line is actually the right person, both in terms of skills and temperament. It's assumed, for example, that the top salespeople should step into the manager's job when it becomes vacant. But the top salesperson may not have a manager's talents or temperament. The result: the company loses its best salesman in return for an incompetent manager; and the person who got the promotion has to go from performing a job with excellence to one he or she must muddle through.

How can this be avoided? For one thing, the criteria for promotion should reflect accurately the demands of the job, and the criteria should be made clear at the time of hiring. In the case of sales, volume should not be the sole factor, as it so often is. Other criteria should include a certain number of management courses taken at a university, or training new employees and new sales representatives. These criteria ensure that the candidates are devoted to acquiring the skills needed to manage. In addition, they provide a face-saving way of saying *No* to the promotion offer—candidates simply don't fill the appropriate criteria.

If you are being groomed for a position that you decide you'd rather not have, let your boss know before he has committed time and energy to preparing you. If you don't, he might feel let down, and your future relationship will be jeopardized.

How can you tell your boss that you aren't interested in a promotion without making it appear you are unambitious or lazy? Be honest and upbeat: "I really like working here and living in Novato. I have strong ties in the community, and I want to raise my family here. I'm aware that the usual move for someone in my position is to district manager. Since that would involve relocating, I want you to know that I'm not a candidate for the job. I would gladly consider a lateral change or a promotion, as long as I can stay here."

Or: "The job I have now is challenging and absorbing. It makes use of my talents and gives me an opportunity to excel at what I was trained for in school. I enjoy working with you very much. These things mean more to me than money and status. Therefore, I'm not interested in becoming head of the department when Hansen leaves next year. I thought you should know that."

How To Hire the Right Boss

We've looked at a number of ways to increase your chances of getting raises and promotions. Let's now look at how to find and hire the right boss.

The best time to begin managing your boss is before you are hired. Find the right boss. Your goal, in most cases, should be to find a "develop" leader. Check his rate of turnover before accepting the job. If he has a solid track record of creating winners, it means your chances will be greater. Remember, winners spawn winners.

The question of how to handle job hunting is of vital significance to any ambitious person, and should be approached with creativity, diligence, patience, and care. The key element is an upbeat attitude. The first step is to assess your strengths and weaknesses, your personal and professional goals, your likes and dislikes. Before you begin your search, you should know precisely what you want and be equipped to present yourself as a valuable employee. You will then approach potential employers from a position of strength—as someone who has a lot to offer an organization and who is looking for an organization with a lot to offer in return.

If you have difficulty determining what form of work you are suited for, and how to find the right place to do it, consult *What Color Is Your Parachute?* by Richard Nelson Bolles (Ten-Speed Press, 1978), and *Go Hire Yourself an Employer*, by Richard K. Irish (Anchor Press/Doubleday, 1973, revised and expanded, 1978). In evaluating what you really want out of a job, you should clearly think through and answer a number of questions: What is your attitude about relocation? (Many organizations require it, although fewer now than in the past.) What is your attitude toward promotion to different forms of work? (Some organizations still punish the person who refuses to accept a promotion.) How will certain work integrate with the work of your spouse? What hours will give you the opportunity to enjoy activities that are personally important to you? How much travel are you willing to endure? Project five years into the future. Try to assess what you would like to be doing then. Very often, by looking into the future, you can have a much better picture of the type of job you should seek now.

When you are evaluating an organization, find out as much

as you can about the particular job you are applying for, and the person who will be your boss. Visit the company, or the actual department that you are considering working in. Ride the elevator at lunchtime and quitting time. Have a cup of coffee, if possible, in the employee's cafeteria. Listen to conversations; look at the faces. Are the people happy? Are they relaxed? Are they bored, tense, angry? If possible, watch how the management people interact with subordinates. Do they communicate well?

You might be able to speak with some of your potential boss's employees. People like being asked for advice, and they may help if you explain that you are considering a job and want to determine whether it is right for you. You might even be able to arrange an interview with the person you will replace if you take the job. Why is that person leaving? What has his or her experience been with the boss?

Find out as much as you can about the company. If its stock is publicly traded, look over its latest annual report. Read trade journals. Call the Better Business Bureau to see if there have been complaints about the company in the past. If possible, talk to competitors, suppliers, and customers to get a feeling for how others see the organization's strengths, weaknesses, and problems. You may also be able to find out pertinent information about your prospective boss: how is he or she perceived by peers? This kind of information will not only give you some feeling for the boss and the organization, but will increase your chances of being hired, should you choose to apply.

Before applying, search for creative ways to meet a high-ranking person in the organization—the higher the better. You might, for example, find someone who knows the person, and have a meeting arranged. Or write a letter expressing interest in the work he or she does, and requesting a very brief meeting. Few people will turn down someone who politely asks for help; the person may even be flattered. Your letter should be to the point. Don't sell yourself—sell only the importance to you of a brief meeting. I have been contacted by many people aspiring to be public speakers. When the request is clear, and they are willing to meet at a time that is convenient for me, I often see them. In this way, I have helped guide several of them to successful speaking careers.

If appropriate, you can use the brief meeting as a first job interview. But never violate the stated purpose of the meeting—to ask for advice and information. Never overstay your visit unless the other person requests it. Armed with what you have learned in this initial meeting, you'll be in a better position to begin the standard interviewing process.

Having done your homework on the prospective job and boss, you are now ready to present yourself creatively. At the meeting, act naturally. Nothing else works as well. You are not only helping your chances of being hired by being yourself, but you're ensuring that there will be no "hidden contracts" that can lead to problems after you're hired. Don't be deferential. Your attitude should be: "We are both involved in something important. He's hiring an employee, and I'm hiring a boss." Don't be afraid to surprise the boss with a question or two that he or she is not used to hearing from a job candidate. You should ask what qualities he is looking for in a subordinate, or why the present person is being replaced. You should also ask what reason he has to believe that his organization will prosper and grow, and why it offers an opportunity for an ambitious, valuable person.

These types of questions are usually asked only by the *interviewer*. But if you ask them, you will not only stand out but might also find out some things that you should know. Don't be afraid to say something like: "What is it really like to work for you, Mr. Jaeger?" Many bosses are so interested in getting the hiring process out of the way that they whitewash the job requirements so as not to scare off the candidate. Or the boss may simply not know how to express clearly what he expects; or he may be under stress and preoccupied with other matters.

Make sure all your questions are answered clearly; there should be no hidden contracts when you start to work. Ask the prospective boss his policies on anything that concerns you, and determine those concerns clearly before your interview:

—Do you like someone who can make decisions and follow through, or do you like to have everything checked with you?
—Will you want me to write letters based on my understanding of the situation and the person to whom they are being sent, or will you dictate everything?
—Am I going to answer all phone calls, with discretion about buzzing you?
—Am I going to be asked to travel?
—Will I get to deal directly with the customers?
—If I have to see the dentist or drive my son to camp, can I take time off if I make it up later?

—Would you be willing to use a dictating machine instead of having me take shorthand, so I can use my time better for both of us?
—How will I be evaluated? Will we both have a clear idea of how to measure what I'm supposed to do?
—What is the company's policy on paying for higher education?

Such questions are legitimate. *Don't hesitate to ask them.* As long as you make it clear that you're willing to work hard and that you appreciate the fact that you are there to produce, it is legitimate to express your own needs. Be sure, however, to put your questions in the proper context and not to sound pushy or demanding. Let the boss have his say before you have yours. And preface your remarks with a statement that says more or less: "I'm asking these questions because it's important that I understand fully the nature of the job. I don't want to take a job that is inappropriate for me, or in which I couldn't deliver what you expect. These questions will help me decide that, and I think they will help you decide if I'm right for the job."

Be candid about your own needs. Don't disguise them in hopes of creating a good impression. "Mr. Ritchie," you might say, "I enjoy being a productive employee, and I have the qualifications to handle the type of work you have in mind. The organization seems to have a bright future. In most matters, I'm very flexible, and I thrive on being given challenging work. But there is one area in which I can't be flexible. As a parent with two young children to care for, it's important that I be home at a fixed time. Under emergency conditions, I can arrange to have my sister help out. But on a day-to-day basis, I must leave the office at five. I can come in early when necessary and I will deliver a solid day's work every day. But if you need someone who can stay late often on short notice, I'm afraid I'm not the person."

Doing preliminary research and making creative use of it during your interview will pay off. If you want the job, chances are other people do, too. Give yourself an edge and get off to a strong start by earning the boss's respect during the interview. Being able to speak intelligently about the business, the industry, economic conditions, and related matters will impress the prospective boss. If, in addition, you can hone in on some of his specific problems or pet projects, he will be much impressed. Indeed, if the boss is *not* impressed by imaginative initiative displayed before you are hired, you've learned something vital already. This may not be the boss you are looking for.

Cahlil Morrissey wanted an editorial job with a book publisher. She searched for information in the publishing community and read recent issues of *Publisher's Weekly* and the *New York Times Book Review.* From her research, she learned about a prominent executive who wanted to strengthen his company's relationships with movie studios. He was interested in joint ventures on properties that could sell as books and as movies. Even though no position was then available in his department, she landed an interview with the executive. When her questions uncovered that he was a movie buff, she managed to let him know of her interest in movies, of her screenwriting course in college, of her familiarity with the prospects of book/movie tie-ins, and of her favorite directors. The executive went out of his way to help her get an editorial position in another department, in hopes of one day creating a slot for her in his own department.

Joseph Flake, president of Flake Travel, told me what happened to him recently. He interviewed five candidates for a regional representative's job. His standard procedure was to interview each applicant twice, consider them further, and make his selection within a month. One of the applicants, Cindy Julian, questioned Flake extensively during the first interview. She asked about the future of the industry and the company, about the exact skills and requirements for the job, and precisely what her duties would be. She took down careful notes. At the time of the second interview, she had a professionally prepared presentation that recapped every major point made in the first interview. Then she showed exactly why her skills, interests, education, and experience suited her for each of the requirements mentioned. In all his years of interviewing, Flake had never seen anybody take that much responsibility and present such a carefully documented case for being hired. He waived his own procedures and hired her on the spot.

Knowing some of the prospective boss's interests, points of view, likes and dislikes can also help you make your evaluation and create a good impression during an interview. If, for example, you find out the boss is chairman of the local Big Brothers, and your husband does volunteer work for the organization, you might want to mention it during the interview, as long as you don't use the affiliation unfairly but simply to establish some common ground.

Jeanette Manes was one of four pianists applying for a job at an elegant cocktail lounge. Each of the other candidates let the prospective employer tell him or her what type of music to play during the audition. By the time Jeanette came in, the manager was tired. He had one of the first three in mind for the job. Jeanette didn't wait to be told what to play. "If I had this job," she said, "here is how I'd approach it. If I saw a lot of people in their twenties in the audience, I'd play this type of music." She played some contemporary songs.

"If," she went on, "I saw an older group, I'd play some of this." And she played some standards. "If the audience seemed lively, I'd play like this. If they seemed quiet or melancholy, I'd play like this."

The manager was impressed with her initiative and her versatility. Then Jeanette played her trump card: "And if I looked over at you, and saw you'd had a bad day, I'd play this." She moved into "Smoke Gets In Your Eyes."

"That's my favorite song," said the manager.

"I know," said Jeanette. "I asked the bartender." She got the job.

Once you hire your boss, get off on the right foot by demonstrating your talent and your good intentions. But be careful not to come on too strong. Remember that you are not your boss's only concern. While you may be eager to prove your value, don't demand too much of his time. Let him acquire his impressions of you gradually; don't let him perceive you as someone who will drain his time and energy.

Act naturally—be yourself. Don't let your ambition tempt you into creating a false image of yourself or adopting a style that is unnatural for you. Your boss will see through it. You can't live a masquerade forever.

Be positive and upbeat. Be seen right from the start as a positive force—a problem solver, not a problem creator. Don't be critical when you discover, as you surely will, that the boss or the organization is less than perfect. Take nothing for granted. Don't assume the boss has your best interests in mind—he or she may be well intentioned but may not understand your goals and your desires. It is your job to keep him or her aware. If, for example, you have your sights set on a particular promotion, or are looking forward to being given a particular responsibility, see that your boss realizes it. But before expecting understanding from your new boss, set out to understand him. If the boss doesn't provide feedback, ask for it.

Three months after being transferred to a new department, Donald Nelson married his assistant and decided to risk asking his boss how he felt about the wife continuing to work as his assistant. He discovered that his boss had strong negative feelings. Donald and his wife decided it was in everybody's best interest for her to work elsewhere. By asking for feedback, he avoided a possible crisis.

While it is risky to ask for feedback, the risk you take by not asking is often greater.

Remember, it is easier to create an attitude than to change one. The impression you make on your boss at the beginning will be far more important than any you will make in the future.

6

Communicate Effectively

"The effectiveness of your life is determined by the effectiveness of your communication."

—Earl Nightingale

Effective communication means getting across the meaning you want to convey. In this chapter, we will look at some exciting ideas for creating effective communication. They will greatly enhance your ability to manage your boss, your work, and your life.

Unclear communication leads to the familiar cycle of resistance-resentment-revenge. If the people with whom you are communicating don't understand what you are doing, or how you are doing it, or what you are trying to get across, they will resist you. Before long, they will begin to resent you. And because of their confusion, or lack of understanding, they will ultimately get revenge by not doing what you want.

On the other hand, if you are clear in getting your meaning across, you will have achieved the first step in the cycle of clarity-cooperation-commitment. When two people establish clarity between them, they create a high level of effective cooperation. Out of that comes commitment to each other.

Increase your effectiveness by taking full responsibility for the communication between you and your boss. It has been said that communication is a fifty-fifty proposition, a two-way street. That is not accurate. Communication is a 100–100 proposition. Each party must assume *full* responsibility for understanding the other, and for causing the other to understand him or her. To say that communication is fifty-fifty is to imply that each person is to go only halfway. Each must go all the way so that there will be no barriers between them.

Four Modes of Communication

There are, essentially, four categories of communication: underwhelming, imposed, feedback, and confluent.

The *underwhelming* mode is practiced by subordinates who are so timid that they either say nothing or hedge their comments with so many clauses that they have no power. The underwhelming subordinate is afraid to express his or her feelings or ideas. An extreme example would be: "Mr. Kleeman, my co-workers think I deserve a raise. What do you think?"

Imposed communication is the most irresponsible, as it consists of the boss imposing his views on the subordinate. The boss does all the talking; you had better do all the listening. The boss is, in effect, telling the subordinate: "No disagreement allowed; no comments necessary." If the subordinate speaks his mind, the message that comes back is crystal clear: "I disagree with what you say, but I respect your right to be punished for saying it." Afraid to relinquish control, the imposing boss creates an immediate and long-lasting breakdown in communication.

The third mode of communication is the *feedback* style. A higher form than the first two, but still not ideal, it is practiced by bosses who are not threatened by any form of feedback, including different approaches, viewpoints, or even disagreement. The boss does most of the talking, but the subordinate is free to respond. The boss, in turn, responds well to the clues and signals conveyed by the subordinate.

Only the fourth category, *confluent* communication, comes close to removing the barriers that characterize most communication. It occurs when both parties take one hundred percent responsibility for communicating clearly. They do not make value judgments about the feelings, attitudes, or ideas of other people; they allow others to be who they are. The boss who practices confluent communication encourages others to express their feelings, hopes, resentments, and beliefs, and feels equally comfortable discussing the relevant parts of his or her job with subordinates. In essence, each party in confluent communication is saying: "I can tell you who I am and what I feel, and you can tell me who you are and what you feel, and neither of us will be damaged for having done so."

It is important for each party to be able to express his or her feelings. In reference to work subjects or business problems, both boss and subordinate should be able freely to discuss their feelings. It is the only form of communication that is truly responsible.

Before we discuss the elements needed for creating confluent communication, make an evaluation for yourself. Think of a person with whom you have never been able to communicate effectively. Hold that person in your awareness. What caused the poor communication? Most likely, you will discover that the person tended to listen *against* you, that he or she had erroneous assumptions about you, and made value judgments about what you were saying. As a result, there was no acceptance and no trust; you were unable to express your feelings.

Now think of someone with whom you *have* been able to communicate well. What made that possible? Most likely, this person accepted you, listened *to* you, not against you, and evaluated what you had to say without value-judging and without making assumptions. Trust and acceptance made it possible for you to express your feelings.

Language without trust is an empty jangling of sounds; language *with* trust comes close to being a sacred bond. If you can establish acceptance and trust, you are well on your way to creating successful, confluent communication. Whether you are a boss or a subordinate, it is critical that you get across the fact that you really are who you communicate you are, and that what you say is really what you believe. When people learn you can be relied upon to back up your words with actions, you will be effective in winning trust, creating allegiances, and getting things done.

Learn to Communicate with Yourself

A major portion of the 90 percent of our time we spend communicating is spent communicating with ourselves, via dreams and silent dialogue. The better you communicate with yourself, the better you will be in communicating with others. Here are five ways to avoid crises in self-communication.

* * *

1. Stop value-judging yourself, and don't accept the value judgments of others. First of all, listen to what you say to yourself and about yourself. The next time you find yourself getting angry or upset, listen. Do you hear yourself saying: "Here you go again, you hothead?" The next time you are afraid, will you really be telling yourself: "There you go again, you coward?" Do you say things like, "You can't do that," or, "You'll never learn, you jerk?" Such negative value judgments about yourself limit you, destroy your self-esteem, and trap you in the past. If you continue to rehash the past, you can't deal effectively with the present, and will be unable to influence the future. Let the past go. Use it to hone your judgment to deal with the present and prepare for the future.

When listening to what you say about yourself, you can intervene and make appropriate changes. Instead of the value judgments, you might say something like: "That particular area of my life is not working the way I want it to. What is there about my state of awareness that prevents me from handling this the way I would like?" Take responsibility for your own inner communication.

It is equally important to stop accepting the value judgments of others. Take the case of a woman who applied for a news reader job at an ABC station a number of years ago. The executive who interviewed her said that she had no chance. He said she had a speech defect and the wrong energy level. As everyone knows, Barbara Walters now works for that network, and she earns much more than the executive who failed to hire her. Had she accepted his value judgment, she might have communicated with herself in such a way as to cause failure instead of success. The next time someone tells you that you can't do something, remember it is just their value judgment; it is not necessarily accurate. As a matter of fact, almost without exception, highly successful people have succeeded in spite of what many people predicted for them.

2. Take your own counsel. Because of low self-esteem, we sometimes give a lot of power in our lives to other people. There are actually people who go to plays on opening night and don't know whether the play was good until they read the critic's review the next day. If two critics have opposing views, those people never know if they liked the play or not. Listen to your own inner voice, learn to understand what it is telling you, and make your own decisions. Inside each of us is a highly creative mind that can be communicated with, and from which ideas can be liberated to make us more effective. Listen to your internal "wizard," but don't be whimsical like the person who says: "If at first you don't succeed, the hell with it."

"The Strangest Secret," a cassette recording by Earl Nightingale, has helped more than a million people to learn to rely on themselves. Get a copy and play it once a month for a year. It will expand your competence and creativity. (It is available from the Nightingale-Conant Company, 3730 West Devon Avenue, Chicago, Ill. 60659.)

3. Practice new responses. Many communications mistakes are based on old, outmoded habits. Practice new ways of responding to situations that have caused problems in the past. Mentally rehearse the preferred way of responding. Often, the way we imagine ourselves to be is the way we turn out. Practice by visualizing while in a state of relaxation the way you'd like to perform. Many athletes have broken world records by visualizing the performance before doing it.

4. Operate from calmness. There is no greater barrier to communication—inner or outer—than anxiety. If you evaluate your past errors in communication, you may find that many, if not most, occurred when you were nervous, overworked, or under great stress. If you want to achieve high levels of competence, learn to cultivate inner calm, even in the midst of chaos. The section on managing stress in Chapter Eight *(Prevent a Personal Energy Crisis)* will provide some suggestions.

5. Develop a genuine sense of humor. The single most essential life-survival skill is to develop the capacity to laugh *about* yourself, while not at yourself. A genuine sense of humor means more than being able to laugh at a funny joke. Throughout history, it has been proven that men and women who can laugh even in the midst of tragedy are better able to survive and to grow. Norman Cousins, in *Anatomy of an Illness,* shows how he developed a genuine sense of humor and helped reverse a terminal illness. He obtained old "Candid Camera" films, and as he watched, he found that the more he laughed, the more he was able to sleep without pain. He used laughter to save his own life.

One of the best examples of a person who has found humor in adversity is the blind jazz pianist George Shearing. Because handicapped passengers are boarded first, they sometimes sit on airplanes a long time with no one to talk to. One day, aboard a 747, Shearing grew bored. Then he got an idea. He asked a stewardess if he might speak with the pilot. When the pilot asked if he could be of service, Shearing said: "Yes, I wonder if you could exercise my Seeing Eye dog before takeoff." And so, while passengers crowded on board for a crosscountry flight, they were greeted by the spectacle of their pilot walking down the aisle led by a Seeing Eye dog. It made Shearing's day.

Shearing's wife shares his sense of humor. Asked what she would do if her husband upset her, she replied: "I'd rearrange the furniture while he was away."

Develop the skill of laughing *about* yourself. It will help you communicate with yourself and others, and it will help you make both a living and a life. Remember, the absence of a sense of humor can be a sign of mental illness.

Listen To, Not Against

Several years ago, a major university surveyed fifteen thousand poeple throughout the United States about the things that upset them most. The single biggest gripe was: Nobody listens to me.

If you watch closely, you will see that most listening between people is what I call listening *against*, as opposed to listening *to*. The listener is often on the alert, not to understand what the speaker is saying, but for ammunition. He is either trying to prove the speaker wrong, or in some way to score points for himself.

Caused by lack of skill in communication, this form of listening conveys an absence of trust, and it creates an adversary relationship between the two people. There is a powerful antidote to listening against: "Active Listening." Developed by the pioneering educator and psychologist Carl Rogers, Active Listening proves to the speaker that you are devoted to understanding his or her views and feelings. It saves time, reduces errors, and creates a climate of cooperation and trust.

Active Listening gives the speaker the opportunity to surface, evaluate, and clarify feelings that might otherwise remain buried. It also makes the speaker responsible for his or her feelings, while making the listener more aware of what is really being communicated. A powerful tool for smoothing out sensitive situations, Active Listening pays big dividends. Once the speaker knows you are able to understand him, he becomes more willing—or less *unwilling*—to understand you. Here are the six basic steps in Active Listening.

1. Begin with a clear intention to understand the other person before you seek to have him understand you. (It is vital to understand the other, but remember that you are not required to *agree* with him or her.)

2. Match the tempo and tone of the speaker. If you are full of energy and enthusiasm about an idea, but the other person is slow and his tone is sober, you might make a serious mistake by overpowering him with your faster tempo and upbeat tone. Slow down to match his tempo and tone. An excellent way to do this is to synchronize your breathing with his. By so doing, you can create a strong connection, and then slowly move him toward the enthusiasm and excitement you feel.

3. Listen carefully *to* the person. Refuse to be blinded by your own prejudices. Do not assume you know what the other person means to convey. Too often we listen against other people, twisting their words to fit our own purpose. Here is a good example.

Lou Witt was traveling on a plane and struck up a conversation with the stranger in the adjacent seat. At one point, Lou remarked: "All violence would end if people would live by the golden rule—do unto others as you would have them do unto you."

"I agree with you completely," said his companion. "An eye for an eye and a tooth for a tooth."

That's what can happen when a person doesn't really listen.

4. Watch for what will never be said out loud. Read the nonverbal signals of others, and use nonverbal communication to reinforce your own message. The way you look at someone, walk, or sit, the way you dress, the way you hold a piece of paper—all these and thousands more contribute to your effectiveness in communicating with other people. For example, a liar is usually caught, even if he is not aware of it, and even if the person who caught him is not consciously aware of having done so. The liar betrays himself unknowingly with microsecond-quick responses to his own lies. His voice might break, his skin flush, his pupils dilate; his face might twitch, or he might turn his body as if to protect himself. The listener may not be aware of it on a conscious level, but he may begin to feel uncomfortable below the conscious level, where the discrepancy is perceived clearly. If it happens, say, in a sales presentation, the salesman will wonder why the customer did not buy. Indeed, even the customer might wonder: "That salesman seemed to have what I wanted. Why didn't I buy?" The liar is caught, but nobody knows why or how.

5. The meaning is in a combination of content and feeling. Be aware of both. If you catch *only* the content or the feeling, you will receive only half the message. *Remember, feelings are neither right nor wrong; they just exist. Don't make a negative judgment of someone because he or she expresses negative feelings.* We each have whimsical, contradictory, and negative feelings, and if they are not expressed, they get buried deeper and deeper. Don't let uncomfortable feelings deter you from understanding.

6. Restate without repeating. Translate what the other person says into your own words, but try to convey the meaning without being obvious, and without merely repeating the other person's words. In fact, at times, this can be done without words—by a simple, silent nod, or a question asked in order to clarify the person's message.

Here is an example of how Active Listening can defuse a person's anger and allow for a resolution of a conflict that both sides can accept. It also demonstrates the high risk of making assumptions.

It happened while I was conducting a morning seminar on communication to all 160 employees of Sherman Industries in Palmyra, New Jersey, in a catering hall not far from the company's headquarters. I had just finished explaining Active Listening and was about to have the audience break up into small groups to practice. Suddenly, the back door was kicked wide open, and in stormed a huge man in a long blue coat with silver buttons down to the knees and a hat shaped like those worn by the Royal Canadian Mounted Police. He thundered out at the top of his voice: "That's a two-hour parking zone out there and your cars have been there for three hours. The other merchants are on my back because people can't park to get to their stores. I'm sick and tired of this happening. Get those cars the hell out of there!"

Considering the uncanny timing and the man's appearance, I quickly assumed that the president of the company had played a joke by hiring an actor to pose as a policeman. So I laughed in the man's face. I then looked over at the president seated in the front row, expecting to see him laughing. Instead, he looked as if he were questioning my sanity. And the 160 employees were looking up at their guest speaker as if to say, "Go ahead, Slick. Show us how to communicate."

I turned back to the intruder and realized I was dealing with a genuine police officer. By this time, he had unbuttoned his coat to reveal a badge and a revolver. I also realized that by laughing I had made a bad situation much worse. Here is how Active Listening defused the situation.

I realized that the policeman was under a great deal of stress. I looked at him and said, with feeling, intensity, and high volume: "You feel you have no other choice but to make us move the cars right now."

This caused him to let more of his feelings out. He said: "Yes, that's what I want. I've been called in off my beat before because of cars parked outside this hall and I'm tired of it."

"You've been put in the middle before," I said, "and you haven't been able to resolve this."

"Yes, that's right," he said, much more calmly. "And I'm not going to allow it to continue."

At that moment, he seemed to realize he had grossly overreacted to the situation. He suddenly took responsibility for his feelings because he realized that I accepted those feelings and understood them. He then became as interested as I was in solving our problem. In a few more seconds he was smiling. "But it's no big deal," he said. We were given another twenty minutes before having to move the cars.

Active Listening is not a miracle, but it is a very valuable tool that can work in a wide variety of circumstances. If you want to create alliances with other people, master the technique. You can't create the Three C's without being able to listen to others, and you can't truly listen to others except by Active Listening.

Let's look at an example of a work situation in which Active Listening was used. Bob Jenkins was a supervisor in a plant that had a pattern of unexpected overtime. One afternoon, he said to his foreman: "Alfred, I'm sorry, but we've got to complete an emergency job. You and your men can't leave until we're finished." Angrily, the foreman burst out: "This is a lousy place to work! I can't ever plan my evenings. I'm getting sick and tired of taking all the brunt of other people's mistakes."

At this point, Bob had a choice—to pull rank or to use Active Listening. Many supervisors would have replied: "Look, buddy, it's a pretty good place to work. Shape up or I'll replace you." Instead, Bob said: "Alfred, sometimes you feel that the other departments don't really understand what we're required to accomplish. Instead of handling their own responsibilities, they make promises that we have trouble delivering on."

"Yeah, that's right," the foreman responded. "Sometimes I feel like we don't even count."

Once Alfred saw that his supervisor understood his feelings and allowed him to express them, he felt less upset. He focused on how to get the work done. He still had to work late, but he knew his boss clearly understood his feelings and hadn't criticized him for expressing them. Had the supervisor responded in an authoritarian, uncomprehending way, Alfred's negative feelings might have been even more deeply imbedded, and the Three-R cycle would have begun.

Let's reverse it now, and show how an employee used Active Listening on her boss. Yvonne Henning's boss came roaring into her studio, shouting: "I thought I told you to have those illustrations finished by ten o'clock."

Yvonne's response was: "It must really mean a lot to you to see those illustrations before your meeting with the client."

That sufficiently defused the boss's anger and allowed him to put his attention on what really mattered: solving the problem in cooperation with Yvonne. Had the artist responded to the outburst defensively by saying something like: "How could I get it done by ten o'clock when Mr. Conrad comes in at nine with an emergency touchup? It's his fault, not mine," the boss's anger would not have been curtailed. Had she just said: "Sorry," that too would not have been enough. Had she misused Active Listening by saying something like: "Now, Mr. Huff, I understand you're angry," she would have made things worse.

By responding as she did, Yvonne acknowledged her boss's anger and the cause of it. She demonstrated that the message had gotten through. No longer did the boss have to vent his wrath. With Active Listening, trust and acceptance are conveyed, and people can turn from a display of emotion to a discussion of content and solutions.

How can you immediately begin to employ Active Listening? Here is a way to test personally just how powerful it is. The next time you and another person have very strong opposing feelings about something you'd like to resolve, try this: Sit down with that person and allow him or her to make a thirty- to sixty-second statement. Then restate what was said until that person agrees, "Yes, that's what I was trying to communicate to you." Then switch. You make a statement and have that person restate it to your satisfaction. This way, each time one of you makes a statement, it's absolutely certain that you're understood by the other person. Continue making statements and switching. You'll come very close—if not all the way—to a solution by quickly resolving strong feelings and understanding one point at a time.

It's truly amazing how people are willing to understand as soon as they feel understood.

The Empathy-Impathy-Ampathy Triangle

To a large degree, good communication requires mutual understanding and adequate information about the subjects and the persons involved. To achieve these, practice empathy, impathy, and ampathy.

Empathy means situating yourself to understand your boss. Your communication will improve to the degree that you can see, sense, and feel what the other person is seeing, sensing, and feeling. Your communication should convey this attitude: "I want to understand everything you want me to understand."

One way to acquire empathy is to tell your boss: "I'm interested in learning all I can about working here. I'd like to be as valuable as possible to you and the company. In order to contribute more, I'd like to know the areas of *your* job that are most critical, and what the major demands of your job are." In addition, you should watch and observe your boss as much as possible. See what it means to be him or her, and examine all the factors we discussed in Chapter Three.

Impathy means situating someone so he or she can understand you. Once I had an associate who drove as though he were in the Indianapolis 500; driving with him was a harrowing experience. One day we stopped for lunch and my stomach was so upset from the drive that I realized I had to do something about it, since we were due to drive together the rest of the day. After lunch, I got behind the wheel, and proceeded to drive recklessly, switching lanes like a halfback. Within minutes, he was gripping the dashboard. "What the hell are you doing?" he cried.

"I'm showing you how you drive," I said.

It was essential for my associate to know what it felt like to be in the passenger seat with him at the wheel. The demonstration really impressed him, and he drove carefully for about a week. Impathy is not a one-time experience. You have to create continuing opportunities to use it.

Involve your boss in a variety of different ways, so that he will have a first-hand understanding of the reality of your work. Have him spend time with you on the job, if possible. Invite him to attend some of your staff meetings, tape segments of meetings for him to listen to, or route minutes to him.

Some bosses are open to this, and in fact some companies so well understand the value of impathy that they build it into the work situation as a matter of policy. A car rental company, for example, responded to a request by divisional managers and now has the president and all vice presidents work for one week a year at a rental counter. They do this anonymously, to see what the life of a representative is like. Some organizations extend the practice to the families of employees. A number of police departments have the officers' spouses spend time with them in their cruisers, so the spouses can better understand how the officers' work affects their home lives.

Be imaginative, and you will cause your boss to understand better what your work day is like. Here is an example of how a group of handicapped workers at a manufacturing plant got their point across. They had been unable to get management to see the necessity of improving the ramps and other special facilities that allow disabled workers to get around better. So, on the occasion of a board meeting, the workers rented extra wheelchairs and requested that the board members ride them for a tour of the plant. They got the needed changes. You may not be able to be quite that dramatic with your boss, but you might find appropriate opportunities to create impathy if you look for them continuously.

Creating impathy can bring important and immediate results. Elliot Friedland worked for a major consulting firm. He had a chance to land an important assignment, but in order to do so, he had to complete the first phase of the project within ten days. However, his firm had such a backlog of commitments that it would take Friedland ninety days just to get the information he needed. This was a case of the boss's understanding being critical. Just telling him about the situation was not enough.

Friedland got the boss to join him when he met the prospective client. In that way, the boss heard straight from the source what the pressures were, and what was in it for his company. The boss responded by juggling other deadlines and bringing in extra people. Elliot saved the account as a direct result of involving his boss.

Ampathy involves understanding the reality of the world in which you live. Are you making the most of the information sources available to you? Can you speak definitively on all vital matters that relate to your work? Avail yourself of a wide range of sources; even information that seems only peripheral to your concerns can prove valuable.

Stephanie Kersey had a meteoric rise to the top of an international organization. I asked her what her secret was. She explained that when she took her first position, she began immediately to expand her range of knowledge. She subscribed to the international edition of the *Herald Tribune*, to the London *Financial Times*, and to major news magazines from other parts of the world. She regularly read book reviews on subjects with international themes, and then read the books she felt deserved her attention. At one point, her department's main concern was Japan, so Kersey joined a local Japanese cultural club. All these attempts to establish a widening information base paid off.

Evaluate what you must be informed about to understand your job completely. Approach new information with a receptive attitude, determine its value to you, develop and improve it according to your needs. Ultimately, you yourself determine what you will get out of any experience or any particular source of information. A marvelous source of information is the cartoon section of *The New Yorker* magazine.

Support, Don't Criticize

Bosses and subordinates are both ideally situated to spot weak points in each other's performance; they often see ways in which the other can improve. The problem comes when those ideas are expressed in the form of criticism. Sometimes, sound ideas that the person could benefit from are never put to use because they were improperly conveyed.

Constructive criticism is almost always destructive. Even well-intentioned criticism can be destructive, because what really matters is how the person receiving the criticism experiences it—not what the criticizer's intention is. So, even if your intention is to help, it is not effective if the person feels put down or diminished by your criticism.

In our seminars, I often ask the audience: "How many of you use constructive criticism with your subordinates?" Almost everyone raises his or her hand. Then I ask: "How many of you enjoy *receiving* constructive criticism?" Hardly any hands go up. "That," I say, "is how much your subordinates enjoy your criticism."

Although I never liked to be criticized myself, I used "constructive criticism" as a way of getting people to do things the way I felt they should be done. I had no alternative. Then, during a discussion with one of my executives, my criticism turned the meeting into a violent argument. Leaving the office with my stomach in knots, I suddenly saw another way. It has since worked well for me and many others. It is called the "mutual support agreement." Here is how I used it after that violent argument.

One at a time, I explained to the people who worked for me: "I'd like you to know that for as long as we work together, you have my permission and my encouragement to comment on how I can be a more effective executive. I'd also like you to give me the same permission. If we work in a mutually supportive manner, helping each other improve our work, we will each benefit."

Because I was seen as a criticizer, it took some time before they accepted the idea. Each time I worked with one of them, I would conclude by asking for ideas on how I could improve my performance. The feedback I got enabled me to see certain of my weaknesses for the first time, and it showed me I had strengths that I had neither understood nor utilized. I quickly became a more effective leader. After four or five such meetings, most of them felt comfortable enough to ask me how they could improve their performance. The entire context of our relationship changed. Now each meeting consisted of two people raising their own self-esteem and working out ways for each to be more competent. Our individual and group productivity improved substantially. We had replaced criticism with mutual support, and could now be competitive and cooperative simultaneously.

With a mutual support agreement, each person's suggestions are supported by the other person. It gives each person not only the right but the *responsibility* to comment on how the other's performance can be improved. Mutual trust, respect, and cooperation will be established and continually enhanced. If you are in charge of others, carefully create a mutual support agreement with each of them individually. Attempt to establish a mutual support agreement with your boss as well. If you handle it creatively and responsibly, you will find your boss's feedback more agreeable, and you will be able to improve your boss's effectiveness as well as your own, in a way that you will both value.

Remember, a mutual support agreement is not a license to criticize or express feelings inappropriately or to behave like a watchdog. Also, don't view a mistake as a reason to discontinue the agreement. I recall an assistant of mine with whom I had a mutual support agreement that worked quite well, except for one unfortunate mistake. During a meeting with my sales staff, my assistant interrupted to tell me I had an urgent call. The caller was the one salesperson not at the meeting. I was disappointed and angry over his absence. Since I wanted my assistant to listen in on all but personal and confidential calls so she could follow up intelligently and quickly, she was on her extension when I excused myself from the meeting to take the call.

Blinded by anger, I made no attempt to understand the salesperson on the phone. I berated him for not being at the meeting and hung up on him. A minute later, my assistant, visibly upset, stormed into the meeting to which I had returned. "Mr. Hegarty," she said, "you were rude and unfair to that man. It sounded like he had a legitimate reason for not being here."

Afterward, exercising *my* rights under our mutual support agreement, I informed her that what she had done was not appropriate. Her response was important and accurate—I *had* been unfair and rude—but it should have been communicated in private. Even with a mutual support agreement, you must provide your feedback in such a way as to let your boss save face.

Establish a mutual support agreement only if and when it is appropriate. Not every boss will be open to the idea. Suggest it only when and if you are convinced that the boss will not feel threatened, and will not think you are presumptuous. Explain it in a way that shows the benefits your boss will receive.

If you're a boss as well as a subordinate, an excellent way to get your own boss to establish such an agreement is first to establish one with your subordinates. Then, when you suggest it to your boss, you can demonstrate results: "I'd like to tell you about something that's worked well in my department." You can even sow the seeds indirectly by sending one of your peers a description of how your mutual support agreement has increased your group's productivity. Present it as an idea he or she might find valuable, and carbon your boss.

Another way might be to tell your boss a story. This strategy can work with any procedure you want to propose, if you feel a direct proposition will not be well taken. In a relaxed moment, you might say: "I recently learned about an idea called mutual support agreements. It provides an alternative to criticism. I always thought you had to be critical of people if you wanted them to shape up. But I tried this idea with the volunteer group I manage for my church, and it worked. I get along better with the others, and we get more done than ever before. My brother is using the idea in his real estate firm, and he says it's done wonders."

There will be times when your boss does something with which you disagree. He may, for example, promote someone you think is wrong for the job, or commit the company to a capital investment you think is unwise. How can you disagree without appearing to criticize if you *don't* have a mutual support agreement?

The first thing to do is make sure you understand completely why the decision was made. Was your boss under pressure from above? Are there facts you are unaware of? If, in the final analysis, you still disagree with your boss, be sure to express your dissenting view without letting your emotions get in the way. You may be hurt or disappointed, but keep to the facts, and keep your emotions out of it as much as possible. Your feelings can, and should, be expressed; but that can be done without displaying negativity. Most bosses are uncomfortable with such displays, and they tend to think ill of subordinates who are what they might term "thin-skinned."

Back up your opinions with as much evidence as you can. Offer alternatives. Remember what we said about going to your boss with solutions, not problems. Telling him you disagree with a decision, or disapprove of an action, gives him nothing except more aggravation. Spell out your suggestions and alternatives clearly, don't just disagree.

Don't Embarrass or Ridicule

Never underestimate the importance of saving face. To save face, people have been known to cheat, lie, and kill. Nations have gone to war in order to save face. To save face, people have stayed in bad marriages their whole lives. And people have destroyed relationships with bosses by trying to save face or by not allowing the boss to save face.

In all your communications with your boss, never forget that his or her need to save face is as great as your own. Build him up, don't put him down. Sometimes the temptation to criticize or point out a fault will be strong. Determine whether your motivation is based on wanting to improve effectiveness or to get even. We all want our day in court, but where your boss is concerned, it is often better to forego justice for the sake of having the freedom to do your job.

For example, suppose your boss has been issuing ambiguous directions that have caused problems in your department. A careless way of expressing that would be: "Mr. Goren, we're having a lot of trouble understanding you lately." A less threatening way of putting it would be: "Mr. Goren, the staff is unclear about what you want us to do. How can we create higher levels of clarity so we can back you up better?"

Suppose your boss comes down on you because you gave him the wrong data. You are enraged because the mistake was not really your fault. Don't defend yourself or argue. Don't immediately point out the boss's error. Wait until the crisis passes, and then explain, politely, in a noncritical way: "Mr. Dyson, the most up-to-the-minute data doesn't get to us until the fifteenth of each month. I gave you the most recent figures available. If it's ever again necessary for you to have up-to-the-minute data, please give me notice, and I'll have the accountants run it down."

You let him know you were not at fault and you allowed him to save face. Without cornering him, without looking for revenge, you showed him there is a better way to handle the situation.

Even if your relationship with your boss is warm and cordial, be careful. In fact, we tend to be off guard when a relationship is friendly. Bosses can let you kid them, they can be buddy-buddy, but if you cause them to lose face, you may discover a huge barrier between you and your boss. If you have a relationship that permits teasing, be sure to kid him up; don't kid him down. Don't make jokes or careless remarks about areas of sensitivity, such as his sexual capacity, family, popularity, wrinkles, bald spot, athletic ability, professional stature, or whatever. Like all human beings, every boss has his or her vulnerable areas. Be aware of them.

Be careful, too, of subtle ways you might make your boss feel put down. Bear in mind his or her particular insecurities; never phrase a remark that might even remotely be construed as an insult. For example, you might say, in passing: "Business is sure tough these days. You really need a strong mind and body to keep afloat." On the surface, there appears to be nothing wrong with such a remark. But if your boss is sensitive about aging, such an off-handed statement might easily be taken personally.

Be alert to potential face-losing situations and help prevent them. Protect the boss, if necessary, from his or her own tendency to look foolish. You will earn the boss's appreciation, and prevent yourself from becoming the target when he or she feels required to do something to make up for the loss of face.

Here is a good example. Mary Ann Haines was the head accountant in a regional office. She was aware that her boss seemed to be padding his expense account and that the auditors at the home office were concerned about his large expense submissions. They demanded exact records from Mary Ann's boss. But she didn't say: "Mr. Stone, the auditors believe that you are padding your expense account, and they want me to verify every dime." Instead, she said: "Mr. Stone, the auditors at home office are making us look at all expense accounts. We have to verify everything. I know it's a bother, but can I ask you to supply receipts for all your expenses? I have to authenticate all accounts, even yours."

Consider your own need to save face as well as your boss's. That too can cause problems. How do you respond to your boss's putdowns, both intentional and unintentional? Is your need to save face so strong as to lead you to destructive reactions?

If your boss has a need to put you down, remember that it is his or her problem, not yours. You are not the real target, even if your boss uses you as one. But no matter who or what caused the situation, you are responsible for changing it. By using one or more of the techniques in this book, you may be able to mitigate the boss's inappropriate putdowns. But if his intention is to destroy his subordinates, do your work with excellence and look for another job! Better to be unemployed than to work for a boss who is bent on destroying people.

How To Say No To Your Boss

Archie Tucker's boss called him on the phone toward the end of the day. "I want you on a plane tomorrow morning," he said, "You're to deliver some important documents to our representatives at the contract meeting in New York."

"It must be very important that the papers get to our negotiators by tomorrow," said Archie. "But there's no way I can be on that plane unless you're willing to shift some other priorities around. If I take the plane, I can't talk to the marketing department at their ten o'clock meeting and I won't be able to finish that advertising prospectus by Friday, as you requested."

Archie did not stop there. "But I have an idea," he added. "I happen to know that Joan Finch, over in sales, has to be in Newark tomorrow afternoon. Maybe she could leave a little early and get the papers to the meeting for you. Shall I ask her?"

Then Archie went on. "If that doesn't work out, I'll find a way to go myself, as soon as you get someone to take over the marketing meeting, and if you'll give me until Monday for the prospectus."

That is a good example of how to say No to your boss. Archie did so with a minimal risk of causing resentment, and without demeaning his boss's order. Let's analyze the components of his reply.

1. Acknowledge the importance of the issue. That was the first thing Archie did. He did not let the boss feel as if his request were trivial or foolish; and he showed no sign of resenting the request.

2. Answer with an unequivocal No. Archie let his boss know that he absolutely could not go to New York under the present conditions. This is important. If you equivocate, as many subordinates do, you open the door for resentment when you don't fulfill the request. "I'll see if I can get to it," or, "I'll try," is almost the same as making a promise. If you do not do what was asked of you after saying you will try, the boss will be disappointed, if not angry. Make the situation absolutely clear, stating the precise reasons why you have to say No.

3. Assist without getting involved. Archie gave the boss an alternative, Joan Finch, and offered to make the call himself. By so doing, he demonstrated his loyalty, gave further credibility to the boss's request, and indicated that he was willing to help.

4. Declare your availability on your terms. Archie said he was willing to fulfill the boss's request, and outlined the conditions under which it would be feasible for him to do so.

These four steps, of course, cannot be followed in all situations. But in most cases the approach will not only get you off the hook, it will raise your esteem in the boss's eyes. It is respectful and to the point. Further, if the boss ends up forcing you to take on the assignment despite your refusal, you have covered yourself for having postponed the completion of your other tasks.

Here is another example. Your boss says: "We're promoting a new line of matching leisure outfits for husband and wife. We want you to help manage the exhibit in Seattle this weekend, and we'd like your husband to accompany you. Here are two plane tickets."

Your response might be as follows.

1. "This sounds like a great idea and an important one. I can see where having a couple at the exhibit will make a big difference."

2. "There's no way in the world I can get my husband to disrupt his plans. As a matter of fact, he wouldn't like my going alone either. We try to keep our weekends for ourselves."

3. "Perhaps Mary and Jack would like to do it. I know they love to travel, and I'm sure they'd do an excellent job."

4. "If Mary and Jack go, I'll be happy to cover some of their responsibilities for them in their absence. And if you need my husband and me for a future trip, perhaps we can arrange it if you give us more notice, and allow me a day or two off on either end of the trip to be with my family."

Don't Make Assumptions

Two men, each of whom had seven children, were riding an elevator and discussing their common problems of raising a large family. A man standing behind them said, "I'd like to have seven kids myself." Another passenger, overhearing the remark, attacked the man. "In this age of ecological imbalance, when the world population should be curtailed, why do you wish you had seven children?"

"It's easy, lady," replied the man. "I have twelve."

The woman had made an assumption, and as is very often the case, the assumption was wrong. On the elevator, the result was only mild embarrassment. In some instances, however, the consequences of making a wrong assumption about another person's intended meaning can be disastrous. On Tenerife Island, an air traffic controller said "Okay" to a pilot. The second man assumed what the first man meant by "Okay." He was dead wrong. As a result, almost six hundred people were killed when two jets collided on the ground.

Think of the many assumptions you bring to your interactions with other people. Think of the many things you assume about your boss or about your boss's attitude in a particular situation. When she turns down one of your suggestions, is it really because she is afraid to be shown up, or might she have sound reasons for saying No? When she asks you to stay late on Monday, is she really being unreasonable, or did she work things out in advance so you wouldn't have to stay late on Tuesday as well? If she says she can afford only a 10 percent raise, is she being stingy or can she really afford only a 5 percent raise and is willing to stretch it for you? Find out the facts before making a determination.

You should also be wary of assumptions your boss might be making, or that you might be making about your subordinates. While on the phone with the national vice president of sales for a large company, I could tell he was so upset he could hardly speak. I asked what was bothering him. "I rehired a regional manager," he said. "I put him out in a territory. He recruited two new people, worked with them three days, and went on to another district. It takes at least seven days of training before you can leave a new person in a territory. I'm trying to reach the guy now. I'm so angry, I may fire him."

I said, "How many times did you tell him that you feel it takes seven days of training?"

"What do you mean?" asked the irate vice president. "I'm going to hang that guy. It takes *at least* seven days!"

"That's not what I asked," I said. "How many times did you inform him that you are convinced it takes seven days?"

This stopped him cold. Then, in a much different tone of voice, he said, "I never told him."

"You made the assumption," I said, "that your regional manager held the same belief as you without even expressing it to him. You have no reason to be upset with him. You assumed he knew what you believed. When you reach him, communicate your concern clearly."

"I will," said the vice president. "And you're right. I have no reason to be upset with him."

Do not assume that the other person understands or even cares about your needs. Many crises come about when one person feels his or her needs were not understood or appreciated. In most cases, it turns out that the offended person did not make his or her needs clear. Before communicating with anyone, remind yourself that no one—not your spouse, and certainly not your boss—will always have your interests at heart. Often, they do not even know what your interests are—unless you clearly communicate them.

While it may be difficult to suspend the assumptions you bring with you to an encounter, try to keep in mind that even premises that seem perfectly logical are often incorrect. Go slowly and check out your assumptions by listening to others and asking questions.

Be Careful of Neutral Statements

People have a tendency, particularly in highly charged relationships, to translate a neutral statement into a negative one. Follow this rule: Make your positive statement first, and if necessary follow it with a neutral one.

For example, a husband sits down to dinner. He tastes the soup. "You've never made this soup before," he says. What does his wife think? In many cases, "Oh, no. He doesn't like my soup."

In reality, the man might have thought the soup was delicious. He might have intended to add: "It's really great." Unfortunately, he made his seemingly neutral statmeent first, and the damage was done. Had he said, "Darling, this soup is great. You've never made it before," the impact might have been entirely different.

A man bumps into an old friend, who says: "Boy, have you changed!" What does the man hear? Probably: "I've gotten so old. He thinks I'm over the hill."

The old chum might have thought the man changed for the better. But what was heard, filtered through the man's own self-esteem, was negative. What a difference if the man had used his positive statement first: "Joe, you look fantastic! You've really changed. Time has been kind to you."

And what if he actually *did* think Joe looked awful? What if the husband actually *did* feel the soup was terrible? They should not have said, "Boy, have you changed!" or, "You've never made this soup before," if they were interested in having the listener save face.

Let's look at some business examples. The boss says, "I watched you with that last customer." The subordinate hears: "Oh, God. I blew it."

The boss's intention might have been quite different. If so, she might have done better to say: "You're doing a fine job. I watched you with that last customer."

Here are two examples of how a subordinate might unknowingly create a crisis by issuing a neutral statement in place of a positive one. In an example used earlier, a subordinate said unthinkingly: "Business is sure tough these days. You really need a strong mind and body to keep afloat." If she meant it as a compliment, she should have said: "You really are remarkable, Mr. Young. You have to have a strong mind and body to make it in business these days."

Here is another example. The subordinate says to the boss: "That sure was a tough meeting you just held." The boss hears: "I was too harsh. He's complaining again."

What a difference if the speaker had said: "I'm really excited. I'm sure things will be a lot better around here after that tough meeting you just held."

An ambivalent statement leaves too much room for a negative interpretation. If your intention is positive, make sure you express yourself in a way that makes the point clearly.

Practice and Empathize

Learn to be as word-effective as you are cost-effective. Your prepared statements should be lean; don't waste words, don't ramble. Get right to the point. Practice your statements, listening to yourself on tape if possible. If really crucial, find a way to rehearse with videotape equipment.

Anticipate your boss's response and be well prepared for each contingency. Get someone to play the part of your boss, and encourage him to play devil's advocate. In this way, you can practice your responses to your boss's possible arguments. Then flip the situation around. You play your boss, while your friend takes your role. Attack your own argument imaginatively; that will acquaint you with a wider range of possible responses from your boss.

A well-prepared, carefully considered statement might turn out as follows: "Many of us are considering requesting extra time off before Christmas. From your viewpoint, I can understand why you would be very concerned about our getting the job done if a lot of people took off. I'd like you to know we're all prepared to do whatever is necessary and have already taken steps to get ahead of our work so we won't cause a crisis. In fact, you may not realize it, but we often stay late or come in early so we are sure not to cause problems by taking extra time off before Christmas. I believe the company's goals will be met more than adequately, and we can have a little more time for our families."

Get Immediate Feedback

A lot is lost trying to convey a message to another person. People tend to think in pictures and speak in words. It is naive to think your pictures, translated into your words, will create the same pictures in someone else's mind.

One way to get around the problem is to cause feedback from your listener. Have him play back your message in his own words, to be sure there are no discrepancies between your meaning and his interpretation. While it might not be appropriate to ask your boss outright to repeat what you said, there are ways you can get his views without making it appear as though you are testing him or her.

For example: "This is how I plan to present our financial statements to the bank in order to try to extend our line of credit. I'm having our financial vice president bring our books up to date so I can present them to the branch manager. With reference to cutting down on accounts receivable, I'm issuing this memorandum to the sales force, which changes our credit terms according to what we discussed at yesterday's meeting. Is that how you want me to go about it? Can you tell me what you think of my plan and any changes you would like me to make? How do *you* think it should be done?"

You are asking the boss to respond directly to what you have said, and at the same time asking for input. The boss must share the responsibility for the communication and the subsequent action.

By the same token, you should make sure you fully understand your boss's remarks. Give him feedback whether or not he asks for it. "Let me make sure I've got this right. . . ." Or drop him a memo after your meeting, listing the main points and stating that you want to be sure you fully comprehend his intended meaning. Asking the boss to respond to such a memo might appear too demanding. So you might conclude by saying: "I will take immediate action to complete the assignment as outlined in this letter, unless you advise otherwise."

Don't Feel You Have To Have the Answers

One of the quickest ways to start the cycle of resistance-resentment-revenge is to feel you always have to have an answer. In many instances, there *are* no answers, certainly no easy or simple ones. Sometimes the other person has come to you, not for an answer but just to have a problem acknowledged, or to use you as a sounding board.

If either the boss or subordinate feels compelled to come up with an instant answer to every problem, it will not take long for trust and openness to diminish. It's all right to say you don't know, or that you would like some time to think the problem over. Often merely acknowledging the problem is the only—as well as the best—thing to do.

The 0–10 Scale

Quite frequently what people agree about causes more chaos, confusion, and communications breakdowns than what they disagree about. We tend to go along with one another, only to discover later on that we really had vastly different perceptions of the situation. Both parties may agree on a course of action—but for different reasons, or with varying degrees of conviction.

Avoid such breakdowns by having each party clarify his or her exact position. That means how much, or how strongly they feel about something, not just a cut-and-dried Yes or No. Get in the habit of ranking your own convictions on a scale of 0 to 10. Not everything you think should be done deserves the same level of priority. Do the same for your requests—how badly do you want something? Ask your boss to do the same. For example, a boss might go along with a subordinate's ideas because he was not given the opportunity to explain the precise degree of his convictions or agreement.

I had an employee who asked me, "Should I go through the files and bring them up to date?" It was a task I had mentioned in passing one day, but it was not a high priority. The subordinate took it as such, however, and grabbed the first opportunity to get it done.

When she mentioned it to me, I assumed that she needed to clear the files in order to do her own work better; I also assumed she had time to do it, or else she would not have volunteered. In reality, she overestimated the importance of the job to me and was doing it at the expense of something I considered much more important.

Communicate the "Write" Way

You can significantly reduce communications breakdowns by putting as much as possible in writing. Memo your boss about all important agreements, instructions, recommendations, policies, promises, and anything else of significance. Phrase your memos carefully and express the reasons for them in terms the boss will understand and respect. Let him or her know that your intention is to ensure perfect clarity and avoid misunderstandings.

Jim Brown once decided to spur the activity of his sales staff by telling them that excellent performance would be rewarded by a paid vacation. After a while, a salesman demanded his trip. But according to Brown's understanding of the criteria he had outlined, he had not earned it.

That led Brown to realize that many communications crises result from problems inherent in verbal interaction. He established a new company policy in which no agreement of importance was to go into effect unless committed to writing and signed by all parties concerned. A typical letter would review each major point discussed, and would then conclude: "This is my understanding of our agreement of May 7. If your understanding is the same, please sign and return. If you differ, please explain."

Putting things in writing is especially important with bosses who change their minds or who cover their mistakes by denying them, as in, "I never said that," or "That is not what I meant."

Naturally, memos can be overdone. Beware of "paper overload." If you work closely with your boss, if you are in constant communication, if you are in a setting in which instructions have to be given and acted upon quickly, then you obviously cannot commit everything to writing. Save the strategy for situations of importance and in which there is potential for misunderstanding. If you dash off memos too often, or use them for trivial concerns, you might be looked on as someone who doesn't have his or her priorities in order.

At one of our management seminars, the vice president of a large organization told this story. Like many organizations, his was being "memoed to death." He had tried to convince people that most of the memos being circulated were not necessary, and that most were ignored because there were so many. He had no luck. Then, in an attempt to prove his point, he distributed a ten-year-old memo. Everyone on the executive committee signed it. He showed the memo at a meeting, and as a result the organization revamped its procedures and reduced paper communication by 50 percent.

Memos should be word-effective. Long, elaborate memos find a quick route to the wastepaper basket. Most of us like to recieve notes that are brief, easy to understand, and to the point, saving our leisurely reading for material that interests us personally. Yet, when we are the writers, we often forget what the reader prefers. If words were gasoline, most of us would get very poor mileage per memo. For an excellent course on economical writing, pick up a copy of *The Elements of Style* by William Strunk and E. B. White (Macmillan, 1959), a slim paperback that anyone who has to put words on paper should read at least once.

Of course, there are times when the subject is complex and requires a precise, detailed, lengthy presentation. In such an instance, supply a brief statement to accompany the needed documentation. Suppose, for example, you want to prove to your boss that one of your products may soon become illegal because of pending legislation. Don't send a seventeen-page memo. Send a concise statement, such as: "Our investment in the Herrell furnaces is in serious jeopardy, as the enclosed report indicates. Here are the major points [list them]." Additionally, remember to accompany this with your best solution to the problem.

Mind Your Body Language

According to Professor Albert Mehrabian of UCLA, there are three things that create an impact when you communicate: The words you speak, the way you say them, and your visual signals. Mehrabian claims that the words you speak constitute only 7 percent of your impact. The way you say them constitutes 38 percent. The other 55 percent is made up of nonverbal signs, such as the way you stand, the way you gesture, the expressions on your face, what you do with your hands, how you hold a microphone or your notes, how you walk and sit. In all, there are thousands of nonverbal signals. People scream at each other in silence. If you are alert to nonverbal signals, you will be much more effective. Remember, many important things will never be said out loud. Be sensitive, and you will hear them anyway.

For some basic tips on nonverbal communication, we called on Merlyn Cundiff and Amy Heebner. The author of *Kinesics: The Power of Silent Command* (Parker, 1972), Merlyn Cundiff has shown thousands of people in seminars throughout Europe, Asia, and North America how to improve their communication skills. She provided us with these common nonverbal signals and their customary meaning. Be alert to their expression in other people, and use them to give added power to your communications. Keep in mind that these nonverbal signs can appear in clusters. Don't accept any one sign as significant by itself.

Stroking the chin: Usually accompanied by a relaxed smile, this indicates that the person has made up his mind. You can stop persuading. By contrast, indecision is usually evidenced by a strained expression.

Folded arms: The meaning can vary, depending on the manner and location of the folded arms. If they are folded high on the chest, it indicates refusal; leaning forward with arms folded indicates strong resentment. If the arms are loose and folded gently across the lower part of the torso, a relaxed, pleasant mood might be indicated (although some people fold their arms just to hide their bellies).

The eyes: Looking up at the ceiling and rapidly blinking is a sign that the person is considering your proposition carefully. He might have already made up his mind and be working out the details. In addition, watch the pupils—reportedly, they dilate to as much as double their size at something emotionally interesting.

The eyebrows: Raising one eyebrow signifies disbelief; two usually indicates surprise.

The shoulders: Hunched or casually raised shoulders indicate indifference. If, in addition, the lips are curled downward, the indifference is very strong.

Posture: An erect body with head held high indicates determination and energy. Contrast this with the tired, timid look of stooped shoulders.

Rubbing the nose: Usually indicates an attitude of disapproval, disagreement, or resentment.

Drumming fingers: Usually accompanied by resting the chin on the other hand, it indicates that the person is mentally absent.

Fingers together before the chest: Hands in front of the chest, fingers touching, signifies confidence.

Amy Heebner is a specialist in speech and drama who has worked with lawyers and business people, as well as actors. She points out that employees often reinforce their subservience through nonverbal behavior. While subordinates should make certain concessions to avoid causing the boss discomfort—such as not infringing on the boss's "personal space"—many people make themselves more compliant than is necessary. Here are some ways to use your voice and body to assert a more confident image.

For a more assertive physical presence:

1. Use more relaxed, expansive movements. Don't be afraid to use your space liberally.
2. Work toward an erect, relaxed posture, with a comfortable sense of being "grounded" confidently in the earth.
3. Take a stand physically in conversations. Don't shift position constantly, don't skitter around with tiny steps, don't restrict your movement by standing with your legs pushed together. When you take a firm stance, you communicate that you are a strong individual with a point of view, not someone to be pushed around.
4. Don't smile unless you feel like it.

For a more confident vocal demeanor:

1. Practice breathing deeply in the body, so that the muscles of the abdomen and back respond to your breath. To test yourself for shallow breathing, watch yourself in the mirror as you breathe. Do your shoulders rise as you inhale and fall as you exhale? If so, you are accustomed to shallow "chest breathing," and need to practice using the abdomen and back for breath support.
2. Practice supporting your sentences to the last word with plenty of energy.
3. Use more low pitches in your speaking voice. More breath support will help, as will singing, or oral interpretation of poems and prose.
4. Use more falling inflections. Don't end sentences on an upward pitch, making declarative statements sound like questions.
5. Project your voice energetically. Don't be afraid to use your voice, even if it might sound a bit loud at first. Practice by reading a poem aloud to an imaginary audience ten feet away. Then place the audience twenty feet away, then fifty.

Using space to assert yourself:

1. Don't be afraid of a more relaxed, expansive positioning, when you are seated in a chair, for example.
2. Don't always lower or cock your head; use more direct eye contact.
3. Take advantage of subtle ways of saying, without words, "I'm listening, I respect what you are saying, and I have my own viewpoint." For instance, if you enter your boss's office and find that a chair is carefully placed in front of, or to the side of, his desk, move the chair just a foot or so before you sit down. This conveys a sense of establishing your own space.

Confront a Crisis at Once

If a crises arises, confront it immediately, and seek a quick resolution. If you don't, the crisis can easily turn into a catastrophe. In fact, it might become a catastrophe even if you do confront it, but at least you will be there to deal with it. It is easy to hope that a crisis ignored will correct itself or go away—but it seldom does.

Here is an example of how this advice paid off double for one businessman. I was conducting a two-evening seminar, part of which was devoted to communication strategies. On the first evening, I made the point under discussion here: Confront crises immediately. On the second night, one participant stood up and said he already had learned two important lessons from the seminar.

His biggest client, he told us, had been on the verge of taking his business to another company. For weeks, the man had been losing sleep, for the jeopardized account represented 40 percent of his firm's total volume. He had tried in subtle ways to keep his biggest customer, but nothing had worked. After learning about crises in communication, he decided to confront the situation head on the next day. He arranged to have lunch with the client. He then discovered that he had been wrong about the reasons for the proposed shift. Armed with clear, accurate information, he quickly resolved the problem.

"And specifically, what were the two things you learned?" I asked him.

His answer: "One, confront crises before they become catastrophes. And two, it's foolish to do 40 percent of your business with one client."

Time does not heal *all* wounds; in some cases, those left untreated get worse. If you have a communication crisis with your boss, solve it as soon as you recognize it.

Yet, while confronting crises is crucial, *preventing* them is an even better policy. We have looked at a lot of ideas that can make your communications more effective. No matter how bright and creative you are, you need to prevent crises in communication and create the Three C's to have the greatest chance of success. Start today to listen, watch, speak, and write with understanding and clarity. Improve the effectiveness of your communication and you will improve the effectiveness of your life.

7

Strategies for Women

THAT WOMEN now have a wider range of career possibilities and greater opportunity for financial independence and self-expression is a victory for all of us. They have brought a bright new dimension to the world of work—a reservoir of skill, energy, and resourcefulness. In my executive development seminars, there has been a dramatic increase in the number of women attending, and I have found very often that their level of interest, competence, and creativity is considerably higher than that of most of the men. Any organization that does not actively pursue women for all levels of employment is making a very costly mistake.

History will probably determine that our society has managed a period of titanic change with relative grace—in the last decade, we have witnessed nothing less than a wholesale transformation of established traditions. Yet we have a long way to go. Inequitable salary distinctions are still widespread, and in many organizations the door is still hard to open on the higher executive levels. Nonetheless, overall the progress has been significant, but there is still a long way to go.

But, like technological revolutions, social changes bring mixed blessings. For many women, the workplace is, while challenging and exhilarating, a source of tremendous stress. For some it is like playing the Super Bowl every day: fans and teammates expect superhuman performances, management has its eyes peeled for every mistake, and opponents are doing all they can to keep them from the goal line. Adding to the pressure is the fact that women in business have fewer role models and peers on whom to rely for support and guidance. Further, for most women, the responsibility of raising children is not conveniently assumed by another person while they devote their attention to a career. Balancing the responsibilities of home and work is a Herculean task. A woman can easily demonstrate this to an unaware husband by having her spouse take over her household duties for just one week. He will never again underestimate the demands of managing a home and an outside job simultaneously.

For some men the adjustment is difficult. Behavior based on sex-related images and assumptions cannot easily be erased by government pressure, media exposure, or even personal convictions. The day-to-day interaction of men and women in a professional setting is mixed with the patterns that for so long characterized their interaction on the social level. The two don't mix well, and it is a continuous challenge for men and women to balance both. The process, therefore, is often bewildering, sometimes frustrating, and always challenging for everyone concerned.

The conflict between social and professional expectations is strongly felt by women and their bosses. It is hard to relate to a person in two separate ways, especially when doing so runs counter to long-standing habits. This chapter addresses the problems created when women find themselves working for an old-line chauvinist boss, and offers sound strategies for women interested in improving their working relationships with their bosses and their subordinates. It is important that you use empathy and skill to make these men aware of how to deal with you. Do not make their problem your problem! We spoke to a number of women executives, consultants, and workshop leaders who have extensive experience with the dynamics of women and work. Their expertise formed the crux of this chapter.

Assumptions and Stereotypes

The erroneous assumptions that complicate most boss-subordinate relationships are compounded when male-female stereotypes are added. Consciously or unconsciously, some bosses, even female bosses—who often feel that they are the exception to the stereotype—harbor the belief that women are not as strong or as agressive as men. He has been conditioned to believe that women don't care as much about promotions and salary; that they are not willing to travel, relocate, or otherwise sacrifice in order to get ahead; that they will get pregnant and quit, or stay home when a child is ill; that they just don't have the stomach for managing or selling. While some of these premises are true, there are many women who are totally willing and superbly able to meet *all* those requirements, and it is crucial that your boss knows exactly where you stand.

We discussed these assumptions with Vicki Kramer, Marcia Kleiman, and Peg Callahan, consultants with "Options for Women," a ten-year-old career advisory service in Philadelphia. They pointed out that men had always kept women from outside sales positions because they believed women weren't tough enough to handle difficult clients or push through a sale.

Interestingly, those assumptions are being destroyed by women who have been enormously successful in sales and by the corresponding increase in men who refuse to relocate or be away from their families for long. Indeed, selling is an excellent way for a woman to begin her career, as her competence can be quickly and easily measured.

Old, erroneous assumptions about women are still held, of course, by many male executives. However, don't make the mistake of automatically assuming that your boss holds those attitudes. In my experience, most men are much more open to evaluating each woman on her own merits. "Not all male managers have those beliefs," says Vicki Kramer. "Find out what the boss is really thinking. If you just go along, unaware of what the boss's assumptions are, you have no way of knowing how they affect his decisions, and what you can do to change them."

She advises women to open up effective lines of communication with their bosses, and warns against adopting an adversary point of view. Having established good channels of communication, a woman can guard against stereotyping by simply setting the record straight. "End the guessing games right away," advises Kramer. "If you have certain goals, make them clear. If you are willing to travel, or relocate, or take courses, or work overtime, make that clear. Express your level of commitment. Let him know what your goals and aspirations are. Make sure he understands you as an individual, and doesn't lump you together with all other women who fit his stereotype."

In her excellent book *Taking Stock: A Woman's Guide to Corporate Success* (Contemporary Books, 1977), Dr. Sharie Crain makes the same point: "Many of us assume that our bosses or other executives know that we want to move upward in the company. Too often, this is not the case." Dr. Crain relates the story of a woman who unwittingly changed the boss's assumption that she was unwilling to make sacrifices for her career. The woman enjoyed her work, and found she could accomplish more if she stayed an extra hour or two at the office in the evening. She was unaware of the fact that her boss took notice of the one light that remained on after all others were turned off for the day. When the boss checked it out, he was astonished to find a woman working there. In that one instant, says Dr. Crain, the woman broke through a deeply rooted stereotype that would have kept her from getting ahead. Instead, she was rapidly promoted.

The message: Look for direct and indirect ways of making your goals and your level of commitment known.

But, it might be asked, isn't there some truth behind those assumptions? Isn't a woman more likely to have family responsibilities that take precedence over work? "In any particular instance, the assumption may be valid," says Peg Callahan. "The important thing is that the reality for each person be brought out, so that no one is operating on false assumptions. The same is true for women who *do* have a limited commitment, or do *not* care about promotions. It would be just as bad to have her boss assume incorrectly that she has great ambitions."

What about stereotyped character traits presumed to be "feminine"? How can a woman let her boss know that she won't break out in tears the first time she is backed against the wall by a tough customer or a hard-edged executive?

"You counteract those assumptions by your behavior," says Callahan. "Demonstrate that you are not the type to crumble under pressure. We've learned that you can't easily change attitudes. But if you can change people's behavior—both men and women—ultimately the attitude might change.

Deanna Scott is a Chicago-based management consultant who has been training women for fifteen years. She agrees that overcoming stereotyped assumptions is a key factor in a woman's relationship with her boss. Scott adds that business success also requires "reengineering" the woman's own assumptions, and her own learned behavior patterns.

There is a big difference, Scott explains, between the nurturing, harmony-oriented behavior that is successful in family and personal relationships, and the behavior required to win respect in the corporate world. Because the woman's learned responses are to nurture, respond to feelings, and keep everyone happy, one classic male question with respect to promotions is: "Can she be decisive?" For example, could she fire someone if she had to?

While it might sound chauvinistic, the question has some validity. Before the women's movement, young girls were considered to be future wives and mothers, and were trained to provide love and support. You don't dismiss your children if they don't meet your standards. Boys on the other hand, are taught to be goal-oriented. They are taught to judge by actions and performance. From Little League on, you produce—or you're out.

But isn't compassion a virtue? Isn't it good business to create harmony? "Of course," replies Deanna Scott. "In fact, a shortage of those qualities in men has become a big concern. Being supportive, especially as a subordinate, is important. But harmony is useful in the business world only as a means to achieving a goal—it isn't an end in itself, whereas to women it often is. When she becomes a manager, she has to add the male characteristics of being clear, decisive, tough, analytical."

Unfortunately, the women who pick up the necessary managerial attributes often find themselves in a double bind. Two messages come in: one demands the demeanor of a manager; the other demands that of a "typical" woman. "Her boss expects certain behavior from his managers," Scott explains. "He wants her to play by corporate rules. But he too expects a woman to be supportive. Psychologically, he may have a hidden agenda. He feels more comfortable with women who act in a "feminine" way. Insecure, he may subconsciously demand feminine behavior, and resent its absence."

The pressure is also internal. Because women have few role models to emulate, they often learn appropriate business conduct only from their male superiors. Then they might develop a conflict about their own femininity. Am I losing it? What is femininity in the first place? What are my real choices? The confusion appears to men as lack of confidence, thus reinforcing the old assumptions.

Men also encounter two sets of demands, but theirs are neatly separated into home and office. Women have to deal with both sets of expectations while at work, and that can make it twice as difficult.

Today we are beginning to see signs of yet another conflict. For women who value both career and home, there is pressure to fill both roles to perfection—a task that calls for superhuman ingenuity, endurance, and perseverance. Then there are the women who reached maturity about a decade ago, when women's rights first hit the headlines. Now aged thirty or over, they are well on their way to success. But they begin to wonder: "Will I ever have children? Must I forsake mothering? Or must I give up my career gains?" The conflict between home and office, often exacerbated by economic pressure, can be devastating. The result, in many cases, is emotional turmoil.

Your Own Assumptions

In her day-to-day interaction with a boss, the woman's stereotypes about men can also get in the way. Some women, Deanna Scott points out, see male authority figures as either Supermen who will solve all their problems, or Superprotectors who will take care of them. A woman may transmit subtle signals that play into those stereotypes. This makes men feel good on a personal level, but not from a corporate point of view. The professional conflict is reinforced.

Her own sterotyping can lead a woman subordinate astray in other ways. She may, for example, have a strong need to be accepted by the male authority figure. If the boss refuses a request, she might see it as a personal putdown, or a rejection. If to combat this she resorts to the feminine wiles that previously have brought success in winning over men, the stereotype is reinforced. The ideal relationship in the corporate world is based on mutual trust and respect. Friendship is not required and in some cases may create problems.

For similar reasons, a woman might refrain from disagreeing with her boss, even when doing so would be appropriate. She cannot say No to unrealistic or excessive demands, because to set limits is to risk disapproval. Similarly, a woman may find it difficult to make her career goals known.

Says Scott: "Recognize that your boss is not Prince Charming, who will ride in on his white horse and give you everything, as long as you stay nice and pretty and true. He is a human being, assigned to a certain role in a formal hierarchy. He cannot understand your concerns unless you bring them to his attention. He is likely to interpret silence as approval of the status quo."

If what you want is respect and advancement, learn to take intelligent risks: make your objectives clear; play by the rules. Don't be impatient, and don't skirt formal channels. It might take six or seven repetitions before your boss really gets the message. Don't take the lack of an immediate response as rejection. Issue reminders, spread out over a long period of time, and cut the length of the intervals as you go along.

But before you do, our sources advise, think very hard about what your goals really are. Don't make the same mistake that millions of men have made of assuming that promotion and status are inherently worth sacrificing for. Often they lead to less fulfillment, not more. Look hard at what will be expected of you if you are promoted. What skills and behaviors will you need to acquire? Can you adapt to the new way of life? Do you really want to? Moving up can be difficult for anyone, and is often especially tough on women who have been reared as followers, not leaders.

The game is wide open. But before you sign up, make sure you understand the rules, and make sure you are aware of the consequences—both desirable and undesirable—of winning as well as losing.

Feedback and Evaluation

Make it clear that you want feedback. Let your boss know you can take criticism, and that you realize its importance to your development. You should know how you are doing in his eyes, and how you can improve. If possible, establish a mutual support agreement.

Don't be reluctant to take the initiative. Women who feel confident and competent, not only in identifying problems but also in offering viable solutions, have the ability to gain respect for themselves and become valued as an integral member of the organization.

Because they lack the informal channels of communication that have served men well, it is even more important for women to establish practical feedback procedures with their bosses. Men have the so-called old boys network, the golf course and locker room, and the formal mentor relationship. Somewhere along the line, they are taught the ropes, and they are given coaching. For these reasons, the sudden proliferation of women's associations is seen as an important development. A number of women's associations have already achieved high levels of value and stature. Evaluate those appropriate for your goals.

It is your responsibility, say our consultants, to sit down with your boss and make sure both of you are absolutely clear on what your tasks are and how they are to be measured. Keep your boss's attention on results. Make sure you are being judged by your performance, not your personality traits. Your boss's appraisal should not include, "She's a nice girl," or, "She's an attractive girl."

While you are at it, make sure your boss doesn't go too easy on you because you are a woman. Researchers believe this type of overprotection can be harmful, since women do not learn about unsatisfactory work until it is too late. They form an unrealistic opinion of how their bosses view them.

Open feedback channels can be difficult for many women; the fear of male rejection runs deep. You have to realize that going about it correctly can only be beneficial. The worst that can happen is the boss will not cooperate, in which case you are no worse off, and you are that much wiser.

Too Little, Too Late

"Bosses who find themselves supervising a managerial woman for the first time," writes Sharie Crain, "are often inclined to be cautious and overprotective. Supervisors win points by developing good people and lose points if they don't, so they probably want you to succeed. But they may have some typically male doubts about your ability to do so."

They may also have doubts about their own ability to manage women. Men are trained to be protectors; women are trained to support and inspire their protectors. This arrangement can keep women down in the business world. A protective or overcautious boss will fail to give you the opportunity to prove yourself.

The problem can be manifested in a number of ways. The boss may send a man to represent the company at a conference to save you from facing the wolves. He might keep you away from difficult clients or hard-to-handle subordinates. He might not let you travel, or see customers in rough neighborhoods, or do physically demanding work. It boils down to not letting you take risks, and not giving you autonomy. But risk-taking and autonomy are essential if you want to get ahead.

Protectiveness creates conflicts on both sides. As a man, your boss may feel comfortable being protective; but as a manager, he wants subordinates who can take care of themselves. From the woman's side, being protected can feel awfully good; it satisfies one's security instincts. But it can keep you from growing in promotable qualities. Deanna Scott warns women with aspirations: "If it feels too good, if the relationship is too comfortable, you may be locked in to an overprotective boss."

Marcia Kleiman agrees. "The woman has to be aware of being overprotected," she says, "because in her own mind she may like it. The problem is, she may not associate it with the obvious conclusion—when salary or promotion time comes, it's going to affect her adversely. She has to realize that in order to be rewarded, she has to accept responsibility. She has to be willing to do what other people are doing, and she can't accept protectiveness."

Protectiveness can stand in the way of a competent person's career goals. Deanna Scott feels that gaining authority and autonomy are so important that women should use any legitimate strategies they can to win them. One way, she says, is to obtain "incremental authority and incremental risk-taking." In small steps, establish your independent identity. Don't let your boss dismiss your request to discuss a report with: "Leave it on my desk and I'll get back to you." Reply: "I think I'll hold on to it. When can I discuss it with you?" The small measure of power implied in your response should not be lost.

If you are responsible for answering your boss's calls, don't just answer with: "Hello, Mr. Fetzer's office." Say, instead: "Bill Fetzer's office, Deborah Dyson speaking." By so doing you begin to carve out an identity of your own, and some measure of autonomy. If your boss is unavailable, you might even make a tentative decision in his stead, subject to his approval: "I'm sure that will be all right. But let me check it with him and get back to you."

Slowly but continually take over more and more of the responsibilities brought in by the phone, and keep your boss apprised. He'll continue to give you more discretion. You should be able to cover at least half your boss's calls yourself, handle them well, and go up in esteem. But you must mind the rules.

Bosses are often threatened by subordinates of either sex who overstep the established boundaries.

Sharie Crain advises being direct with a protective boss. "If you feel that your boss is being overprotective for your own good, tell him that you appreciate his concern and his desire to have you succeed in your work. Then tell him you strongly feel that your career development depends on your ability to demonstrate that you can stand on your own two feet, and that you would like to have the opporunity to do this."

The overcautious boss may withhold promotion until he is certain you can do everything backwards and forwards. Some women, lacking the confidence and assertiveness required to take risks, collaborate unwittingly. They want to be so thoroughly prepared for the new position that they can't possibly fail. The problem, of course, is you might get stale waiting for certainty. Without risks, advancement is next to impossible. Establishing a support system through peer allegiances is valuable; risk-taking is difficult without someone to turn to.

If, in the end, you feel your boss is keeping you down, you may have to move on. Before you do, however, make sure your boss understands your position. Make sure there are no surprises when you tell him why you are leaving. Leave behind no enemies. One of men's fears is that women don't know how to play by the rules. Therefore, make your move through acceptable channels, and let your boss know you are loyal, but you can't let your career stagnate.

Too Much, Too Soon

On the opposite end of the spectrum are bosses who are overeager to promote women, and women so impatient that they plunge in over their heads.

Ten years ago, women were fighting to obtain management positions. Now, for a number of reasons—for example, affirmative action—in some work settings women are sometimes pushed ahead before they are ready. Like many men, they find themselves in charge of people with more experience than they have. The obvious pressures are compounded by the resentment people have toward anyone promoted only because management needed or wanted a woman in a high position.

While some bosses promote too quickly because they truly want to help, others do it for cynical reasons. "Sometimes," contends Vicki Kramer, "the boss is actually setting the woman up for failure in an attempt to prove that women can't handle management jobs."

Whatever the reason, it is important for the woman to determine whether the time is right for her to move up. She might want to learn more, or develop specific skills. Each person has to determine where to draw the line between excessive caution and impatience. Take no promotion before its time. For anyone, both men and women, the fear of success is often as great as the fear of failure. When you receive a promotion the pressure is on—now you have to perform!

"Women are very impatient these days," says Geraldine Rhoads of *Woman's Day*. "I think many of them miss out on the real experience they should be getting out of their jobs. It is important to master the job you have, and grow in the ability to cope, so that you can grab on to the next rung and hold on. Some people think there is a sharply inclined ladder, and that you should move up a step each year, like in school. It's not always that way—for men or women. If you are too impatient, you will be perceived as pushy, unsophisticated, or unworldly."

What can you do if you find yourself in over your head? Deanna Scott advises honesty. She tells of a woman with no engineering background who was put in charge of an engineering department. Realizing she had walked into a potentially explosive situation, she addressed her new staff with total candor. She explained the situation and asked for their help and support. At the same time, she pledged her trust and respect to them. The group fell in behind her, helped her learn the technical aspects of the department, and supported her managerial decisions.

Had she tried to overcompensate with authoritarian methods or pretend to know more than they did—she most likely would have failed to establish a supportive relationship. Ironically, she did so well that her boss soon promoted her to another position she knew nothing about.

One alternative to moving up too quickly, or to stagnating too long, is a lateral promotion. Geraldine Rhoads points out that lateral moves provide the opportunity to acquire professional acquaintances; a wider perspective on the company, the industry, and the boss; new skills and information; and new peer alliances.

Demeaning Tasks

"If he says, 'Make some coffee, sugar,'—CREAM HIM!" So read a picket sign at a demonstration by an organization called Cleveland Women Working. While the group had a general point to make, the specific target was the editor of a local newspaper who was in the habit of sending only copy girls, not boys, for coffee. Publicly ridiculed, and gifted with an eight-foot diagram of how to make coffee, the editor now has both men and women handle the coffee assignment.

Women everywhere are speaking out about the demeaning jobs that bosses—both men and women—often hand out with undersized paychecks. Secretaries and others in supportive roles commonly complain of being asked to do trivial things not in their job descriptions—buying theater tickets for the boss, arranging vacations, decorating the meeting room, shopping for gifts, serving lunch, making coffee.

They have a point, our experts agree. But they advise putting things in proper perspective. "There are lots of problems in business that women have to contend with," writes Sharie Crain, "so let's channel our energy toward the important ones." She points out that men also do legwork, and take care of odds and ends for bosses; they even make coffee and pick up theater tickets. "They don't feel demeaned by that," says Dr. Crain, "because they recognize the value of their time and their boss's, and because they know that their willingness to do what needs doing will be an important element in the boss's perception of them."

Don't make the mistake of thinking that getting coffee is a demeaning experience. There are other ways of knowing whether you are really being held in low regard. You have to distinguish between unfair or demeaning treatment and a logical divison of labor. Perhaps the key factor is: Are you being treated the same way as men, or are you being given menial tasks just because you are woman? If it *is* a case of sex-related stereotyping, you should nip it in the bud. But getting too upset over relatively trivial matters like coffee may soon give way to behavior that can jeopardize your career goals. But it is important to treat the situation without creating animosity or tension. Your boss may have no bad intentions and may be acting out of habit. Always ask yourself what is more important, freedom or fairness. By making a big issue of small matters, you run the risk of being labeled a troublemaker and of having your freedom to work effectively curtailed.

Vicki Kramer cautions against overreaction to minor issues. She suggests waiting until you have objectively assessed the situation. Don't jump on the first sign of a demeaning task; it might be normal treatment even for men in the same position. Many women are so on guard for discrimination that they find it everywhere.

We also suggest placing the boss's requests in a larger context. Look behind the action to the intention. Is there have a one-sided attitude about service beyond the call of duty? Or are you allowed to take time off when a family problem arises? Do you get to take unauthorized breaks, or leave early when things are slow? Ask yourself if you want a relationship that goes strictly by the book, in which neither party is entitled to ask for anything beyond what is written in the company manual. If your boss makes concessions for your personal needs, he or she may just be expecting payment in kind by asking you to do something you consider demeaning.

Your goal should be a mutually supportive relationship, in which both parties' needs are met.

Meetings

As a result of deliberate sabotage, discomfort, or old habit, male bosses frequently exclude women from key meetings. This, of course, can deprive the woman of important information and visibility. Deanna Scott suggests first evaluating the situation to see whether you really belong at the meeting, and whether male peers are also being excluded. If you decide you are being discriminated against, and that as a result you are at a disadvantage, Scott advises: "Fight to the death to get in. If the meeting is critical, get invited even if you have to volunteer to take notes in order to do so. You can always deal with that later on."

"Persuade your boss in a pleasant way," says Geraldine Rhoads. "Tell him you can't produce what he wants because of your exclusion. It is difficult for a woman in that position to learn how to play the game."

One way to conquer any tendency of men to exclude you is to find an influential and supportive male, and work to gain his confidence and respect. He might then serve as your entré to important meetings and informal gatherings.

Once you are invited to meetings, be prepared for strange things to happen, particularly if you are the only woman present. (The sense of intrusion, and the urge to don courtly manners, hits men harder when only one woman is present.) The men might seem uncomfortable; they might stand up when you enter, make a fuss over who sits next to you, worry over whether they should pull out your chair for you. They wonder if they must defer their usual banter, curtail the dirty jokes and the foul language they are accustomed to. They might even remark, seemingly in jest, about having to mind their manners.

You can handle it with a light touch and a sense of humor. But one form of special treatment is more serious and more difficult to deal with: they may not take you seriously. It is not uncommon for a woman to present an idea and be met with indifference, only to hear a man offer the same idea and have it accepted with enthusiasm. Dr. Crain suggests these strategies. First, speak in a "clear, clipped voice"; a woman's soft tones are easily ignored by busy men. Second, be direct and concise; women are stereotyped as blabbers who drag everything out. Third, observe the men who are effective in getting ideas across, and learn their style.

I am finding that in many executive seminars women are playing vital roles, and often are the people who give direction to the meetings. Don't fall into the trap of thinking that all men are stereotyping you. Be careful to present your ideas professionally, briefly, and clearly in order to gain the ear of everyone present. Be certain to back up every point with evidence. Many men have the same problem of not being heard; it has to do with technique.

If a significant idea of yours is usurped, find a way to get the credit. But not during the meeting itself—that would be too threatening. If you put yourself in a win-or-lose situation with your boss, the odds are you'll lose. Discuss it privately. If your relationship is a good one, you can be candid about your desire to gain credit when it is deserved. You might have to use more sublte means, such as declaring in another context: "You remember when I suggested . . . ?"

In line with communicating the "write" way, reinforce your ownership of an idea by distributing it in a memo. The written word has a different impact from face-to-face encounter. You should also be prepared to back up your recommendations with facts and figures. In the end, the accuracy of your judgments will earn you credibility despite any resistance you may encounter.

While meetings with groups of men can often be uncomfortable, don't discount the advantage you have if you are the lone woman: no one at the meeting has a better chance to stand out.

Seize every opportunity to make people aware of your thinking and your solutions to problems. Participate in meetings you aren't required to attend. Spend time with peers in other departments. Broaden your view of the issues, so you can act as a highly productive, bottom-line contributor.

Sexual Harassment

A very difficult and delicate issue for many women is sexual harassment. In a variety of forms ranging from verbal banter to explicit propositions, there have been a significant number of cases where women have been sexually harassed by male bosses. It is very important for you to determine clearly what you feel is appropriate and inappropriate behavior, and to allow no violation of that code. If you feel you are being taken advantage of, or treated in a manner that is offensive or degrading, you have legal recourse. A growing number of women who have had this problem have brought the issue into the public's, and the court's, awareness.

Before taking legal measures, however, there are several things you can do that might put a stop to the behavior. If you have a good job and an otherwise sound relationship with your boss, make it crystal clear to him that you are not receptive to sexual advances. But try to do it in a way that doesn't embarrass him. Allow him to save face by clearly and politely stating that you value him and the job, but that sexual contact is out of bounds. If you've stated your views clearly and the harassment is still repeated, communicate clearly and candidly that you feel you are being intimidated, and that if it continues you will have no choice but to seek legal action. For further information on sexual harassment, contact your attorney or send a request for information and a self-addressed, stamped envelope to Working Women's Institute, 593 Park Avenue, New York, N.Y. 10021.

Women Bosses

Deanna Scott tells us that most women at her seminars say they would rather work for a man than a woman. Why? Women, the feel, are too tough.

How to explain such a surprising discovery? Scott offers two reasons. First, the woman subordinate cannot elicit the protectiveness she can with a man, and is thus forced to gain acceptance through her work performance alone. Since she has little training in that, the subordinate might perceive the boss as overdemanding when in fact the boss might just be doing what bosses should do—evaluating by results.

The other reason, Scott suggests, is that women traditionally have seen each other as competitors—for men. They are trained to use every device they can to stay ahead of other women, and never to share success with a competitor. Young girls seldom band together in teams. While women are now breaking through this barrier by creating networks and allegiances, much of the ingrained competitiveness remains.

Vicki Kramer adds that women bosses can harbor the same erroneous assumptions about women as men do. Both sexes, after all, have been nurtured in the same social milicu. Successful women may see themselves as exceptions to the rule. Or they may assign the stereotypes even to themselves, and treat female subordinates in a way that reflects their own insecurities.

Some time ago, I was contacted by a major trade association to create and present a seminar entitled "New Dimensions for Women in Business." I suggested to the association director that they use a woman instead of me, and I recommended a woman on the board of that very association who was an extraordinary executive. They turned down my suggestions twice, and I finally accepted the assignment. I then contacted Susan Stein, the woman I had recommended. She provided me with the issues around which the seminar was organized. At the conclusion of the seminar, which was enthusiastically received, I publicly acknowledged her as the author of the seminar and recommended that next year's program be conducted by a woman.

By the way, the executive director of the association, who had insisted on using me instead of a woman speaker, was a woman. You will sometimes find it more challenging to deal with other women than with men. Some women made it to the top before the days of the women's movement and affirmative action; they did it before women had widespread support for career advancement. Because they had to do it on their own, some are unwilling to provide support for younger women. That, plus subliminal competitiveness, might make a woman boss feel more threatened by a female subordinate than by a male—they don't want to be passed by another woman. There are only a limited number of vacancies at the top, which must be shared by both men and women.

In their zeal to make it in a man's world, certain women overcompensate. They might deny their femininity, adopting extreme forms of the characteristics generally felt to be managerial. To prevent being accused of using feminine cunning, and to reduce the possibility of being viewed as emotional or passive, they go overboard in the opposite direction. They become very technically oriented, quantitative, rigid, tough. So careful are they to display no nurturing or supportive instincts that they lose the one attribute no manager should be without—empathy.

Her perceived toughness may also be attributable to the extraordinary pressure such a woman faces. She lives in a glass house; male peers are on the lookout for her every mistake. She might not get the support she needs from peers; in a conflict, a male subordinate might be given the benefit of the doubt by other men. If she errs, the men will attribute her mistake to the fact that she is a woman, not to the kind of human frailties that men are permitted.

Being a boss represents a challenge to anyone, particularly a woman who has learned to play a passive, supportive role. When in charge of men, a woman can have problems being assertive. Be consistent, and make sure the men who work for you treat you as a professional. Don't vacillate between being emotional and logical. Be especially careful to deal with male subordinates so that they don't feel threatened. Be aware that some men are extremely sensitive about working for a woman. Again, don't make their problem your problem!

As a subordinate, you should note that there might be definite advantages in working for a female boss. They tend to have more empathy, and a greater ability to see what is going on beneath the surface level of communication. Male and female subordinates alike can have their awareness expanded and their ability to evaluate people and events enhanced by learning from a competent female boss. Men will also gain tremendous insight into the problems and challenges of women in the work setting, and that can pay big dividends later on, when they have women working for them.

For women subordinates, a female boss can provide a number of advantages. Deanna Scott believes that such an arrangement forces the subordinate to behave in a professional manner, as she can't use the passive-supportive behavior she might find advantageous with a male authority figure. Further, it provides the opportunity to acquire a genuine role model. Peg Callahan adds: "There are an awful lot of mid- and upper-management women who are taking motivated people under their wings and bringing them along."

Kathleen Maloney, senior editor at Times Books, told us how important her first woman boss was for her career. She had been fortunate enough to enjoy good professional relationships with a series of male bosses who went out of their way to coach her and introduce her to the right people. "But," she recalls, "there were things I could not learn from a man, such as what to wear and how to act at cocktail parties, or luncheons, or business trips."

For women in management positions, the challenges are big, and the resistance—particularly from male subordinates and peers—is often still strong. But the opportunities are there, and if a woman can learn how to succeed in the organizational world, she and everyone with whom she works will benefit.

Priscilla Poindexter Smith is the president of three corporations and a well-known seminar leader. She has followed a four-step formula that's enabled her to be highly successful. It would work for anyone, regardless of sex. "One, be clear about what you want to achieve and communicate it clearly to others. Two, be consistent in the way you deal with people and events. Three, be confident by understanding what you do thoroughly; and finally, be calm in front of others no matter what is happening." I recommend to both men and women to remain calm during a crisis—fall apart later if necessary.

Play By the Rules

While the business world is changing rapidly, your organization may still operate under the old axioms. If you want to move ahead, you have to play by the rules. For many women, the adaptation process is difficult.

Without acting like a man, and without sacrificing her feminine qualities, the career-oriented woman is required to deemphasize some of the caretaker/nurturer traits and develop some of what Deanna Scott calls "promotable behavior." For example, there is a vast difference between doting on your boss or worrying over whether he eats or not, and picking up a sandwich for him because he is too busy to leave the office. The former is the sort of mothering behavior that can perpetuate the female stereotype and keep you from looking professional; the latter is common teamwork and cooperation of the sort men routinely provide one another.

Let's look at the positive aspects of having these two sets of traits. The woman who can successfully balance them will bring to work a dimension her less-balanced male colleagues will be unable to match. Not only are some of the feminine characteristics acceptable in business, they are vitally needed.

For example, women are more empathetic than men, an outstanding trait for a manager. That trait can be used to establish and maintain harmony within a group. Remember to distinguish clearly between empathy and sympathy. Don't let your ability to empathize cause you to overreact on an emotional level and sacrifice sound business decisions. Since women can be more intuitive than men, they are often well equipped to combine the faculty with logic to make excellent decisions.

Conversely, some of a woman's culturally induced behavior patterns can work against her career development. And they are hard to let go. A woman executive who conducts seminars for women describes a turning point in her own career:

"I was attending a conference, and arrived back at the hotel late one night after going out for dinner. Realizing I was out of shampoo, I asked the desk clerk where I might find some. He told me that the only place open at that hour was ten miles down the road. To get there would take about twenty minutes each way, and about eleven dollars in taxi fare.

"Just then a man who was also a conference participant came

by. 'I have shampoo,' he said. I automatically fell into a classic female routine—the helpless damsel in distress. Without even thinking about it, my voice and demeanor became flirtatious, even though I had no romantic or sexual interest in the man whatsoever. I asked him if he would bring the shampoo to the desk. 'No,' he said. 'My room is too far away. Why don't you come with me?' When I suggested that a bellhop get the shampoo for me, the man refused.

"At this point, I had a clear-cut choice. I could reject his offer and forego the shampoo, or I could go to his room, and, when he made an advance, pretend to be shocked. I could then walk out—without the shampoo. I thought to myself, 'You are an executive, training other women to become self-sufficient and not use their feminine wiles. Don't be a hypocrite.' So, in a straight, businesslike manner, I said to the man, 'I really need shampoo. No games.'

" 'Then you'll have to take a cab,' he said."

Without a doubt, the man's behavior was out of line. But the woman acknowledged that she had started the game, and if you start it, you have to keep playing. "Those feminine ruses are terrific," she explained. "They allow women to get away with murder, and giving them up is tough. But if you want to get ahead in the business world, you have to retrain yourself. In the long run, those little tricks to manipulate men will work against you."

Most of the women we consulted agreed. Deanna Scott says that when she first started giving seminars, she would have men set up and operate the movie projector. As an attractive woman, she could get away with being too dainty to know how to operate a machine. Men loved coming to the rescue. But she realized that even that small male-female interaction affected her credibility as a speaker with something to offer. She chose to learn how to operate the projector herself.

"Either keep getting the feminine feedback you enjoy," she says, "or equality at work. You can't have both. Which is not to say you can't be feminine. But your primary signal should be, 'I'm not using my femininity in order to get ahead.' "

While toning down on certain traits, the aspiring woman should cultivate promotable qualities. Here are some points made by our sources:

—*Think team.* From an early age, men learn to value teamwork and to place group goals ahead of their own. Those values are alive and well in most organizations.

—*Think organization.* As much as possible, understand the "big picture." Apparently, women are prone to focusing all their attention on the immediate job, without perceiving the organization as a whole. A myopic view will hold you back.

—*Think bottom line.* When it comes to decision making, the bottom line is the final arbiter. As you advance, you'll be expected to be analytical and objective. We know an excellent editor, lauded for years for her impeccable taste and skillful handling of authors. But promotion to higher management has always eluded her. Why? She had openly expressed an indifference to finance. The consensus was, if she had more power, she would likely produce great works of literature and have happy authors, but the company would risk going bankrupt.

—*Learn to take risks.* Deanna Scott asked fifty women in upper management: "What is your biggest regret?" The most common answer: "I wish I had taken more risks." They had been too cautious, they felt. Many experts feel that women are overly cautious for two reasons: they internalize the notion that they don't have what it takes; and they are not reared, as men are, to feel that risk-taking is acceptable.

—*Curb the need to be liked.* Separate your self-esteem from your work. As they grow up, women are taught to win the affection of men at almost any cost. Popularity is the ultimate, as any high school wallflower will painfully testify. The need for masculine appreciation lingers, but in the business world respect is more important than being liked. Don't be fooled by verbal niceties or chivalrous gestures. Many a woman has gotten her hopes up because her boss treated her nicely, only to be disappointed when promotion time came around. The boss was responding as a man to a "nice girl," but he ignored her as a potential executive.

—*Understand the power structure.* As part of becoming traditional conciliators and producers of harmony, women are taught to treat everyone the same, and to view all men as power figures. In a typical organization, women often fail to comprehend status distinctions. They don't appear to respect rank. They might, for example, make an inappropriate "end run" by going around or above their bosses. Learn the ropes and show you understand rank and protocol.

—*Communicate professionally.* In a business setting, certain characteristically feminine speech patterns can create a passive, nonconfident image. For example, a woman might introduce a request to her boss with: "Would it be okay if

I. . . ?'' Deanna Scott recommends the more assertive: ''I think that . . .'' or, ''I have looked into this, and my conclusions are . . .'' Followed by, ''What is your opinion?'' or, ''How do you feel about it?'', those statements project an aura of confidence rather than meekness.

Another thing to look for is a propensity for being overapologetic. Why say, ''I'm sorry,'' when you can just as easily say, ''I made an error. How do you think we can correct this?''

Put the Boss at Ease

A male executive was a panel member at a seminar on women in business. During the first segment, he encouraged the audience to hire women for management positions. The rest of the program went downhill, because the executive lost favor with the moderator when he made a careless remark during intermission. The moderator, a feminist, asked about a mutual acquaintance. ''Oh,'' said the man, ''Mary's a wonderful girl.''

The word ''girl'' so infuriated the woman that she remained hostile through the rest of the conference. The executive, of course, had meant no harm. His choice of words was simply habit, and certain habits take time to change.

While women should be alert for signs of residual sexism, our experts tell us, they should be careful not to overreact. Doing so will make your boss, and your other male colleagues, uneasy, and it might lead to more serious forms of discrimination. Not without justification, many well-intentioned men are weary of being criticized for actions or remarks that can only remotely be branded sexist. If the woman's rejoinder is an emotional one, the effect is double-barreled: not only does it create tension but the woman is branded a troublemaker. And the stereotype of the over-emotional woman is reinforced—a big problem in a world where feelings are viewed as unfavorably as red ink on a balance sheet.

''Not every obstacle is a sign of discrimination,'' says Peg Callahan. ''The term is used too loosely. I would say that eight of every ten complaints I've seen have *not* been rooted in actual sex discrimination. Often the word is a convenient scapegoat for incompetence or impatience. In some cases, the woman may have been treated unfairly, but not because she was a woman—the boss was treating men unfairly too.''

Before you jump the gun, evaluate the situation objectively. Become familiar with the company's personnel manual; understand your job description and the jobs of people who seem to be favored; know what is going on in other departments; assess the salary levels and promotion policies in your organization and in similar ones; compare the way men and women are treated. In other words, gather evidence before you make an accusation.

Most important, guard against putting men on the defensive over relatively trivial matters. "Some men are uptight about how to act with women around," says Vicki Kramer. "They don't know which words to use, or what standards of manners to apply. When they do something like use the word 'girl,' it is important to treat it lightly. Let them know it doesn't mean that much, and that you understand that we're all in it together, trying to adapt to a changing world."

Deanna Scott thinks that women should accept the responsibility for being pioneers and help their bosses adapt to the new reality. "If men are uncomfortable," she says, "it is our responsibility to show them they can deal with women in the business world. Train them. Educate them. If you do, you make it easier, not just for yourself but for all other women your boss will have to deal with."

Although the organizational world is still no rose garden for women, there has been extraordinary progress in improving opportunities and conditions. While continuing to work toward improving things still further, it is important, all our experts agreed, that everyone concerned maintain one vital quality: a sense of humor.

You can make it easier for everyone, Peg Callahan adds, by keeping your boss's focus on job function and results. "Show them that, with respect to work, men and women are more alike than they are different. Everyone is in it for the same reasons; they share similar goals."

The good news for the future is that many companies are no longer advocating a strictly authoritarian (task-oriented) style of leadership. The leader of the future will have attributes such as sensitivity, empathy, and the ability to build and function as part of a team. More and more often, women will be rewarded for their special strengths. The future belongs to the competent, regardless of sex. In an industrial society, strength meant brawn. In an information society, strength means brains, sensitivity, and an ability to adapt to ever-changing needs.

8

Making Your Own Work Work

What You Seize Is What You Get

IN THE FINAL analysis, you are your own boss. Your raises, promotions, and professional and personal satisfaction all hinge on your ability to create allegiances and get your job done. If you do your job competently, your boss will take you seriously; if you do it with excellence, he or she will find you irresistible. Create and follow a lifelong agenda of learning new skills and your future will be bright.

Each of us has extraordinary capacity for creativity and accomplishment, and each of us is personally responsible for using and developing it. Are you making maximum use of your potential? In this chapter, we will discuss ways to attain self-direction and the ability to channel your talents toward the successful achievement of your goals. Are you self-directed? This quiz will help you evaluate where you are now.

Self-Direction Test

________ 1. Do you *not* have clearly defined aims in all aspects of your life?
   a. Professional or business________
   b. Personal________
   c. Family________

________ 2. Is boredom a large factor in your life?

________ 3. Are you unable to rely on yourself in a crisis?

________ 4. Have you *not* benefited from your unsuccessful experiences?

________ 5. Have you *not* benefited from the unsuccessful experiences of others?

________ 6. Do many of your actions depend on the approval of others?

________ 7. Are you dissatisfied with your life's accomplishments?

________ 8. Are you dissatisfied with your interpersonal relationships?

________ 9. Do you often suffer from indecision?

________ 10. Do you often suffer from indifference?

________ 11. Do you often say: "Someday I'll do the things required to get what I want from life"?

________ 12. Do you tend to put yourself and your achievements down?

________ 13. Does your planning depend on some future event (e.g., when the kids are in school, or when you get your next raise)?

________ 14. Do you find yourself saying such things as: "If I had only accepted that transfer," or: "If I had only finished college"?

________ 15. Do you often leave projects undone until the urgent takes precedence over the important?

________ 16. Are you highly anxious when late for an appointment?

________ 17. Are you almost as anxious when someone else is late for an appointment with you?

________ 18. Have you *not* put your talents to work in their best ways?

________ 19. Have you *not* pursued the kind of life you would like to lead?

________ 20. Do you leave many projects unfinished?

________ 21. Do you often feel frustrated by lack of time?

________ 22. Do you feel you have little or no impact on your life's events?

HOW TO SCORE: If your answer is Yes to more than seven questions, you are not exercising a high degree of direction over your life.

If your answer is Yes to more than fifteen questions, you are primarily reacting to your environment rather than exercising direction over your life. You are "other-directed."

Regardless of your score, if you choose to, you can begin immediately to exercise dominion over your life. Let's examine potent, proven, practical ideas that you can use to cause immediate results.

On Becoming Self-Directed

Self-direction begins with a close look at yourself and your life. However, many people are reluctant to look at themselves, and/or their future. It's easier to look elsewhere.

Are you serving time? Or is time serving you? Before going to bed at night, ask yourself this question: "I exchanged a day of my life for what I did today. How do I feel about what I gave and what I got in return?" Your answers may surprise you.

Writing down the answers to the following questions will help bring your life, and your use of time, into sharp focus:

1. What do I want to do with the rest of my life?
2. What do I want to do with my family?
3. What do I want to do with my own physical, mental, and spiritual development?
4. What do I want to do for my community, church and country?
5. What contribution of my time and energy do I want to make, and to whom do I want to make it?
6. What are the five highest priorities of my life?
7. What are three things I've wanted to do, but haven't yet done?
8. What people in my life do I want to spend more time with?
9. What people in my life do I want to spend less time with?

10. What can I do right now to bring my attention in line with my intention?
11. What changes am I willing to make right now?

Completing these sentences will help you to focus even more:

12. I procrastinate most frequently when I____________

____

13. I am less efficient and effective when____________

____

14. I am most efficient and effective when____________

____

15. I don't want to be disturbed when____________

____

16. I welcome interruptions when____________

____

17. My time serves me when____________

____

18. I serve time when____________

____

19. I create my own distractions by playing the following "games"____________

____

20. I am most creative when____________

____

Timepower means making sure what you do is the best thing for you to be doing at that time. Be both efficient and effective. *Efficiency* means doing things right; *effectiveness* means doing the right things. Will the activity help you achieve one of your high-ranking goals?

People usually do the things they will be recognized for doing, or those they will be punished for *not* doing. But in many cases those activities are not the most important ones; they don't necessarily bring the best results. Often they cause you to be sidetracked from what you really should be doing.

Here is a technique for checking the use of your time. Purchase a stopwatch that records hours. Cover the hour indicator with a strip of masking tape. During the week, turn the watch on only when you are involved in a high-priority activity. Shut it off as soon as you stop that activity. Don't delude yourself—turn the watch on only when you are truly involved in a highly productive activity. At the end of the week, remove the tape and look at how many hours have been invested profitably.

The Difference Between Persistence and Perseveration

To persist means to strive for something worthwhile; *to perseverate* means to chase around in circles meaninglessly. Some people are confused between the two. They strive and drive for things that are no longer important. Therefore, persist—don't perseverate. Continuously assess what you are striving for, and eliminate activities that are unimportant.

Good use of time requires being well organized in advance. But self-direction doesn't mean following a prearranged schedule rigidly. Clearly defined goals and priorities should not be carved in stone. Reevaluate constantly; use schedules and lists to give you more flexibility, not less.

There is a simple, practical system now used regularly by more than a million people that can help you organize your professional and personal goals and keep you up to date, with the help of an operational manual that can fit in your pocket or purse. Write to Mr. Keith Snyder, DayTimers, Allentown, Pennsylvania 18001, for literature describing the DayTimer system. It's a valuable aid in achieving timepower.

Why Do You Waste Time?

More than likely, you already know most of the things that cause you to waste time. The issue, then, is to find out why you allow them to continue.

In order of priority, list the persons or things that waste your time:

Now, list the reasons you have allowed these time wasters to continue:

Now, state a solution for each reason:

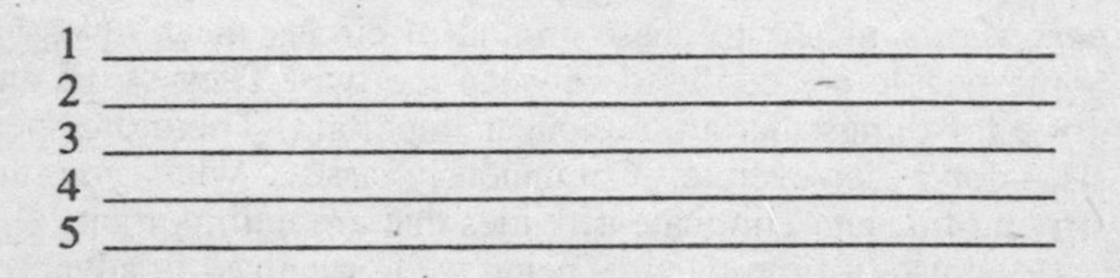

You have just demonstrated that you know how you are wasting time and that the secret rests in fact facing, not fact finding. Instead of hoping to discover new facts, face the ones you already have. Make changes now—even if it's uncomfortable to do so. For example, if you've allowed people to consume your time, remember patience is a vice when it destroys your timepower. Say No—be disliked for it, and enjoy the benefits of more time with your family or however you wish to use it.

In addition to fact facing to use your time *effectively,* here are a number of blocks many people have to *efficient* use of time:

The Telephone

Researchers placed several groups of men and women in a laboratory setting. They were hooked up to biofeedback devices designed to monitor a variety of stress responses. The group was aware that there was no way they could receive an outside call, so it was not possible for them to receive any bad news. Then the scientists rang the telephone in the lab. The mere sound of the phone ringing set off an acute stress response in many of the subjects, even though they knew the calls couldn't be for them.

The telephone has a powerful influence on us. Executives who would think nothing of having someone wait outside their office often feel compelled to pick up the phone as soon as it rings. Even powerful people allow the phone to intrude on their time. During a meeting with a British ambassador, Franklin D. Roosevelt repeatedly interrupted his visitor to answer the phone. Finally, the exasperated diplomat stepped out of the office and called the President on an extension phone. Roosevelt was startled. Explained the diplomat: "You seem to work well on the phone. I thought we could continue this way." Roosevelt got the message. He shut off all calls and concluded his meeting in person.

How can you conquer phoneaholism? Manage your phone; don't let it manage you. Use a switch that shuts off the ring, so you can control when you hear it. You might also attach a timer to the phone to see just how much time you devote to particular calls, and to *all* calls over a given period of time. Then set reasonably flexible limits on your calls, and use the timer to signal the end of your allotment.

If you have an assistant or secretary, he or she should be able to handle 60 to 70 percent of your calls. Your assistant should be able to field most inquiries, or save you time by asking callers to put their messages or questions in writing. This will ensure that unimportant matters don't take up your time. It also ensures that messages are presented in an orderly fashion, and can be considered at your own convenience—so many phone calls arrive at the worst possible times. Teach people who call you that they will get better and quicker results by dealing with your assistant. Teach your assistant to take more and more responsibility for the calls.

At my seminars, most people dash to the phone during the break. When they return, I have them evaluate whether the calls were really vital, or simply validated the person's sense of importance. We make many calls just to prove to ourselves and others how important we are. How many of your calls are vital?

Drop-ins

Joyce Williams, an executive who attended one of our timepower seminars, decided to log her time at the office. She became aware of the constant barrage of people who dropped in on her. Most were nice, congenial people, but they seemed to believe in an open-door policy, whether Joyce's door was open or not. Once inside, they talked about ideas and issues that were "obscurely relevant"—they seemed important, but were really not.

Joyce became resentful. But, with her new awareness, she realized the problem was *hers*, not the drop-ins'. She realized she had taught them how to treat her time. Her past behavior caused the visitors to feel it was okay.

Whether spoken or unspoken, you too have made a clear agreement with your drop-ins. You have, in some way, clearly communicated that it is okay to drop in and be "obscurely relevant." You may have communicated tolerance, and perhaps even the impression that you accepted, even invited, the dropping in.

Now that you realize you have an agreement you don't like, how can you change it without resentment? Be perfectly candid, without attacking anyone. Tell them you are falling behind in your work and would like their help in allowing you more time to fulfill the requirements of your job. Set clear guidelines, and ask for their support. Restrict your socializing to appropriate times, such as lunch or coffee breaks. When someone who used to drop in regularly leaves you undisturbed for a day or two, thank him or her for helping you get your job done. This will reinforce the good behavior.

Joyce tried this strategy, and it paid off for her. She rewarded herself by leaving the office early on Fridays, knowing she wouldn't have a big stack of work waiting for her on Monday. (Always reward yourself for increasing your competence.)

The In Box

Bill Docherty was fed up with the pile of memos, papers, mail, and reports that made his desk look like a recycling plant. He began to have his assistant look at everything sent to him, and told her to expedite as many requests and answer as many letters as possible. The assistant sent Bill copies of the correspondence she handled, and copies of her replies. The arrangement freed time for the things he really needed to give attention to.

While most of what reaches a manager's desk should never get that far, handle what does reach you effectively. Your assistant should make you immediately aware of anything too vital and urgent to delay. Then you should avoid procrastination. Some people see the same items day after day, but succeed only in moving the whole pile from one point on the desk to another, while adding each day to the mess. Ignore your in box until you are prepared to deal with its contents. When you do pick something up, complete whatever must be done. Most of it should be handled the first time it is picked up.

Here is an interesting and even enjoyable way to test yourself. The first time you handle a particular item, make a tic-tac-toe frame on it. The next time you pick it up, place an *X* or an *O* in one of the boxes. Continue to make a move each subsequent time you pick up the same material. When you complete a game, the message that you are wasting time should sink in.

A major source of time-wasting is "problem memos." Take a lesson from your own boss-management techniques, and don't allow subordinates to memo you on problems unless they add a suggested solution rated from 0 to 10. This alone will reduce by more than half the number of problem memos on your desk, and those that do arrive will be more easily dealt with.

Take Time To Think

Edward H. Harriman, the railroad magnate, once unexpectedly popped into the office of one of his executives and found him with his chair tilted back and his feet up on his desk. Afraid the boss would think him lazy, the terrified employee bolted upright. To his surprise, Harriman said: "I'm glad you take time to think."

In one poll, 72 percent of company presidents surveyed said they had no time to think and plan. Yet they are paid to do these things, not to stay busy. We are so ingrained with the idea that being busy is good that we equate *not* being busy with being unproductive. Many executives wonder what went wrong when they find themselves with five spare minutes. Instead of realizing that the free time is a reward for having done a good job, and an opportunity to replenish their energy, they panic. They think they are worthless if not under pressure. Unfortunately, a great many bosses reinforce this dangerous pattern by rewarding time spent on an assignment instead of results, and by being impressed by outward displays of busyness instead of measuring only results.

Competence is not necessarily correlated to the number of hours spent on a task, or the amount of energy expended in doing it. Work compresses to the time allotted. In fact, the person who labors excessively may be doing so because he was inefficient or uncreative earlier. A young executive told me of an incident that had a powerful impact on him. He came into the office on a Saturday to get some work done. Coincidentally, his boss stopped by to pick up his golf clubs. The young man was quite pleased; he thought he would impress the boss with his dedication. But the boss said: "What did you do wrong during the week to require being here today?"

Don't feel that the best use of your time means spending every available minute on your work. Recreation and "creative idleness" are very valuable. Research on creativity clearly demonstrates that the best ideas come to a mind that is refreshed, and unengaged at the moment with the problem in question. The mind needs time to assimilate and incubate. Take time to fly a kite, or relax in a tub of hot water.

Prevent a Personal Energy Crisis

A thirty-five-year-old executive is doing the family shopping on a Saturday morning. He is wheeling his son around in a shopping cart and trying to keep the child quiet. As they walk up and down the aisles picking merchandise off the shelves, the man is heard to mutter: "Please, Billy, be good. Behave yourself. Don't lose your head, Billy. Just calm down. Don't do anything embarrassing, Billy. I promise you, if we can just get out of here without a scene, I'll buy you something nice."

"Excuse me, sir," says a woman passing by. "I just wanted to compliment you on the gentleness you show to your son."

"Lady," says the executive, "you've got it all wrong. I'm Billy!"

Billy was a highly stressed person, one of a common breed in American organizations. Each year, American industry loses $10 to $20 billion through absence, hospitalization, and early death among executives. Heart-related diseases cost business about $15.6 billion in wages and 32 million work days. And figures such as these say nothing of the incalculable cost of diminished energy, bad decisions, avoidable errors, interpersonal tension, alcohol and drug abuse, and other insidious killers of productivity—all caused and complicated by stress.

Clearly, your single most important resource is your own reservoir of vitality, adaptability, and energy. Protecting your mind and body against the ravages of personal and professional stress is critical if you are to use your energies productively. The ability to operate from calmness even in the midst of chaos is a key factor in determining success. For that reason, anyone interested in managing the boss and getting ahead needs to understand stress as well as the technical nuances of the business.

Stress isn't synonymous with nervous tension, nor is it the

same as a tough situation. It is defined as the internal response(s) to a demand by a *stressor*, the outside agent that creates an impact requiring a response.

In and of itself, stress is neither good nor bad. Indeed, it is an indispensable defense mechanism, the body's way of responding to changes in the environment. The problem arises when the stress response is set off too often or lasts too long—then chronic high blood pressure and other dangerous conditions follow, threatening your health and vitality as well as your mental powers.

The key is not to try avoiding stress (life would be bland without it, and we'd suffer the stress of boredom), but to manage it successfully. Turn stress to your advantage, and learn to channel it constructively, avoiding the extremes of too much or too little stimulation. The same stimulus can lead either to *distress* or *prostress*. Distress is the relentless expending of energy and ability in a destructive way, which "uses up" the resources of the person and may lead to "burnout" and/or premature death. Prostress is the expenditure of energy and ability in a productive way that "uses" those resources effectively and efficiently. Research on stress clearly demonstrates that the person, situation, or event that sets off the stress response is *not* the key variable.

The central issue is *your response to the event*. There is a measurable physiological difference between the way one person responds to a stressful demand and the way another does. One person's distress is another person's turn-on; one person's threat is another's challenge. By learning to manage stress, you can become the kind of upbeat, confident, calm individual bosses like to have around, as opposed to the nervous, panic-stricken person who sees danger everywhere. You will, in addition, produce better results, because you'll be able to operate from calmness when all about you are panicking.

Whether you are the servant or the master of stress depends on a variety of factors: heredity, physical well-being, mental stability, lifestyle, attitude, environment, and others. All of these factors—with the exception of heredity—can be managed by you. Two excellent books about stress and how to handle it are *Inner Balance* by Dr. Eliot Goldwag (Prentice-Hall, 1979) and *Executive Health* by Philip Goldberg (Business Week Book/McGraw-Hill, 1978).

In investigating the wide range of available advice, be certain to adopt only proven, reliable information. Be *seclectic*—a combination of selective and eclectic. It's important to exercise discrimination along with variety; health and stress are not one-dimensional matters, but can and should be approached from many angles at once. Here are some areas to look into:

1. A regular physical examination. An important safeguard against illness, a good exam, employing the latest diagnostic procedures such as stress treadmill testing, can spot early warning signs of disease before they turn to actual disorders. Further, a good prevention-oriented physician will alert you to habits and behavior patterns that might be draining your energy, or dangerously affecting your heart and other key organs.

2. Recognize the stress response. Each of us responds to excessive stress in our own way; learn to recognize your own response, so that you can take steps to stop the process before it goes too far. Watch for rapid pulse, pounding heart, tightened stomach, tense muscles, gritting teeth, shortness of breath. Watch for these signs of prolonged stress: headaches, insomnia, poor digestion, irritability, lethargy, abuse of alcohol or drugs, reversals of customary behavior, excessive anger.

3. Exercise regularly. There is no doubt that exercise, properly designed for individual needs and propensities, is one of the best ways to maintain energy and vitality and strengthen the body to withstand the impact of stress. With the aid of a physician or skilled exercise specialist, devise a program combining cardiovascular endurance (aerobics), strengthening, and flexibility.

Approach your exercise with a blend of joy and caution. Don't just dash out to jog; for medical reasons, jogging isn't right for everyone. Good alternative aerobic exercises include jumping rope and swimming. But if your exercise is a competitive experience in which you must beat another person or beat your previous performance, it could become distressful. Keep it noncompetitive.

4. Sleep. Insufficient sleep—whether from insomnia or overwork—has robbed many an aspiring person of the clarity and energy needed to perform. Insomnia can be doubly debilitating if you try to cure it with sleeping pills. They cause harmful side effects, are addictive, and actually interfere with natural sleep patterns. While sleep may seem a waste of time, it is still nature's most potent restorative.

5. Relaxation. You can't be relaxed and stressed at the same time. Research in laboratories throughout the world has established that meditation is a simple, effective way to eliminate the build-up effects of stress, and to strengthen mind and body against the impact of stress in the future. Brainwave studies have further demonstrated its value in enlivening and integrating the mind.

Another good method for relaxing is deep breathing. For practice, place your hands on your abdomen, right below the navel; the fingertips of each hand should touch each other (after you master the technique, this isn't necessary). Breathe in through your nose. Silently say: "Relax." Inhale very slowly and gently, pushing the abdomen out as though it were a balloon filling up with water. Your fingers should separate.

As the abdomen expands, fresh air will enter the lower part of the lungs. Keep your back straight throughout the exercise. As the breath continues, expand the chest. Your lungs will continue to fill up from the bottom. Now, contract the abdomen slightly, raise your shoulders and collarbone; the rest of the lungs will fill. Hold to the count of seven and slowly exhale. As you exhale, say: "Letting go." Within sixty seconds you will be centered and calm. A vital fact to remember is that you cannot be stressed and physically relaxed at the same time, so relax through the day by using the breathing technique and you will not suffer from distress.

6. Nutrition. Recently, the U.S. Senate completed an extensive research project and concluded that the average American should reduce fat and cholesterol, sugar and salt, and meat, and increase the consumption of fruits, vegetables, whole grains, and nonmeat protein sources such as fish. While diet is, of course, an individual matter, those general guidelines are sound. Next to air, food is our main source of energy, yet we tend to ignore the dangers of rich, heavy meals.

7. Positive mental attitude. Nothing saps energy more than negative emotions such as fear, suspicion, anger, resentment, and worry. There is always a more positive way to interpret an event. Without being fanciful or unrealistic, adopting a positive perspective saves energy and puts you on the track toward a solution. Upbeat attitudes and values turn a potentially distressful situation into an opportunity or a challenge. Aside from its obvious benefit to your health and work, a positive attitude makes you attractive to your boss.

An associate of mine told me about an experience he had that illustrates the difference attitude makes. He was watching news coverage of an earthquake. A reporter was wandering through the ruins of a ravaged area, interviewing people whose homes had been destroyed. At one home, a man was sitting on the stoop with his face buried in his hands. "I'm wiped out," he moaned. "I don't know what I'm going to do." The interviewer prodded, trying to get the man to speak, but all the victim could do was hang his head.

Next door, another man was digging in the rubble of his ruined home. The reporter asked him what he was going to do. "I'm going to rebuild my property," the man asserted. "This is my home, and my children will be raised here."

"How will you do it?" the reporter asked.

"I don't know," the man replied. "It won't be easy, but this is our home and I'm going to rebuild."

Same situation, two different responses. Which man do you think will find the energy to set the situation straight? Which will find satisfaction in his efforts? If you were an employer, which would you rather have in your office?

Remember, your best bet is to rely on yourself. No other person or organization can ever guarantee you anything. The only real security is self-reliance. For example, look at the employees of W. T. Grant & Co. Many of them had worked for the company for more than twenty-five years to "guarantee" their retirement security—the company went bankrupt and all retirement benefits were lost. In *The Wisdom of Insecurity* (Random House, 1968), Alan Watts drives home the point that it is wise never to count on anything as permanent and secure. Believe in yourself rather than any external object.

In the 1980s the world is going to be more changeable and unpredictable than ever before. Under those conditions, the ability to handle stress becomes as important as any skill your boss could ask for.

Learn to manage stress in two ways: internally, by monitoring your response to stress, and externally, by managing the events that cause stress. If the stressors you are dealing with are the same ones you have been dealing with for some time, resolve to take action. If you are stressed by the same things as a year ago, you are headed for serious problems.

The Difference Between Hard Work and Workaholism

To miss the joy of working hard, taking risks, and striving to accomplish something you consider purposeful would be to miss one of life's greatest experiences—but be very clear as to the difference between *hard work* and *workaholism.* Hard workers do their jobs—workaholics are done in by their jobs. Workaholics often look like hard workers with their sights set on a goal. But more often than not the work is an end in itself, a way of keeping busy, a way of deluding the person and others into believing he or she is doing something valuable. Only by engaging in nonstop toil can a workaholic feel significant. Dreading inactivity, they cite the virtues of hard work, sacrifice, and dedication to company and family. In truth, they are driven by a fear of failure based on low self-esteem.

Long hours and hard work do not a workaholic make—it's one's relationship to work and to recreation that makes the difference. A workaholic has an anxious relationship with his job. He is obsessed with the need to be busy, fearing that if he slacks off for a minute, failure will darken his doorstep instantly.

Perhaps the best clue to whether or not a person is a bona fide workaholic, not just a hard worker, is his or her relationship to leisure time. A truly successful person can work long and hard for years but will also enjoy his leisure time, no matter how limited it is. In fact, a thirty-five-year study on the careers of Harvard graduates proved that all work and no play might, indeed, make Jack and Jill dull. Psychologist George Vaillant found that "those who were successful did not achieve success in one area of their lives at the expense of other areas. Contrary to the common mythology, it was the very men who enjoyed the best marriages and the richest friendship who became company president."

True workaholics can't tolerate free time. They get tense and angry on vacation (if they take one at all), call the office hourly, and drive their families crazy. Billy, in the supermarket, was a workaholic on the verge of burnout. So was the colleague of mine, a New York-based executive, who asked me to stay over after a Friday conference to join his family on a picnic upstate. Not only did he want to talk business all night and the next day, but he somehow got it into his frenetic mind that the picnic party had to be across the George Washington Bridge by 8:10 on Saturday morning. When we drove across at 8:20, he was so upset that he ruined the day for everyone.

The bottom line is this: workaholics—not hard workers—simply do not produce as well as they might. Someone of equal competence who knows how to manage his energy—who knows how to pace himself, organize himself, rejuvenate himself—will have a better relationship with his boss, get better results, move up faster.

True, some bosses like to have workaholics around. Usually workaholics themselves, they have bought the notion that a subordinate can be judged by the amount of sweat on his or her brow. Such bosses put their employees under tremendous strain. Yet, in the end, you stand to lose if you allow a workaholic boss to turn you into a clone of himself. Show him the wisdom of measuring you, himself, and others by results.

Always ask your boss exactly what he or she is trying to accomplish. Make sure the objectives are crystal clear, otherwise you too might end up working for the sake of working. There are an increasing number of executives who have seen through the workaholic myth, and have come to value subordinates who produce real results, not just a whirlwind of activities. If your organization has not learned this, and is not creative enough to measure by results only, you should consider leaving.

Here is a list of questions to ask yourself to determine if you do your job or if your job does you. More than three Yeses might indicate workaholism and a misuse of energy:

1. Do you feel uneasy—perhaps guilty—when not working?
2. Do you regularly take office work home at night or over the weekend? (Instead of going home *from* the office, you go home *with* the office.)
3. Are you reluctant to go on vacation for fear things at the office will fall apart?
4. Do you take phone calls even when trying to complete a difficult job or to relax on a coffee break?
5. Do you require others to put in the same hours as you?
6. Do you avoid delegating work because you feel you are the only one who can do it right?

7. Is your desk so piled with paperwork that often you can't find things?
8. Are you an obsessive memo writer?

If you've determined you are a workaholic, many of the ideas discussed in this book can help you to shift from a commitment to work based on guilt and/or duty to one based on purpose and responsibility. Being a recovered workaholic, I have examined carefully how to continue working hard without being a workaholic. I now do my job. When I was a workaholic, my job did me. For a cassette tape, "Workaholism, the Cause, the Cure," write to C. J. Hegarty and Co., P.O. Box 1152, Novato, California 94947.

Expand Your Awareness Level

Everything you do is influenced by your level of awareness. In turn, your awareness is determined by a combination of all your past experiences and the current condition of your nervous system. We don't see things the way they are so much as we see them the way *we* are. The more distress, the less accuracy. The more you are calm, the clearer your ability to understand.

Let's look at how you can expand your awareness, and thereby increase your effectiveness.

1. Stay in touch with your feelings. Since mental and emotional distress can cloud your ability to evaluate a situation, it's important to recognize anxieties. Then you can learn to deal with them effectively, and prevent outer and inner pressure from dimming your awareness and weakening the resulting action.

2. Avoid pseudo-pleasures. Do you go to the same old restaurants, attend the same old functions, visit the same old people? Are you engaging in activities that were once pleasurable but are now, in fact, a bore? If so, break out and find new people, new sources of entertainment, new encounters. Above all, seek out new sources of information and insight.

3. Alter your work patterns. Break the set and setting of your activity, even if you have to begin by simply driving to work over a different route. Investigate new and different ways of doing your job, new ways of contacting clients, new equipment, and other means of adding freshness to your approach.

4. Explore opposite ideas. Spend time with people who have different religious, political, and personal beliefs. At work, explore the ideas of people who do things differently. Your efforts may result only in reinforcing your own ideas; but you may, in fact, change or refine some of them.

5. Examine your habits. Any habitual activities can hamper your overall effectiveness. You may find it worthwhile to try changing some habits while refining or reinforcing others. Many of our habits prevent us from giving adequate time and attention to high-priority items.

6. Practice empathy. Recognize that every person you deal with has a unique personal point of view. Accept the fact that each has value, and expose yourself as much as possible to variety.

7. Don't blindly trust experts. In 1948, *Science Digest* polled the top minds in the country, asking when we might land a man on the moon. If everything went right, said the experts, and we made it a national priority, we could do it by the year 2148. In 1899, experts predicted that the horseless carriage would become a luxury for the wealthy, and never be as common as the bicycle. The price of blind faith in experts has often been high. IBM discovered this when they decided not to buy Haloid Corp., based on a survey of future market potential. Haloid retained its independence, and later changed its name to Xerox.

In our age of specialization, we have become ever more dependent on experts. Properly used, experts are valuable. They should be considered sources of information—means to expand awareness, and to help you make your own choices.

One of the problems with experts is that they are often quite narrow in perspective. They tend, almost by definition, to focus their attention on one small corner of the universe. Another difficulty with experts is that they often begin to defend their viewpoints and stop exploring new ideas. They get the disease of having to be right. Yet another risk is that experts are too busy working to review new breakthroughs. A study by a major university, for example, found that 35 percent of doctors are two years behind breakthroughs in their own fields.

It's up to you, therefore, to test their information and explore other options. When possible, get a battery of opposing views. And *don't try it until you've knocked it!* Before using any idea, be sure it satisfies the Three P's: practical, proven, and potent. A *practical* idea is simple, easy to identify and show to others, and will gain the cooperation of your boss, peers, and subordinates. A *proven* idea is one that someone else has used and proven valuable. You know in advance it can work. More than just a sound idea, it has been used successfully. A *potent* idea is extremely cost-effective, and has a high payoff—it leads to measurable, bottom-line results.

One of my client companies was once nearly ruined by a partner who was enamored of experts. Convinced by a personnel expert that psychological testing was the key to personnel selection, he began to treat tests as if they were messages from an oracle. He ignored all other aspects of selection and evaluation, even going so far as to pore over test results to explain every mistake a subordinate made. The result was mis-hiring and mis-evaluating—a bottom-line disaster.

What should the partner have done? He should have used the tests as *a* factor, not *the* only factor. But he forgot all about the applicant's attitude, experience, appearance, and his own impressions during the interview. Fortunately, he became aware of his folly in time to avoid destroying the firm.

8. Learn to use new information. Resist the temptation to resist. While you shouldn't try it until you've knocked it, you should still be open to new information. Threatened by the unfamiliar, we get stuck in ruts. We like to protect our old beliefs and perceptions, and the people around us tend to reinforce that restraint, since any change in you might require a corresponding adjustment from them.

At first a new idea may seem attractive; you get excited by it. But soon the subconscious begins to fight back: "Uh, uh. He's going to pull a switch on me." The past rises up to push the intruder out. Fold your arms for a moment. Now open and refold them, putting the opposite arm on top. The feeling of discomfort is similar to how we feel about other new things, as well. Remember it's okay to be uncomfortable if you're doing something you'll benefit from.

If you discover new information that has merit, seize it, refine it, improve it. Add your own touch, customize it, adapt it to your needs, and when you feel uncomfortable using it, recognize that that is positive. Comfort is not the ideal state.

New procedures do not always produce instant results. Don't abandon something before you've had ample time to test it out. Indeed, a new behavior may even cause a temporary reversal. Diane Bradley once had a boss with whom she argued constantly. While they respected each other, their personalities clashed and minor disagreements turned to raging battles. At one point, having acquired some good advice, Diane decided to break the pattern. She stopped arguing. The boss resisted. He tried extra hard to push her buttons. He evidently relished the battles, and did not want to change their established pattern. At first, Diane's attempts at being conciliatory upset the boss more than her previous behavior. Fortunately, she persevered, even though she felt very uncomfortable, and the boss finally realized there was no payoff in provoking her. Their working environment became tranquil and more productive. By taking one hundred percent of the responsibility, she changed the boss's behavior.

When evaluating alternative sources of information, keep in mind that we often spend a great deal of time fact finding as a way to avoid fact facing. Many people attend seminars and read books in hopes of finding answers that will allow them to continue avoiding facing up to information they already have. You may have found yourself doing this. Have you been facing the facts? Are you making the most of what you've read? Make sure you're not saying, "I can't," when you mean, "I won't."

9. Be aware of both style and substance. I was riding in a golf cart at a luxurious resort with the chairman of the board of a large company, for which a friend of mine was regional sales vice president. Although he had broken every sales record in the company's history, he was passed over when the national sales manager's position came up. I asked the chairman why he had not been chosen.

"John is one of our most competent and able managers," he said. "But he lacks style."

John didn't have the requisite social graces, which, for that position, were essential. He didn't dress correctly or belong to the right clubs, or know how to position himself advantageously, or possess the refinement and sense of etiquette to mingle, impress, and charm people. All of which may seem superficial. Nonetheless, in certain situations, these skills are crucial.

Success, it is generally agreed, depends on a combination of style and substance. Substance means getting things done in an effective way. It means being bottom line-oriented, understanding costs, procedures, and technologies; it means knowing how to set goals and how to meet them. Style means knowing how to use the social graces to your advantage. Some people make the mistake of trying to get by *only* on style. They often go far, but only *so* far. Ultimately, the lack of substance will catch up with them.

What is the bottom line? Major in substance, and take a minor in style.

Decision Making

A national survey showed that most top executives view a subordinate's level of decisiveness as the single most vital factor in evaluating the subordinate for promotion.

To earn and keep a competent boss's trust, you must be decisive.

Many people make rash decisions by reacting impulsively to first impressions (often because they feel their bosses expect them to know exactly what to do under all possible circumstances). Sometimes quick decisions are the best ones. The test is to evaluate the results of your quick decisions; if positive, continue as before; if not, your quick decisions are *rash.* Slow down and use a different approach.

At the opposite end of the continuum are people who decide by default. They ponder every alternative again and again, but never reach a decision. Gradually, events take over. I have witnessed several companies go bankrupt because the top executives made decisions by default.

You will improve your decision making significantly by following these steps.

1. **Identify the problem.** Discuss the situation with everyone involved, until you have clearly determined what the problem is. This may sound obvious, but the greatest error made by people trying to be decisive is failing to identify the problem correctly.
2. **Identify the alternatives.** Record in writing every possible alternative decision you can make. Be certain everyone involved contributes possible solutions; some of the best decisions come from combining different suggestions.
3. **Identify the consequences.** For each alternative solution, list in writing every possible ramification. When these have been identified, assign a numerical weight to each. Rank them on a scale of 0 to 10, with the higher numbers indicating a desirable outcome.
4. **Compare the scores of each alternative.** Your final

choice now becomes a mathematical equation. To the extent that you have accurately assessed the possible outcomes, you have a numerical weight for each alternative decision.

5. Implement the decision and monitor it. Watch the results carefully. Being decisive does not preclude changing your mind. Few decisions are irrevocable; indeed, reluctance to change a bad decision—usually for fear of appearing indecisive—causes more problems than indecisiveness itself.

Listening and ranking in this way will bring order and coherence to your thinking. It will change what might otherwise be a chaotic process to a systematic one. Even though the rankings are at least partially subjective, the final outcome can be quantified. This rational process, however, doesn't mean you should disregard your hunches. Intuition is a vital, although underrated, factor in decision making. It plays a much more critical role than analysts care to believe. But you must learn when to trust your intuition. If your inner voice is persistent, if something feels particularly "right," you may want to give it extra credence, particularly if your "gut feelings" have paid off in the past. Nonetheless, continue the rational process outlined above, modifying it with an assessment of your hunch.

In all decision making, as in all creative acts, a combination of reason and inspiration is involved. The key is to achieve a balance between the two mental processes; leaning too far in either direction can lead to problems. The overly rational mind turns out neat, predictable decisions, but often of an uninspired nature. And, while deemed safer than intuition, logic often turns out incorrect, since it is incapable of dealing with uncertain variables. On the other hand, a purely intuitive thinker may be prone to impulsive or whimsical decisions, which often ignore the facts.

Ralph Townley was plagued by having to decide whether or not to hire someone. All the evidence pointed to not giving the person the job. Yet, despite this, Ralph was procrastinating. His gut feeling, he said, was to hire the person, and in the past such feelings had turned out right more often than not.

But what was the actual basis of his hunch? Was his inner voice telling him that the employee was capable of doing the job despite a lack of experience and education? Or was Townley hearing something other than intuition? Was he, in fact, listening to his own need to hire someone he liked?

If Ralph's psychological needs were doing the talking, I

would call that desperation, not inspiration. One way of cutting through the morass is to write the question out in longhand: "Should I hire Ellen Hayes?" List the pros and cons, thereby making it a rational process. Then go a step further and use sentence completion, a good way to pull up inner feelings and cut through alibis and self-deception. "The reason I am uncertain about hiring Ellen Hayes is . . ." In the end, your decision should be based on solid facts and sound logic, but it should also "feel right."

Effective bosses do not like wishy-washy subordinates. But they don't like them headstrong either, particularly when they try to impress their bosses with their self-assuredness. "I'm going to try a new recruiting campaign," such a subordinate might say. "It's all worked out. I guarantee it will work, and work big." He's either naive or a fool, might well be the boss's first reaction.

Managing your boss with a different type of approach will bring you more cooperation and power: "I've decided to try a new recruiting campaign. Here's the plan, and here's why I think it will work. This is the budget I need. I'm going to watch it carefully. If, in ninety days, I haven't achieved these intermediate goals, we can reverse the strategy and cut short our losses. Here are the contingency plans in case it doesn't work out."

The second approach showed that the person had the courage of his convictions and that he retained the courage to doubt.

It also showed a rational process at work. While bosses shoot from the hip a lot more than they would like you to believe, they like their people to be as logical as a computer. They feel safer with reason than with intuition. Back up your hunches with facts and figures; demonstrate an awareness of potential problems and ramifications. You should prepare in advance for your boss's scrutiny of your decision.

One other factor the second approach demonstrates is a concern for, and sensitivity to, finance. In the future, anyone who wants to be considered for an executive position will have to have some grounding in finance. No matter how skilled you are in dealing with people, no matter how insightful or creative your ideas, a decisionmaker has to examine the financial aspects of any idea. Decisions must be cost-effective. No matter where you are on the organizational ladder, no matter what your job description, your boss will have infinitely higher regard for you—and you'll show infinitely better results—if you add at least a rudimentary understanding of finance to your other skills. Even if you work for a nonprofit organization, you must understand what is financially feasible and what is not. Through independent study, or a course or two at a local college, learn something about basic business finance. Even if your job never calls for it, the knowledge will help you understand your boss's mind.

Remember, while competent bosses like subordinates to act decisively, they do not expect—and most often will not tolerate—their acting in a vacuum. Involve your boss: "Mr. Jones, I'd like to review something very important with you. I want to increase productivity in our manufacturing plant. I'm evaluating the costs and benefits of moving the entire department closer to our assembly center. The labor market is significantly better and I can hire top people there much easier than here. Here's a cost analysis of all the factors involved in the move. In addition, I've drawn up a study of the quality of schools in the area, the availability of transportation, the tax structure, etc. I've listed the pros and cons of the move, as compared with staying here, and ranked them in terms of priority. Before going any further, I need your input."

Naturally, your boss doesn't want to be bothered with trivia. Go to him too often and he'll see you as indecisive. Go to him too seldom and he might feel threatened, suspicious, fearful, or not needed. Strike a balance. When unsure about whether to check with him or not, check. It's the safest approach.

The Last Word in Decision Making!

"It's okay to change a decision as soon as you have evidence it can't work."

Allow yourself and others the right to make a mistake. Successful people are not flawless in their decision making, but they have another trait that sets them apart: the courage to adapt to new information and change direction if necessary, even if it means admitting to a mistake. In an unpredictable world, it would be ludicrous to conduct business without the courage and intelligence to change one's mind. Make the best decision you can and retain the courage of your doubts. Avoid the disease of having to be right. Don't be blind to new information.

Your Assistant/Secretary

Next to yourself, a secretary or an assistant can be your most valuable asset. Exercise great care in hiring that person. Determine exactly what his or her responsibilities will be, and be sure he or she can meet those expectations. Find someone you respect, who will be competent, creative, and devoted to the job.

Once hired, the assistant/secretary should be allowed the greatest possible authority, autonomy, and involvement. Don't use him in a routine way. Give him latitude. Encourage him to make judgments. Give him the responsibility for getting his job done, and give him consistent, reliable feedback. It's far better to have an assistant make a mistake doing too much than not enough.

Imaginative use of your assistant's energies, along with imaginative incentives, can turn a routine job into a satisfying one. It can also turn a secretary/assistant into a vital asset.

Establish a mutual support agreement in which you each agree to be one hundred percent honest with one another. Who is in a better position to give you reliable feedback than anyone else? People who are unable to accept this kind of arrangement miss out on a great opportunity to improve their own performance. Seize this chance to increase your competence by utilizing fully the opportunity to work with your assistant in a way that will benefit you both

Your Work Group

An important factor in managing your boss is an understanding of how groups interact, as virtually every work setting involves group interactions. Learning how to create a group that causes individuals to compete and cooperate simultaneously will make you an exceptionally valuable asset to your boss and to your organization.

Groups function in three basic ways. Pick out your group as I identify them. Additionally, select the way you think your group would best function and what you can do to move it toward such methods.

1. Low energy-low confluence. In this first group, no one has any interest in doing his or her job and no one has any interest in supporting anybody else. Low energy means the individuals are turned off. Low confluence means there's no cooperation, no team spirit. "I'm sorry, but that's not my job," is a comment often offered by people in this type of group.

Drive leaders create such groups through rigid job descriptions, boss-imposed work, and excessive criticism. Default leaders create such groups through lack of communication and the absence of clear performance standards. Whatever the cause, the results are the same: boredom, stress, low self-esteem, lack of cooperation, low productivity, high turnover, and absenteeism. Because of high levels of resistance, resentment, and revenge, people in the low energy-low confluence group will often do more to get out of doing their jobs than to do the work. They frequently commit sabotage. A computer programmer for a manufacturing firm who was fired erased all the information.

2. High energy-low confluence. Here the members are concerned about doing their own jobs, but have little interest in supporting anyone else. Sometimes the problem is rigid job descriptions that people are required to follow exactly. In other cases, due to an overemphasis on competition, members actually view associates as adversaries when they should be seen as allies. While individuals may produce, the group as a whole falls short of expectations, like basketball teams with shining stars but few victories. In many sales organizations, the last person a salesperson would give a good idea to is a fellow salesperson. When carried to the extreme, as this behavior often is, associates actually build their own empires without any concern for the overall good of the organization. Such organizations actually fail because the individuals are out to get each other; individuals will do nothing unless it's something they view as being in their own interest.

Here's an example of what can happen: A former consultant colleague of mine presented a program to the training and development manager of a major airline that she felt would help his company increase sales. The training manager refused. By chance the consultant met a senior vice president of the airline, who allowed her to institute the suggested program at one reservation center. Within nine months, during a period of declining air traffic, the program resulted in a sales increase of 22 percent with no change in overhead.

The consultant showed the overwhelmingly positive results to the training manager who had earlier turned the program down. Again he refused to adopt it. Why, in the face of irrefutable evidence and virtually no risk, did he reject the suggestion? That training manager had to be the guru—every innovation had to come from him. He was protecting himself by ignoring the consultant's program even though it had already been successful. He was afraid he would look bad if someone else got the credit for a good idea. He failed to realize that a successful innovation, regardless of who thought it up, could only result in benefit to him and his company.

The company, by the way, is now losing large sums of money, and that executive has added to the peril. The business may actually fail because of his action.

That is one example of how an organization is put in jeopardy because of an executive who saw other executives as adversaries rather than allies.

The high energy-low confluence group is caused by drive and default leaders and a management belief that people are not trustworthy.

The results are high levels of suspicion and distrust, high levels of stress (sometimes boredom), high turnover, and low group productivity. The individuals are in the Three-R cycle.

3. High energy-high confluence. In this third group, the members want to do their own jobs with excellence, and are also interested in—and rewarded for—assisting others to do their jobs well. Individuals have high self-esteem, and advance quickly in their careers. Simultaneously, individual and group productivity are advanced.

The remarkable productivity increases at companies like Dana Corporation, Rushton Mining, and numerous other organizations are a result of the high energy-high confluence approach. This group is the most exciting and valuable. The results are high levels of job interest, low turnover, individuals who have high self-esteem, and an entire group operating from the Three-C cycle.

Here's a statement of purpose for a high energy-high confluence group:

"The primary function of each person in our group is to be as valuable as possible to the people our group serves. The secondary function of each person is to do the specific measurable job he or she is paid to do!"

There are a number of ways to move a group toward high energy and high confluence. Seven suggestions are listed here:

1. **Don't just do something, stand there.** Most people can do their jobs better than they do. Often, they do far less than their best because they have no real incentive or encouragement to excel. Let people solve their own problems; cause them to invest their ingenuity in their work. When a subordinate has a problem, many managers either criticize or solve the problem themselves. It is far better to let the person try to solve it, assuming it isn't an emergency. This will build self-reliance while simultaneously contributing to the accomplishment of the group's objective. By allowing people to solve their own problems you cause them to experience a sense of accomplishment and pride in performing with excellence.

2. **Bring people from all levels together.** Don't allow people to work in isolation, cut off from those whose jobs affect them. The finance department, the truck drivers, the secretaries, the shipping clerks, the salesmen—all are in different groups, and all have different functions. But their tasks are interrelated, and your organization will be well served if each understands what the others are doing, where they are going, what their concerns and problems are. You can't achieve confluence if the members of the group are kept in the dark about each other. Some organizations spend tens of millions of dollars presenting their products or services to the public, and do nothing to bring their own ideas to the people who produce, sell, service, and deliver the product.

We do all-day communication seminars where we bring people from various departments into a room, break them into groups, and have them tell each other their concerns, priorities, and feelings. We then facilitate small group discussions of how the various departments and people can function better. This type of program creates high levels of clarity, cooperation, and commitment.

3. **Create a sense of continuity.** On a day-to-day basis, work is full of changing episodes. Underneath that, try to establish continuity with respect to priorities, modes of interaction, and the form the work takes. Avoid hidden agendas and sudden reversals. Mutual support agreements, Vital Tasks Management, and Active Listening—all discussed earlier—will help create a base of continuity.

4. **Respect personal values.** Treating people as equals

doesn't mean treating them the same. SRI International did a major study that identified seven distinct groups of Americans, each with its own value system and approach to life and work. In an age of diversity, you can't assume that people in similar jobs will see things the same way. In addition to the things you have in common with others, be aware of the differences.

5. Give people a voice in hiring and promoting. This is a provocative idea and it will not work in all organizations. Study it carefully to see whether it might be appropriate for your organization. If employees share in this responsibility, they will be personally committed to making the decision work. This idea alone can make the difference between success and failure for a new employee. Originally, when I hired new personnel, my staff did little or nothing to help their new colleague. However, once I gave them a voice in hiring, including even veto power (under certain circumstances), things changed dramatically. From that point on, the staff worked hard to guarantee the new person the best possible chance of success.

6. Use lateral movement. Expose people to different work assignments. There are many responsibilities that require too much specific training and experience for lateral movements to be effective. In situations where it is appropriate, however, creatively managed lateral movements can be a powerful tool for broadening awareness, increasing allegiances, and reducing boredom. Lateral movement will be seen as positive *if* employees understand from the start that it is an expanding, exciting, and valuable part of work.

Does it create inefficiency? Only if the people are inadequately prepared for the switch. One way to prepare people to rotate jobs is to have two people exchange assignments and train each other. Later, both will be available for support and assistance.

7. Hold effective meetings. Most people who attend meetings claim they are twice as long as they need to be, and about one fourth as effective. One of the reasons is the leaders' lack of awareness about how to handle a meeting. They often feel they have to control the meeting by themselves. Members can also subvert the true purpose of a meeting with "hidden agendas"—personal resentments, vendettas, and biases that interfere with communication. Both problems can be solved by the "reverse staff meeting," discussed below.

In a reverse staff meeting, the leader doesn't have a cast-iron agenda. He uses a "meeting process" in which everyone else's interests are brought out. The responsibility for the meeting is equally distributed. If it runs too long, or if important issues aren't covered, all participants share the responsibility; and if it runs well, everyone shares the credit.

The leader should announce at the beginning that the format will be different that day, and that everyone is expected to share the responsibility for making the meeting work. The leader should tell everyone that candor and honesty will be appreciated, and that no one will be punished or criticized in any way. Then the leader should begin by asking one person a question, such as: "Since our last meeting, what has been going on in your area that has worked well?"

Listen carefully to the response. Then ask: "What has *not* been working well?" Or: "What has held you back from getting the job done?" Other questions might be: "What have I done that has helped?" "What have I done that has hindered your work?" "What should I have done more of?" "What conflicts do you have with me or anybody else?" Using this process with each person individually will create the Three-C cycle in your group.

There are numerous benefits to be gained from reverse staff meetings: hidden agendas, resentments, and hostilities that prevent meetings from working are eliminated; the responsibility for the meeting is evenly distributed; if there is a saboteur in the group, his or her power is neutralized—when colleagues know the saboteur can speak freely in a meeting, they will not be influenced by destructive talk at other times.

The first few times reverse meetings are held, the staff might feel awkward. However, once they learn that they can tell the truth without reprisal or penalty, they'll be more willing to speak out. This format is a powerful tool for improving communication and cooperation, but it requires a leader with self-esteem and a willingness to take risks. If you're easily embarrassed, or if you'd feel threatened by hearing comments about how you might improve, use these meetings carefully or not at all. While they should not be used on occasions when the leader has a clear-cut agenda of items that have to be covered, there are many times when a regular gathering can be turned into a reverse staff meeting, if you are willing to take the risk.

Whether the meeting is reverse or ordinary, you can earn your boss's respect by having him or her witness an exceptional meeting for which you are responsible. Prepare for the occasion in advance. Work out the kinks in several other meetings before your boss attends—"don't open on Broadway." Prepare your boss by telling him the nature of the meeting and its purpose. Prepare the participants by telling them that the boss will be attending, and what the boss's role will be. That role should be either participant or observer, depending on which is appropriate.

When the day arrives, your boss will be impressed by seeing a group of highly responsible people deal competently with solutions, not just problems, relating to reality, not just personalities. Goals should be clearly established, along with precise methods for accomplishing them and ways to measure results. Well-organized visual aids such as slides, charts, and graphs can add value and interest. So will imaginative additions like an important guest speaker. A sales manager for a carpet manufacturer invited the vice president of sales to an important meeting, where she had a guest speaker—the purchasing manager from a large hotel chain, a big customer. The woman who organized the meeting rose in stature as a result; she was invited to serve on the company's meeting committee for its annual conference, a boost to her credibility and visibility. And the purchasing agent who spoke increased his carpet purchase.

Create Allegiances

Early in his career, Henry Chapman learned the value of allegiances. At age twenty-two, he became general manager of an automobile agency in a small town. The previous manager had lied to and cheated the banks and finance companies every chance he could. He had one of the highest rates of repossessed cars in the country. During Henry's first week on the job, a representative of the auto agency's finance company announced that, due to the agency's past performance, they were cancelling all credit lines for the agency. This would have meant bankruptcy for the agency and disaster for Henry.

A year earlier, while Henry was a salesman, he had assisted the same finance company arrange the sale of some repossessed cars, even though he wasn't paid for his efforts. In his moment of crisis, he called the executive in charge of the divisional finance office with whom he had dealt the year before. He explained his plan to make the agency successful, and to develop a good working relationship with the finance office. Then he asked the executive to reconsider the decision on the financing arrangement. "Send someone here once a week to check on us," Henry suggested, "instead of the usual monthly visit. Watch us closely, and see if we don't meet your standards."

The finance executive decided to give Henry a chance. In turn, Henry personally saw to it that no misrepresentations were made to the finance company, and he did all he could to make certain that customers financed and insured both new and used cars through the finance office. Within a year, Henry had completely reversed the situation. The agency had the highest percentage of company-financed sales in the entire geographical zone.

The story illustrates the importance of allegiances in two ways. First, because Henry had helped sell the cars the year before, the finance executive reversed his decision about the financing arrangement. Second, because the finance manager demonstrated support for him, Henry worked extra hard to reverse the poor experience the finance company had with the previous manager. The allegiance Henry created worked well for everyone, and created high energy and high confluence.

Paul Dumont, a highly successful investment executive as well as a leader in several national associations, is an example of the results possible through creating allegiances. "It is my choice," says Dumont, "as to how I deal with people. It's easier to be cooperative than difficult. I enjoy dealing in solutions." Held in high esteem by everyone who knows him, Dumont attracts people because of his upbeat, friendly manner. What is your choice about how to deal with people?

Inside your organization, and outside as well, is a network of peers whose jobs have a direct and indirect impact on yours. How strong are your alliances with them? If you found yourself in a crisis, could you count on them? Begin now to create high levels of allegiance. Create an understanding with each of them; take the responsibility to advise each other; alert each other to problems and discrepancies; work together to meet both of your goals. If you first demonstrate your trustworthiness, most people will live up to the trust you place in them, and will honor the allegiance you establish.

BOSS

PEERS INSIDE ORGANIZATION — PEERS OUTSIDE ORGANIZATION

WORKERS

Once a month, create a written assessment of how much allegiance you have in all four categories. (0 to 10; 0 = no allegiance, 10 =

> maximum allegiance.) Your success ultimately may well be determined by your ability to create allegiances that cause people to be competitive and cooperative simultaneously. Your exercise of authority will be greatly diminished to the extent it is not accompanied by significant levels of allegiance.

An important element in establishing allegiances is to practice both empathy and impathy. Go out of your way to understand your customers, suppliers, colleagues, and any other people or groups you deal with. Visit them. If appropriate, sit in on their meetings, talk to their personnel, even examine their budgets, planning schedules, or anything that is acceptable under the circumstances and will give you insight into their work.

At the same time, see that they understand your situation. Strategically place them to see what you are up against. Invite them to your office; give them a tour of your operation; ask them to key meetings; introduce them to your staff. Show them what they should know about you and your work.

Some people will be suspicious of your attempts to create strong allegiances. Carefully communicate that you are going to benefit from doing this, and that they will too. Show them how all parties stand to gain. If they see the value for themselves, most people will join you. But if a person is truly against your idea, don't force the issue.

Your approach might go something like this: "My department has let you down a couple of times. There have been instances in which we didn't do as well as we could have. I think one of the reasons is that my people resent having to do things they don't understand. I find the more I can get them to understand, the more they accomplish. So I'd like to have a joint session with our staffs; together, we'll select the areas to discuss and who will attend. By being able to back up your department better, my department will also function better." Step forward first. Don't wait for a crisis before you demonstrate your support. Ask yourself how you can be of value to the other person. Suppose, for example, your company's printing department is backed up with work. See if you can work out a different arrangement with some of your customers. You can then go to the head of printing and say: "I'm aware of the fact that things are really tight for you. I was able to get several clients to move back their delivery dates. I hope that makes things easier."

Think of the impression that would make on the printing

manager. Had you done the same thing *after* he asked for help, the impact would have been entirely different. Later on, when you are stuck and your biggest client needs a rush order, the printing department is likely to do everything possible to help you.

Another way to create peer allegiance is to avert the danger before it comes. Eleanor Abernathy was head of manufacturing at a cabinetmaking company. She discovered that the paint they were using was peeling shortly after the cabinets left the plant. She knew that soon the service department would be swamped with returns. Wisely, Eleanor didn't wait. She went to the head of the service department and said: "We made a big mistake in quality control. The paint is peeling off these products. You'll be getting a lot of them to refinish. What can we do now to solve the problem? I've already suspended production until the paint is corrected and I can assign three people from my staff to assist you. Additionally, all overtime for your people will be charged against my department."

What Eleanor did, in effect, was to disarm her peer by stepping forward, taking responsibility, and demonstrating a willingness to help. Had she waited until the service department was deluged with unanticipated jobs, she would have had a difficult time neutralizing the manager, who would certainly have been upset.

The same strategy should be applied to peers outside the organization. Tom Daniels owned a small business. He had recently borrowed a large sum of money from a local bank. Then, ten days before his first payment was due, a violent blizzard paralyzed his deliveries. Tom found himself with a serious cash-flow problem. He went to see the branch manager at the bank. He took him to lunch to avoid distraction, and told him: "We have a problem. The blizzard set us back a month and cost us a lot of money. I can't make the payment. How can we work together to solve this?"

Tom and the banker worked out a satisfactory arrangement. Had he let the due date slip by and waited for a call or letter from the bank, he would have been in trouble. Instead, he seized the psychological moment, and created an ally where he might otherwise have created an adversary. Put people on notice as early as possible about a problem and offer to help solve it.

It's difficult to harbor bad feelings toward someone who is communicative and supportive. As a matter of fact, many people enjoy helping someone who is friendly and supportive. I know another public speaker, who gives seminars on subjects I don't cover. We aren't close friends, but when we run into one another on occasion, we enjoy each other's company. From time to time, when he finds himself in California, he'll call me just to say hello. Sometimes he mails me an article or a clipping he thinks I'll find interesting. In his seminars, I have been told, he credits me with some of his ideas. His thoughtfulness has paid off for him. Whenever I am asked to recommend a speaker in his field, he is my choice.

The same idea has worked for me. I nominated a prominent business leader to receive an award that he truly deserved. I have since received a number of speaking assignments for which he was directly responsible.

It's all right to have your own interests in mind—as long as the gesture is sincere, and as long as you do nothing you will regret if it does not "pay off" materially. The gesture should be meaningful in and of itself.

Another way to create allegiances is to be willing to take the blame when a mishap occurs. Blaming someone else creates defensiveness and antagonism. Remember, your goal is to create as much freedom as you can in which to grow and do your job. Demand that you be treated fairly, and you will have people waiting to pin the blame on you. Be big enough to accept the blame, and watch how other people will help solve the problems. You want more power, more cooperation, more trust—not just fair treatment. If you must choose between fairness and freedom, always seize the freedom.

At the very least, accepting the blame will defuse an explosive situation; it might create a lasting bond. If trust and cooperation are as important to you as winning a victory in an argument, you might find it worthwhile to take the blame even if you don't feel you deserve it. "We messed up. I'd like to correct the situation. Will you help?"

Negative feelings toward those you work with can destroy your own ability to function and can rob you of your energy. Imagine a continuum of feelings, ranging from extreme negativity on one side to love on the other. If some of your peers are on the negative side, try to move them closer to the middle, to neutral. The value of doing this was indelibly impressed on me by a remarkable ninety-nine-year-old man named Vincent Stroops.

When I asked him to explain his longevity and his astonishing vigor, Vincent replied: "I discovered early in life that to hate another person would destroy me. I never met anyone important enough to allow them that power. I have always tried to see the good in people, and I always released myself from hatred and negativity."

We each *choose* an approach to dealing with life. We choose to be negative or positive, fearful or hopeful, out to get as much as we can or out to *give* as much as we can. If the choices you have made up to this point are not creating purpose, peace, and success, you can change your life by changing your choices.

What has been does not have to be what is or what will be—we each continue to choose for ourselves.

9

Questions and Feedback

THESE ARE questions about bosses that have been asked by seminar participants in a wide range of positions and work situations. They are representative of the questions I am asked, and that readers might ask.

I value my job and both like and respect my boss, but I'm not clear where I stand. He doesn't criticize me or compliment me. Should I risk asking him how he evaluates my work?

C.H. The risk of asking him is less of a risk than you are taking by working without knowing how your boss feels about your competence. Watch for the right time and ask in a nonthreatening way, such as: "It's important for me to know your feelings about how I'm handling my job. It will make me more valuable to get feedback about the various tasks I perform."

My boss is a former Marine, and he acts as if he's still in the military. The others know his bark is worse than his bite. They giggle behind his back, make disrespectful remarks, and placate him with false displays of loyalty while doing very little work. I don't feel comfortable in such an atmosphere, but I don't want to alienate myself.

C.H. Standing apart from the crowd is often the right thing to do. If you don't participate in putting down the boss, and your peers know that you are equally respectful of them, you may stand out as an exception in everyone's eyes. It requires only that you be consistent. Don't talk behind *anyone's* back, and be supportive of everyone.

In the long run, it is always in your best interests to do the job you are being paid to do. No one benefits from sabotage, except those whose main concern is revenge. But they gain only temporary ego satisfaction. They never go anywhere.

Since you said your boss's bark is worse than his bite, it is especially important for you to do your job well, quietly, and with integrity, no matter how much the boss blusters around. His mannerisms may be old habits, but he might be decent and honorable underneath, in which case he deserves your support and will probably repay in kind. Far better to work for an honest, competent boss with a gruff exterior than a phony who lurks in the shadows playing nice guy until it's time to strike.

Another department has areas of incompetence that are hampering my own department's work. I know how to straighten them out, but my boss rejects my efforts. She doesn't like me to make waves.

C.H. This is a common problem. Your first mistake may be indicated in your use of the words "straighten them out." Each department should think in terms of cooperating with another, not of straightening each other out. Your goal should be working together in a cooperative environment.

If you understand what the other department is doing wrong, see that you clearly identify both problem and solution, and communicate them, without putdown, to your boss. If she resists, suggest holding a combined staff meeting of the two departments (and others, if appropriate), at which the problem can be discussed and a solution determined by the entire group.

If your boss is threatened by the proposed meeting, show her exactly how you are structuring it. Present the benefits she will derive. But if she still vetoes the meeting, don't complain. Work informally to get the people in both departments to understand each other's priorities and responsibilities. The better they understand each other, the more willingly they will cooperate.

My boss is a prince. Everyone loves him. But he is so agreeable that other departments continually take advantage of him. He can't say No, and as a result, our department is always overcommitted.

C.H. Many bosses mistake being a soft touch for "human relations" management. A good manager, however, knows the difference between effective communication, group cohesion, reconciling conflicts—all necessary functions—and just being a nice guy. It is good for a boss to have genuine concern for individuals, but he also has to motivate, inspire, and make tough decisions. Sometimes he has to reprimand; sometimes he has to say No; sometimes he has to get tough. Conflict is not only inevitable in organizational life, it is often quite useful.

You should consider your future. If your boss's need to be liked is a preeminent factor in all his decisions, you may be on a slowly sinking ship—a pleasant ship, perhaps, with good companions, but a sinking one nonetheless. The boss's need to be liked may be so deep that he violates sound management methods because of it. Such a boss is not likely to last.

You should also be concerned about the subtle influence that such a boss may have on you, particularly if you aspire to a management position yourself. Even in a short amount of time, a subordinate can adopt the rhythm of his or her boss. Further, in a too-soft atmosphere, you run the risk of having your own skills go stale. If your boss is replaced by a more demanding leader, you may not be ready.

While under your boss's supervision, try to get him to understand the impact of his policies on the department. Volunteer to take over some of the interdepartmental communication, so that you can say No in his place. Look for ways to help him change by talking about the importance of evaluating by results, the need to be unpopular sometimes, and the risks that executives have to take in order to be successful.

I've been doing my job well for ten years. Now my boss is under pressure and she wants me to come up with something different. I think she just needs to make a show of change to satisfy upper management. My way has always worked.

C.H. True, in many cases, people demand change for the sake of change. But in most cases changes are made for a reason. Are you open to it? Or are you resisting because change is uncomfortable psychologically? As Arthur Koestler wrote in *Act of Creation* (Macmillan, 1964): "The mind likes a strange idea as little as the body likes a strange protein, and resists it with similar energy. If we watch ourselves honestly, we shall often find that we have begun to argue against a new idea before it has been completely stated." Go to your boss and ask: "What is it you are trying to accomplish by these changes? Can I participate in some of the planning so that I will really understand the requirements, and be able to make the best changes? If I can continue to get outstanding results with no harm to the organization, is it okay to continue doing my job the way I always have?"

Examine your attitude toward change. It can be a crisis or an opportunity, depending on your perspective.

My boss is feuding with another manager. As his secretary, I have to type his memos, many of which contain nasty remarks addressed to his foe, or political statements addressed to peers whose support he is trying to enlist. His obsession with the feud is destroying morale, and I don't feel right being an accessory to dirty politics.

C.H. There may not be much you can do about the boss's penchant for battle, his need for revenge, or his preference for clubhouse politics. It sounds like a self-destructive situation. Either your boss or his enemy will probably soon be gone. If the other person goes, your boss may change immediately. Or he may find another campaign to wage. If that happens, you might have to accept the fact that your boss will always be contentious. If you find it intolerable, you have every reason to quit.

In the meantime, you are wise not to be an accessory. Even if no immediate trouble ensues, it can get awkward because other people will know that you have been aware of the fight and the accusations that have been made. You might say to your boss: "I think it might be a better strategy to convey this information in person so that my effectiveness as your assistant won't be diminished because I was involved in the feud. I'm going to be your representative to these other groups for a long time."

I don't like my boss. I can't really say why, but there's something about him that turns me off.

C.H. I don't like driving on rainy days. But sometimes I have to go somewhere and the weather doesn't cooperate. I have no choice over whether it rains or not, no power to do anything about it. What I *do* control is how I react to the rain.

Similarly, you may have little or no power over the boss's personality. But you can determine how you react to him. Are you letting your personal preferences or biases get in the way of your professional relationship? Are your priorities in the right place? It is not important that you like your boss or that he like you. What matters are trust and respect. Where does the boss stand on those matters? You can trust and respect someone without wanting to spend time with him.

In fact, not liking your boss can often be a good thing. Personal friendships sometimes get in the way of a good working relationship; they can distort your perceptions and create unrealistic expectations. And think of the time you will save if you don't have to socialize with your boss.

My boss is an extremely competent person, who moved up quickly from the position I now occupy. My problem is, he doesn't seem to be able, or want, to teach me very much.

C.H. Is your boss's reluctance to teach based on fear of being shown up or passed by? If so, you may be in a difficult position with respect to your career development, and you might want to look elsewhere for support. If, on the other hand, your boss simply is not capable of teaching you, then you might be dealing with someone who is naturally gifted, but has no idea *how* he accomplishes what he does and is therefore incapable of teaching his skills to others. The ideal boss, of course, is a "consciously competent" one who does something well and understands the process well enough to teach it to others.

Your situation is not uncommon; the top ranks are well populated by unconscious competents. You might start by suggesting that you and he practice Vital Tasks Management. That will force him to think of your job in a systematic way, and to identify the actual tasks that it entails. Having taken that step, he might better be able to isolate the skills involved in performing those tasks, and begin to teach them to you.

If that does not work, and even if it does, you might want to isolate for yourself exactly what you want to learn. Then you can question your boss more effectively—some bosses are unaware of the importance of teaching, but respond well to direct questions. You might be able to obtain some of the key knowledge by enrolling in courses at a nearby university; perhaps your boss will see to it that the company pays for them either partially or completely.

In addition, don't discount the possibility that you are learning more than you think you are. A considerable amount of knowledge is transmitted through example. That is, your boss may not be a good teacher in the traditional sense, but he may be a terrific role model whose behavior may well be worth observing and emulating. Learning is as much the responsibility of the student as the teacher; be sure you are observant, inquisitive, and receptive.

In organizational life, two elements are often cited as requisites for success: a sponsor and a mentor. Your boss can be either of these or neither. A sponsor is an authority figure who directly aids a subordinate in the advancement of the latter's career; he goes to bat for you. The mentor is a teacher and a model who imparts information and skills. If your boss is not able to be a mentor to you, but is willing to help you meet your career goals, accept him as a sponsor, and at the same time continue to look for a mentor. In many cases, senior executives enjoy taking on a mentor-like role for ambitious, competent younger workers.

My new boss is someone I worked with for three years before he was promoted. We were part of a group of fun-loving guys who worked well together, even though we didn't always do things the company way. I'm apprehensive about what might happen now.

C.H. First evaluate whether you are jealous of your friend for having been promoted over you. If you are, recognize that the feeling is very normal. You can deal with it in a creative way that will allow you to adjust to the new reality without jeopardizing your job.

Take the lead and go to your new boss. Congratulate him, and be honest about your feelings. You have a right to feel disappointed if you had been working for the promotion, but you do not have the right to hold it against your new boss. Your candor should break the ice. Then express concern for the future: "I'm aware of the fact that we will have to work together differently now. What can we do to make it work for both of us?"

Some day the situation may be reversed. That is, *you* get promoted and are now in charge of your former colleagues. Maybe you were the one who organized the late-night poker games at conventions. Maybe you were the one who taught the others how to pad their expense accounts. Now they report to you—an awkward situation. I suggest being as open as possible. Call a meeting with each of your former peers:

"You and I have been friends and colleagues for a long time. We could have written a book on how to not do what we were told and still get the job done. Things are different now. I've been asked to take over the group. Frankly, I'm concerned about how it will work out. By necessity, our relationship will have to be different. I'm asking for your input. How can we maintain our trust and cooperation? What are your feelings and ideas?"

Or you might address the group as a whole: "I stand before you in many ways the same person who stood *beside* you for three years. But I now have a new responsibility As a result, part of our relationship must change. I admire and trust you, and I'm asking for your help. I want to establish clarity between us. I would appreciate your ideas."

Whichever side of this scenario you are on, take responsibility and handle it with care. The peer-turned-boss can create difficulties for everyone concerned, whether because the new subordinates are resentful or demand special treatment, or because the new boss can't relinquish his buddy-buddy status or tries so hard to project a bosslike image that he goes too far in the other direction. Delicacy and patience, and above all honesty, are needed.

My company is about to merge with another. The rumor is that my department will be absorbed into the equivalent department in the other company, and that my boss will be let go in favor of his peer. What can I do to make the change smooth?

C.H. When the merger is announced, contact your peers at the other company. Express your willingness to help make the merger work. Ask for their ideas and suggestions. Think of ways you can be of value to them, e.g., volunteering to advise them if they are moving to your location.

While the departure of your boss is still in the rumor stage, be as supportive as you can. Let him know, through your actions, that you are not going to abandon him or go behind his back. Once the change is definite, continue to maintain a supportive attitude. Not only are you responsible to your outgoing boss to make his transition smooth, but you owe it to yourself to be seen as loyal. Your old boss may become a valuable friend in his new position, and the incoming boss will likely be favorably impressed by witnessing your loyalty. He will deduce that you will be loyal to him as well.

Find out as much as you can about the incoming boss. Check out his reputation in the industry. Speak to customers and suppliers who deal with him; speak to former employees; speak to your peers at the other company. It pays to be as well informed as possible about the incoming boss's intentions, style, and personality. Then step forward to welcome him. The best way to win his trust and respect is first to demonstrate your own.

I am one of a group of chemists working in a research laboratory. Our boss is leaving, and we are apprehensive because we are afraid we might not have it as good with his replacement.

C.H. Ask yourself why you liked your old boss so much. Was it because he or she was likable, easygoing, undemanding? If so, you may have good reason to be apprehensive. It may not stay that way, and you really have no right to expect it to, if the cordial atmosphere resulted in less than your best efforts. Indeed, the boss may be leaving for just that reason.

On the other hand, if the good feeling was generated because you and your colleagues were treated with respect, and given autonomy that resulted in accomplishment, then you should want to protect what you had. Let the new boss know how much the group achieved, and back it up with facts. If possible, let him or her know that the department had earned the support of the previous boss. Present this information in an open, supportive manner—a written report might be best, preferably awaiting him or her on arrival. Let the new boss know that your intention is to be helpful.

The range of "new boss" questions is wide. Just as frequent as the loss of a beloved supervisor is the opposite—the departing boss was *unloved,* and the subordinates fear a repetition. In such a situation, use your past experiences and avoid the danger before it arises. Let the new boss know at the outset that you are willing to support and aid her, and that you deserve to be treated with respect. Let her know the group is competent and qualified and eager to work. Then let her know how she can get the most out of you. For example: "Dear Ms. Mahren: We look forward to working with you. You can count on us to do our best. In the past, our best performances have come when given clear, challenging objectives that allowed our own approaches to be used. When evaluated by results, we have always excelled. You will find us a good group to work with."

Suppose you don't hit it off with your new boss? Don't jump the gun; give the boss time to settle in and show her true colors. She may feel just as awkward as you, if not more so. You must assess whether she treats everyone badly or whether there is some uniquely bad chemistry between you. If the latter, you may have a big problem. You will have to reevaluate your career plans, perhaps, and ask yourself whether you would not be better off elsewhere. But before quitting, begin with a positive outlook, and employ the strategies described in this book. The overwhelming majority of bosses are manageable; in the case of a new boss, half the battle is learning to adjust to a new atmosphere, a new personality, and a new style. Give it time.

When you don't get along with the new boss, your biggest battles will be fought internally. You must realize that you are not being victimized. Don't feel sorry for yourself, or make yourself feel locked in. If you stick it out, accept the fact that it was, indeed, your choice. Work on your self-esteem; your inability to get along with your boss does not detract from your worth as a human being.

What if the new boss gets along with no one? Then *he* or *she* has a problem. Now it is time to evaluate the organization, especially the boss's immediate superiors. Does the organization care about its people? Can you go to upper management with legitimate grievances? Will they be open to your discussing the situation with them? As a last resort, you might try an anonymous letter, explaining that the newcomer's methods and personality are a threat to the company's well-being. If customary channels prove fruitless and the situation is intolerable, your group might get together and ascend en masse on upper management, prepared to threaten a walkout if necessary.

Such dramatic tactics, of course, carry great risks and should be employed only after all else has failed, and only after the new boss has been given sufficient time to prove himself. He may have been impossible at first because he was nervous, or because he thought he had to establish authority immediately. Whatever strategy is used, management will be more responsive if your arguments are presented as something more than selfish; that is, demonstrate to them that the bottom line is at stake, not just your own pride. Back up your claims with facts and figures.

Most situations with new bosses are not so dramatic. Still,

they are delicate and fragile. Don't come on too strong at the start. Let the boss study the organization, learn who everyone is, become familiar with the terrain. He is under pressure. Give him a chance to settle in. Demonstrate that you are worthy of trust, and that you will support him. Let him know you appreciate his problems; look for ways to be of value to him, such as keeping him well informed about work-related matters, or giving him advice about schools, transportation, shopping, and so on, if he has come from another city.

Give him a complete report on work already in progress. Tell him as much as possible about each person's style and talents. Above all, look for signs that he is doing the right things and reinforce his behavior immediately. Well begun is half done. The first hours, days, and weeks with a new boss are far more important than any subsequent amount of time.

I have a feeling my boss is on the way out. There's talk of a reorganization that will eliminate her position. How can I protect myself while still doing my job?

C.H. Waiting until your boss is in trouble is waiting too long. Every subordinate in a large organization should set out the minute he or she joins the company to build a personal identity. With no inconsistency whatsoever, you can support your boss, satisfy all her demands, and still be seen apart from her. Make yourself visible beyond your department; never stake your career on one person alone. Your mentors and sponsors need not be your boss.

Grab every opportunity to assist another department. Institute ideas. Organize interdepartmental meetings. Do whatever you can to let others know who you are and what you are capable of. Most important, whenever you do something significant, make sure people know about it, without making it seem you are out to gain recognition at the expense of others. If you acquire a showboat image, you may join your outgoing boss in looking for a job.

Hitch your wagon to your own star. Politics have a way of changing—another reason to acquire visibility throughout the organization. No one can ever guarantee you anything. Even if your boss does not fall from favor, she may go to another company and leave you behind. Never be seen as your boss's enemy; but don't be seen as a clone either.

My manager seemed destined to rise quickly in the company, and she told me that I would go along. I've done all I could, therefore, to cultivate the relationship. Now I've discovered that she has been embezzling. I'm torn between my future and my moral responsibility.

C.H. Do you want to place your future in the hands of an embezzler? If so, be prepared to take the consequences, including possibly being named as an accessory. In all likelihood, your boss's ride to the top will suddenly be curtailed when she is found out; you may go down with her. If you know for sure that she is guilty of wrongdoing, I suggest you immediately tell the company president. Your future does not rest with an embezzling boss.

My boss is an old-timer, soon to retire. He is fond of me, and has taken to coming into my office and chatting on and on about the good old days. He is lovable, and I'd hate to hurt his feelings, but I end up staying late to make up for lost time.

C.H. Take a close look at what is transpiring during those seemingly trivial flights of nostalgia. It is not uncommon for old warriors to adopt a favored youth for whom they can play the role of mentor. You may be very fortunate; a mentor can be critical in any person's career development. You may be picking up vital information about the company or the industry during those informal sessions. The boss may also be evaluating you to see if you are ready to take on his job.

If, however, the encounters are eating into your time too much, you must change things without making the boss feel rejected—that could be disastrous for both of you. Make him feel needed. I suggest you see him when he is not in your office, and present an alternative in a face-saving way—in terms of the company's needs, not just your own: "I really enjoy and value our talks; they teach me an awful lot, and I'm grateful that you've seen fit to share your experiences with me. But, as a result, I'm slipping behind in my daily work schedule. Could we have lunch twice a week, so we can talk to our heart's content, and I can use my other time for getting my work done?"

My boss reprimands me in front of co-workers and customers. I realize I make mistakes, but this is embarrassing.

C.H. Your boss may be well intentioned, not out to get you.

He may simply have learned, erroneously, that criticism, whip-cracking, and fear are what make employees get the job done. If you handle it correctly, you can influence him to change.

If you can't negotiate a mutual support agreement, have a sincere talk with him. Tell him that public ridicule, even if deserved, makes you feel less effective. Tell him you don't object to negative feedback, that you appreciate the need to have your mistakes pointed out, because you are as interested as he in improving your performance. But ask him please to wait until you are alone so that you can feel free to ask questions of him. Suggest a regular, private evaluation session, and try to institute Vital Tasks Management.

In addition, use Active Listening. Suppose your boss says: "You're so dumb. I told you to follow that order through and you didn't do it."

You might reply: "You really feel that I don't listen, or that I disregard your directives."

Such a response, administered in a nonthreatening way, can often successfully defuse the situation, and make the critic aware of how he sounds to others.

Whatever strategy you use to reduce the incidence of criticism, be sure not to overreact at any given moment. The worst thing you can do is get defensive, or argue back in an attempt to convince the boss that he is wrong. This is one of those instances that can mushroom into a battle whose furor is way out of proportion to the causes. You have to choose between freedom and fairness. Give up your day in court for the sake of greater autonomy and trust.

I am assistant to a department head who despises red tape and rigid procedures. He is a freewheeling type, adept at getting around regulations. Some of the things he does would anger upper management, but so far he has never been bothered, probably because our department really produces. I'm uncomfortable, however, because I'm afraid we will get in trouble.

C.H. If anything your boss is doing causes you to break a law, or a deep personal conviction, I suggest you don't do it. While the offense might not be as bad as the embezzlement cited earlier, the consequences could be similar.

However, if he is merely going against company policy, your boss may well be right. He may be sidestepping antiquated, obsolete procedures. If that is the case—and your good results indicate it might be—you may want to ride with him, and help him convince others that there might be a better way of doing things. You have to ask yourself whether your boss's actions are in the best interest of the company. If you're still uncertain, you might want to talk it over with your boss. If you and he trust each other, it should be relatively safe for you to discuss it with him . . . but be careful.

Should you decide that the rule-breaking is definitely *not* in the company's interests, and that you might get into trouble for it, tell your boss that while his intentions may be good, he is making you very apprehensive. You do not feel comfortable doing certain things, and would like to be left out of the circle of people required to do it. Admittedly, this is risky—your future under that boss may effectively be ended—but you will have to decide whether going along with something you disapprove of, and fear the consequences of, is any less risky.

My boss is a real bureaucrat. Her rules and regulations are so rigid I have trouble getting anything done. I'm anxious to prove myself, but I feel stifled. I'm increasingly tempted to sidestep the rules.

C.H. This is the opposite of the previous problem and much more common. The way to handle it is more or less the same. The first step is to determine whether your boss's rules are arbitrary or necessary. This requires empathy. What pressures have been placed on your boss, or on the company as a whole, that might make seemingly ridiculous regulations a matter of real need? Is she acting in accordance with orders from the company president, or from a government regulator? Before you conclude that her procedures are petty, make sure you understand the consequences of her not following them.

Sometimes a subordinate is required to do things that he or she cannot understand. I once met a young executive named Barry who was required to submit extensive reports by the fifth of each calendar month. This created a tremendous workload in his department. Barry was enraged over the requirement, because the same information he was asked to compile was provided automatically by computer on the tenth day of the month. Because he felt the assignment was an unnecessary burden, he became bitter and hostile, particularly during the first week of every month.

When he finally expressed his feelings, he found out there

was a good reason for the requirement. His company was one of many in a conglomerate. The parent company made certain financial decisions on the seventh of each month, and the information was essential to the execution of a vital company procedure. It simply could not wait until the tenth.

If you do determine that the regulations are stifling creativity unnecessarily, and that the company as a whole is suffering thereby, try gradually to get some leeway. First, reassure your boss that everything is being done to the letter. Keep her posted, without waiting to be asked. If, for example, she has to be out of town the day your monthly report is due, make sure there is a message on her desk when she returns—or, if possible, leave word at her hotel—letting her know the report went out in plenty of time. Such practices will get her to relax her anxiety about you and your adherence to rules.

Then look for little signs of her easing off, and immediately reinforce them. Catch her doing something good. Suppose, for example, she loosens up on some trivial matter, such as getting back from lunch at precisely one o'clock, or paying for something out of petty cash instead of requisitioning the supply department. Let her know you appreciate the little extra room because it helps you get more done. Gradually, she might learn that she can ease up without disaster.

I am going through a divorce, and it has affected my work. My boss has not been understanding; he seems to think that a true professional should not let personal problems interfere with her work.

C.H. Your boss needs to have his awareness expanded. He should understand how a difficult life situation can temporarily impede performance, even with the best employees. But you should not wait until your performance has already begun to deteriorate. The moment the trauma begins, you should negotiate an understanding with the boss. Make him know that you are going through a difficult and demanding period, with lawyers and children and emotional adjustments all biting into your mind and time. Point to your past record, and assure him that you will resume a high level of effort once the problem clears up. But, meantime, you need personal understanding and professional assistance. You might ask him to lighten your responsibilities on a temporary basis. Most bosses, when confronted in a nonthreatening way in advance of any problem, will be reasonable. Much may depend on your previous record.

In this case, part of the problem may have to do with the fact that the subordinate is a woman. Traditionally, men and women have handled such personal crises differently. Men tend to bury themselves in their work to compensate for emotional loss; they actually spend more time at the office. Women, who customarily have had to maintain responsibility for children, can't do that. Neither have they been trained to keep a stiff upper lip in the face of tragedy—a trait that is not necessarily desirable, but certainly snows a male boss.

A crisis like this is a good test of your relationship. It will help you evaluate whether to stay with your boss after the problem is ended.

I work for a small business. The owner started it from scratch and still runs the show at age seventy. He won't let go. He still does things the way he did when it was literally a one-man show, despite the fact that times have changed and the company has grown.

C.H. Your risk may be even greater than you imagine. Unless your boss has clearly determined what will happen to the company after he dies, you may end up dealing with his heirs—a bereaved widow who wants to sell out for cash, sons and daughters with no interest in the business, a lawyer out to maximize his fees. It is in your interest—if you plan a career with the company—to be clear about the future.

Sit down with the owner and say: "Mr. Peterson, I've worked for you for ten years, and I'm aware that sometime in the future you will want to retire. I'd like to stay on here and be an important part of the company's future. What are your plans and ideas?"

Do your homework, and be prepared to discuss possible alternatives for him. For example, if you know that the lines of succession are unclear, you may want to make a suggestion: "Mr. Peterson, you might want to evaluate the benefits to you, your family, and your employees of an Employee Stock Ownership Plan. Under such an arrangement, you still control the business, and you set it up in a way that is good for your heirs. At the same time, employees can own stock in the company. E.S.O.P. plans improve productivity and can be designed to ensure that the firm will be passed on to the next generation without excessive taxes." (For information about E.S.O.P., write Kelso & Co., 111 Pine Street, San Francisco, Calif. 94111.)

What can be done about the boss's one-man operation when he hates to relinquish control? Often such bosses are reluctant to bring in managerial help, even when the company is too big and too complex to run alone. If they do bring in help, they tend to hire people who will not threaten their power.

Each individual, however, must be evaluated separately. Ask yourself what it is about delegating responsibility that makes your boss nervous. Does he treat everyone that way, or just you? If you decide that it is impossible to get him to change, you have to ask yourself some basic questions: "Is this an environment in which I can carve out a piece of satisfying work for myself? Am I content with being a lower-level employee? They have less pressure and risk; but they also give up a certain amount of autonomy and room to be creative. What is best for me?"

If your old-timer boss has not kept up with changes in the industry and technology, if he is resting on his laurels, you must understand that that is a perfectly normal reaction from a man who has worked hard for many years. Nonetheless, if you believe that his attitude is detrimental to the company, show him face-saving reasons to change: "Mr. Peterson, we have maintained the leading position in the industry for many years. Recently, however, some of our competitors have overtaken us. I have a plan that can put us right back on top and reestablish the reputation that you built so well. Look at these statistics. Our market penetration has declined from 17 percent to 11.1 percent in one year. And, while our dollar volume was up 20 percent last year, which adjusted for inflation comes to about 5 percent, our major competitor, who was behind us a year ago, went up more than 35 percent. Projections indicate that the next forty months may see more changes than the last forty years. We can capitalize on a number of these changes and again be the leader in the industry. When can we review our future?"

This approach combines both evidence and solutions, each of which is necessary. But even then, the boss may resist. One strategy that has worked well is to bring in respected outsiders to reinforce your position. Arrange a meeting with some of his best clients, who will help sell the boss on the need to change.

A person may take any of four stances toward change.

1. The Never Stance. "That's the way it's always been," or, "You know my M.O. That's the way I've always done it," or, "What do you want from me? I'm waiting for the good old days to come back." People who adopt this stance are extremely rigid, and resist change whenever possible. What they are really saying is, "I won't change." They are confusing rigidity for stability.

2. The Reluctant Stance. "I guess I'm going to have to change, even if it kills me. Remember, if it doesn't work, it's not my fault. I didn't want to change in the first place." Even if they know the change is an improvement, they would rather avoid it.

3. The Fickle Stance. "Change is where it's at." These people go from job to job, bed to bed, guru to guru, seminar to seminar, looking for new answers. Their rule for persistence goes something like this: "If at first you don't succeed, the hell with it." They keep all their options open by making no commitments. Here today—gone tomorrow is their view of life.

4. The Creative Stance. People who adopt this stance look very carefully at the areas they have discretion over, and recognize that it is their responsibility to change or not change. They manage the change, or the nonchange, according to their needs and priorities. Then they determine which changes they have no choice but to accept, and ask themselves: "How can I capitalize on the changes that will happen with or without my permission?"

Organizations can be assessed according to their capacity to change. Those capable of adapting successfully to change hold all their answers as tentative. They measure results only, and continuously examine what they are trying to achieve. Their approach to management is facilitative—they know their objectives and purpose and how to pursue results. Such organizations *cause* change; they don't just react to it, and they don't resist it.

My boss told me I had two weeks to implement a new program. That's insufficient time, even if my staff works round the clock. What can I say, and how can I break it to my staff if the boss won't change her mind?

C.H. Try to understand the new program, and the time requirement, as well as you can. If you are totally convinced you can't pull it off, try to negotiate with your boss. But before you do so, think out all the alternatives and come up with possible solutions. Don't just go in with a negative attitude. Break down in clear terms how many extra people, or trucks, or machines, you need to get the job done in two weeks, and what the costs of these additions will be. What other assignments will have to be shelved in order to meet the demand? When you spell out exactly what you need, you not only demonstrate that you are willing to make the effort for your boss, but you are involving her in the solution.

When you break it to your staff, treat them with respect. Listen to their ideas. Let them know that the demand is not being imposed by you personally, and that you understand the sacrifice they are being asked to make. Do this, however, without making your own boss look bad. This is the time to cultivate teamwork and mutual cooperation.

Be careful not to "middle" your boss, or be "middled" by him. If your boss makes an unrealistic demand on you, causing you to drive your subordinates in order to achieve it, you run the risk of becoming the target of the subordinates' resentment. Make sure they know that you are acting on orders from above, not your own arbitrary whims or unilateral decisions.

At the same time, if you accept an obligation and something goes wrong, don't "middle" your boss. If you and your boss agree on a deadline date and you fail to achieve it, don't go to other people and say: "I would have finished on time if the boss hadn't . . ."

If you absolutely cannot perform the task as directed, use the four steps for saying No described in Chapter Six.

I've been lenient in letting my staff come in after 8:30 A.M. I'm satisfied that they work well and get the job done, even if it means staying late. Now I'm being pressured by my boss, who has gotten flak from personnel.

C.H. Unfortunately, many people find it difficult to measure results, so they require procedures like time clocks. In an organization with strict regulations, it is hard to be an innovator, even when it is in the company's best interest. Until flex-time becomes more common, as it surely will in the eighties, you just may have to level with your staff, perhaps compromising by giving them flexibility at lunchtime when it might not be as noticeable. But, first, try to negotiate with your own boss. Try to earn as much flexibility as you can without alienating anyone. Suggest instituting Vital Tasks Management.

My boss says I waste the company's money on unproductive research projects. But I know they will result in profits.

C.H. If you have a track record, dig up proof of the cost-effectiveness of your work, or the return on investment. That should be all the evidence your boss requires. If, however, you have no track record, you will have to be more persuasive.

Researchers, and others who work with their imaginations, are indispensable to an organization, but they must learn to establish allegiances with those who hold the purse strings. Those allegiances must be built on genuine empathy from both sides. Bottom-line bosses sometimes fail to see the long-range importance of research, or to appreciate that there will inevitably be blind alleys and false starts. On the other hand, researchers frequently are unable to understand the need to hold down costs. Evaluate carefully the goals and priorities of the organization. Enlist the aid and support of the top people. Be sure your projects are directly in line with their thinking. Then defend your ideas in their terms, not just your own. Also, by cultivating allegiances with your boss's superiors, you may someday be able to get approval for a project that might otherwise not get off the ground.

The president of the company called me: "My brother's daughter, a nice, bright young woman, is looking for a job. I understand you have an opening for a management trainee. I'd like you to meet my niece." Does that mean I'd better hire her?

C.H. In some organizations, such a call means hire the niece or you're out of a job. In others, it might just mean see if you can use her. Don't hesitate to interview the niece—she might be a superstar. If, however, she turns out to be unsuited for the job, you have to evaluate the ramifications of turning her down. Perhaps the best way to find out is to query peers who have been around for a while. At some point, you may have to decide which risk you are willing to take: putting up with the incompetent niece, working around her and hoping to achieve your goals through political means; or taking the risk of telling the boss you don't think his niece will work out.

One way out would be to discourage the niece from taking

the job. If that fails, ask for a personal meeting with the president, and utilize our four steps for saying No.

1. "I understand how important it is for you to have your niece in the company."
2. "I can't use her in my department. I've assessed her; she has many strengths, but I don't think she is right for the job. It would be a disservice to her and the company for these reasons . . ."
3. "I've checked with personnel. There's an opening in market research that I think will fit her better. It starts at about the same salary, and I think it will give her an opportunity to learn about the company."
4. "If that doesn't work out, I will do all I can to help find a place for her that fits her skills and interests."

My boss is the type who manages by reacting to events, not controlling them. He does no planning. Everything is a crisis.

C.H. Zig where he zags. If he is impulsive and whimsical, take the planning function away from him and do it yourself. Be a steadying influence. If he goes the way the wind blows, show him how you can assist him in adopting planning strategies that will help keep things on an even keel. Do surveys. Obtain advance information from customers and other departments. Keep him informed at all times, and try to arrange things so the jolts are not so heavy.

He should see the value in what you are doing. If he doesn't, he may be beyond hope. A manager who doesn't have time to plan is like a minister who doesn't have time to pray.

My boss does not keep us informed about what is going on in the company or within other departments. Consequently, we can't plan or prepare well. We have to respond to eleventh-hour emergencies.

C.H. Like the previous boss, yours may thrive on crises. She may like to ride in on her white horse to save the day. She might feel bored with smoothly functioning operations.

Nevertheless, you have some questions to answer. Is she keeping you in the dark intentionally, so she takes on greater importance? Or is she really too busy to keep you up to date?

If the former, show her how you can make her *more* important if you are well informed. Play your supportive role well;

give her credit for the things you are able to accomplish when you are informed.

If she is just too busy, take it into your own hands. Volunteer to set up a communications committee with all departments represented. Set up meetings with important peers. Take your staff on a tour of other departments. Establish an interoffice newsletter. Create allegiances for your boss where she has none. These and other strategies will raise your visibility and solve the information gap.

My boss is bright but fickle. He changes his mind all the time. He has great ideas, sets priorities and goals, then shifts before the job is done. It is frustrating never to see a task through to completion. We are not reaching our assigned goals.

C.H. Idea people are extremely valuable to a company, but only when they convert their ideas to bottom-line results. While a quick-thinking, creative person will create a good impression, he will not last unless he passes the real test: What does he get done?

Start by trying to slow him down. Ask him to explain what he is trying to accomplish. Each time he shifts gears, ask him (without threatening him) to clarify his goals. Point out what must be abandoned in order to adopt the new strategy. Make him think things through, by bringing in facts and data.

In a noncritical moment, you might say: "Your ideas are fantastic. Sometimes the rest of us have difficulty keeping up with you. How can we work together better so I can be more valuable to you? I've kept track—we've had seven new projects in the last eighteen months, and each has been abandoned. My staff is getting confused, and I'm concerned with how we're going to look to upper management."

When he fires off a new idea, hold off. Delay getting started until the last possible moment, in anticipation of yet another shift. Wait him out.

In the final analysis, if the frustration is intolerable, you may want to pin him down on a particular project, with an agreement to let you see it through to completion by a certain date. Whatever your strategy, however, make sure you create alliances elsewhere, and make yourself visible to others in power. The ideas man may not be there much longer.

I am a department head. My boss just hired a new manager for a department with which I work closely. I think she made a grave error; the new person is wrong for the job.

C.H. You should think very hard about your own assessment and your own motivation. Is your objection to the new manager a personal one? Were you fond of his predecessor, and therefore resistant to the new person? Are you concerned that your own job will be made more difficult, or do you really have the company's welfare at heart? You might also ask yourself what it is about your relationship with your boss that makes you reluctant to express your opinion; it might be indicative of a communication breakdown with wider ramifications.

The approach you should take largely depends on your current relationship with the boss. The fact that you have asked this question indicates that you don't feel comfortable simply expressing your disagreement openly. You might, therefore, consider who else in the company can bring the information to your boss. Perhaps one of her peers can express it in a way that will not seem threatening. Have a talk with that person.

I recall an instance that illustrates how serious this can be. A man was made president of a company that was part of a large conglomerate. The newcomer ran the place like a boot camp, and created within weeks acute resistance and resentment. Many of the top executives could see a disaster coming, but could not comfortably go to the head of the parent company. So they enlisted the aid of a peer in a client company, who placed an anonymous telephone call to the home office of the conglomerate. "You've made a terrible mistake," said the caller. "You've hired someone who is going to ruin your company. If you don't believe me, poll all the executives who report to him. Grant them anonymity, and I'll bet that ninety percent tell you that the choice was catastrophic. You will lose both clients and personnel."

Less than three months later, the company had a new president.

When I went to work for an investment firm, my boss promised big opportunities quickly. However, I've been there over a year at the same small salary, and haven't yet been taught how to sell.

C.H. Ask yourself, "What is my level of awareness now, as compared to when I started?" If you have learned a great deal, and if you stand to continue learning, your approach should be very different from that if you have been doing routine work with no improvement in your awareness. You should also examine the rate of progress of others in the firm. How fast did they move up to big earnings? Has anyone who started after you moved up? In other words, see if the slow rate of progress is a companywide practice or a personal problem. Indeed, ask yourself if you are actually moving slowly or if you are just being impatient. Quite possibly, you and your boss have different ideas of what the right timetable should be. His definition of "quick" may be different from yours. His intentions may be good. He may believe in bringing people along carefully and slowly, letting them prove themselves over time, rather than throwing them into the deep water too soon.

If, however, you are convinced that you are ready for a higher challenge, and that staying on in your present capacity offers no significant opportunity to learn, it might be time for a talk: "Mr. Scher, I joined this organization with the understanding that I would learn the business and be given the opportunity to earn commissions. I think I can handle selling very well. What can I do now to prove I can be of more value to you? Please give me the opportunity to sell—you can easily measure whether I can handle it. I'm prepared to pay the price to show you I can do it."

If your efforts don't succeed, it might be time to consider moving on. Before you quit, however, assess whether your prospects would be better if you stayed long enough to learn some more, and what your prospects elsewhere might be with and without more training. Finally, remember that the best time to determine what your boss means by "quick" is before you go to work. Next time, have your new boss put in writing the requirements for promotion and higher earnings.

I think my boss is getting a bum deal. He is over sixty, and is being written off by upper management. They are letting him coast until mandatory retirement, but I think he's got a lot of value left in him, and can still make important contributions.

C.H. Clear up in your own mind the difference between being responsible to your boss and being responsible *for* your boss. Being responsible to means being an asset and an aid. It means supporting his objectives. Being responsible for is taking on too much of a burden with respect to the boss's future.

You are wise to be concerned, for your boss's sake and your own. But most likely, while you may be of some help, your boss will have to take care of himself. Being seen as over the hill is tough. If he is not content with his role, he will have to decide his next move.

As for your own future, now is the time to be seen as both a team player and a high scorer in your own right. Become known to others in the company while trying to encourage your boss to be a mentor. Your department could become dull, and the boss apathetic. Your opportunities for creative contributions may diminish. Assess whether or not to move on. Remember, if you stay too long in such an environment, you may find it's too late to break away. It may seem safe and secure to stay, but that could be an illusion.

My boss consistently fails to follow through on requests or suggestions. I don't want to appear pushy, but I feel I deserve a response.

C.H. Managers often don't want to contend with problems that are less than urgent. By so doing, unfortunately, they frequently create more crises than they would otherwise have. I used to delay picking up my dry cleaning because it seemed so trivial. Then it would come time to leave on an important trip and I would have to cut short a staff meeting to pick up my clothes. The urgent takes precedence over the vital.

Sometimes the boss will have a psychological resistance to listening to subordinates' requests. Drive leaders, for example, might feel threatened by them, while default leaders—if they are within earshot at all—may not care. I can't count the number of times employees—even high-ranking executives—have complained about this kind of scenario:

SUBORDINATE: "Mr. Wasely, I'd like to check into getting a different position in the company. I've been here a long time, and I'd like to move up."
BOSS: "I appreciate that. I'll look into it."

And there the matter dies.

Or: "Ms. Jones, I'd like to talk to you about this list of recommendations from the maintenance department."

BOSS: "Fine. Why don't you leave the list with me and I'll look it over?"

And the list goes no further.

Or: "Ms. Olsen, I'd like to have a meeting with you and the secretarial pool."

BOSS: "I'll get back to you as soon as I can fit it into my schedule."

What can you do? First, ask yourself, was your request appropriate? Was it well presented? Was it precise? Did you express how important it was? Are you being impatient? Can it be taken care of without taking up the boss's time? From the boss's point of view, is it really something he or she should spend time on? What will be the consequences of your being ignored?

If you determine that the matter does, indeed, warrant the boss's attention, you must approach him in a way that shows appreciation for his position and the importance of his time: "I know how busy you are, so I don't want to take up too much of your time. I'd like to know when I can have ten uninterrupted minutes to go over something I think is quite important. Is today possible? No? How about tomorrow, for breakfast perhaps?"

When you see him, ask for immediate feedback. Pin him down. Don't let him put you off with an ambiguous response, or with another delaying tactic. If he says: "I'll get back to you on this," counter with: "When can we meet?" Without being obnoxious, try as best you can to set up a specific meeting before you have to leave. If that doesn't work, be sure to follow with a memo summarizing everything that was said, including the promise of setting up a meeting (indeed, even if you are given a specific time, the follow-up memo may be good reinforcement).

If the boss says: "I'll have to think about this," you might respond with: "Is there anything else I can tell you now? Can I track down the information you need?" Try to find out if there is a specific reason for his hesitation.

If the boss says: "I want to check with Christine on this," you might say: "Fine. Shall I call her right now?" If you know in advance who he will want to call, do it before the meeting and get the other person's views.

Always seek closure on any matter you discuss with your boss. And you might conclude your meeting by following the advice of one of the top executives in the insurance industry, James McElvany of Johnson and Higgins. He has always reinforced his working relationships with superiors by closing each meeting with a statement like this: "Between now and our next scheduled meeting, what else can I do to assist you?"

Our new boss is a very ambitious woman with a fast track record in other companies. She seems to be after visibility, and is out to make a name for herself. As a result, she can be quite demanding, and likes to take the credit for things the department does.

C.H. Is she a real winner, or just a fast mover? Remember, winners spawn winners. Often the fastest way up the ladder is to work for a manager on the rise. Such a person is usually tough and demanding. But if she is legitimate, if she gets results, if she is of value to the organization, her very toughness can be an asset. You stand to learn a great deal working with her. Further, if you establish yourself as valuable to her, she may be as demanding of others on your behalf.

Does she want to be visible? Help her do it, and be known as a person who made an important contribution to her success. Is she trying to get permission for a big project that will add several feathers to her cap? Don't resent her for it, help her do it. Make her presentation the best it can be. You might have to relinquish credit in some instances, but there are ways to make your competence known quickly. And if she is truly a winner, she will never lose sight of your contribution. Show your trust and respect, and you will earn hers.

If, on the other hand, she is just a fast mover but not necessarily a winner, be as supportive as you can, and continue to create allegiances with other key people. She may be gone before you know it.

My sales manager once had my job, and was excellent at it. Now he has a tendency to do my work for me, and to take over tasks that I should do. This leaves him insufficient time for his managerial duties, and the entire department suffers.

C.H. Resorting to the familiar is a common trait in many managers. Sales managers are especially notorious for this. They get promoted because of their excellent sales records, and then find themselves in management positions for which they lack the skills and/or training. As a result, they tend to slip back into doing the things they enjoyed and were successful at—they end up selling more than managing.

With such an arrangement, the subordinate loses, because he cannot grow if he is not allowed to do the things he is supposed to do.

A transfer might be in order. Before taking that route, however, you might discuss the problem with the boss, explaining that you are unable to be of maximum value under the circumstances. You might also try to institute Vital Tasks Management. This will cause you both to focus in on what you each should be doing. If you can get the boss to make the next step—focus in on what *his* vital tasks are—you will have taken an important step toward dividing the duties appropriately.

My boss uses advertising copy and illustrations that I think are exploitative of women. I am offended; what can I do?

C.H. Any business person who interacts with the public must be sensitive to public opinion. But don't confront him in an accusatory manner; that will only make him defensive. And don't make it a personal issue; the boss may not care about your opinions.

What will be more likely to hit home is a bottom-line argument. If he thinks the ads are going to lose the company sales, he will be open-minded. If, for example, he thinks an influential women's group is going to protest the ads, boycott the product, or write angry letters to the president of your company, he will rethink his advertising policy. If the product is targeted for female customers, the potential loss of market share will be a convincing argument.

Whether or not you choose to speak with the boss directly, you should first be sure that the ads are not just offensive to you. How accurately do your views reflect prevailing attitudes? If you truly believe you are doing a good service by putting an end to the ads, you might reinforce your arguments by having a representative of a women's group write to your boss. Once, a model train company received a letter from a three-year-old girl, written with her mother's assistance, that changed their policy. The letter read: "Dear Mr. President: My mom gave me a set of your trains, and I really like it. But why do all the pictures show *boys* playing with trains and *fathers* giving them?" The company now has girls in their ads and instructional manuals.

My boss and I have a conflict about overtime. He demands it frequently, but I don't like it. I have been giving in, but it is causing personal problems.

C.H. Examine your conflict with the boss. Is it a conflict of needs? Or a conflict of values? If you are alert and creative, you have a good chance of solving a conflict of needs. A conflict of values, on the other hand, may represent a no-win situation.

To understand the distinction, think of it in personal terms. Suppose your teenage daughter wanted to use the family car for the weekend. If others in the family have to use the car, you have a conflict of needs on your hands. With some compromise and clear thinking, you may be able to work out an arrangement suitable to everyone. But if your daughter wants to use the car in order to go away for the weekend with her boyfriend, you may have a conflict of values on your hands, in which case, a mutually satisfactory conclusion is most unlikely.

Does your boss demand frequent overtime because of his work needs? Or does he demand it because his values require a constant display of devotion? It may, in fact, be a legitimate demand; in certain businesses, the unexpected is commonplace, and everyone understands that their success is dependent on a willingness to stay late at the office regularly. Sometimes that demand is compensated for with liberal vacations, pay bonuses, compensatory days off, or flexible hours during slow periods. If, therefore, the conflict is one of need—your boss's need for results conflicts with your family needs—an arrangement might be worked out. If you can get your boss to isolate precisely what his goals and objectives are, and what he requires of you, then you might be able to demonstrate your ability to produce without having to compromise your home life.

There is a chance, of course, that a conflict of needs can be irreconcilable. In which case you might be in the wrong job. The important thing is to pinpoint the exact problem and try to work out a compromise. With a conflict of values, however, your chances of a solution are slim. If your boss demands you work overtime even when not necessary—get a transfer or find another job.

I like your concept of Vital Tasks Management, and I can see where my boss and I would benefit from such an arrangement. However, I see no way that I can approach him on it. He's not the type to be told how to do his job.

C.H. As you suggest, he might not be able to handle a role reversal. After all, he is the one who is supposed to teach you your job, not vice versa. Try this:

"Mr. Carter, I really want to do my best work, because I know it will pay off for both of us. I'd like to ask you to list for me the most important tasks I can do in order to accomplish what you want. Independent of your list, I will write down what I think are my most vital tasks. I thought we could then sit down and compare lists, so we are both crystal clear on what my priorities should be."

If he agrees to that much, you can, once the tasks have been identified, suggest that you get together the following week and go over the self-evaluation you plan to make. Tell him you want to make sure you are accomplishing your vital tasks and that his feedback means a lot to you.

This informal arrangement is less effective than the formal agreement. Under these conditions, your boss is not likely to refrain from criticizing or imposing solutions. But it will nevertheless help remove some of the mystery in your relationship, and ensure that you both have the same understanding of your job.

My boss is a gossip. He's always whispering secrets to me about who said what to whom, who is sleeping with whom, and so on. It makes me uncomfortable.

C.H. While it is vital for you to be tuned in to the company grapevine, you don't have to participate in malicious gossip. Joining in may seem to give you acceptance, but at the same time it may be shutting you off from those who are not being asked to participate, and from those who are the targets of the gossip. Often gossips are saboteurs at heart. They go from one person to another, slightly bending their stories until the tale becomes a big distortion that they try to work to their advantage.

One way to keep gossips away is simply to look them straight in the eye, deadpan and serious, and say: "Thank you for the information." Never feed the gossip by asking questions, or replying: "Really?" or, "Oh, my!" Often this strategy can be so powerful the person will not only exclude you, but may stop spreading it further.

I'm a superintendent on a production line. My boss makes excessive demands. Now he wants us to go from twenty-three thousand units a week to thirty thousand. I know we can't do that.

C.H. Excessive demands are one of the most common complaints about bosses. Yet, in many cases, workers are performing at far less than full capacity. Where resistance-resentment-revenge has made significant inroads, the workers themselves may not even realize they can be producing more than they are; they simply do not care. Or they have a psychological resistance to doing better work, perhaps based on the fear that improved performance will lead to greater and greater demands.

The point here is: Are your boss's demands really unreasonable? Have you exhausted your imagination for ways to upgrade performance? Have you motivated your staff sufficiently? Are you resisting higher standards for fear of failure, or fear of losing popularity with your subordinates?

To obtain an objective assessment of your production capacity, check out industry statistics. Obtain figures from every available source, and add to it expert opinion on related matters such as safety regulations. Before confronting your boss, build up your case in your own mind and be sure it is accurate. In addition, go to your own staff and tell them about the new demand that has been imposed; ask for their points of view. Perhaps they know a way to raise productivity to the desired level. Or they might give you good arguments to strengthen your case. Or they might suggest a compromise agreement. In any event, the mere fact that you asked for their opinions will stand you in good stead if you must eventually enforce the new regulation against your judgment.

Finally, if you have built up a strong case against raising productivity levels, present it to your boss in terms that he can appreciate. It is not enough to say, "It can't be done." Show *why* it can't be done, and show what the negative impact of trying might be, e.g., morale will deteriorate, overtime costs will skyrocket, the error ratio will inevitably increase, the accident rate will go up. Above all, practice empathy and impathy. Your boss's demands may be based on financial difficulties that could spell danger to everyone in the company. It might be to your advantage to see it from his side and comply as best you can. How would you feel if you talked him out of his demand without sufficient reason, only to discover later on that your attitude has contributed to bankruptcy of the firm?

My boss has always been fair and honest. Lately, however, she has been difficult to relate to. She has become irritable, easily angered, overcritical.

C.H. Evaluate the situation carefully. Is she acting that way toward everyone, or only to you? If the latter, you have evidently been undermined in her eyes—either by something you did, or perhaps by something that has been said about you. If she has changed toward everyone, she most likely has undergone some personal disruption, either at work or at home. Perhaps she is under pressure from upper management; perhaps she has marital problems or difficulties with her children. Identify the problem. Is it yours alone or the entire group's?

If it is unrelated to you personally, try not to abandon the boss. Now is the time to see how helpful you can be. Help her ride out her crisis, even though you may be the target of misdirected anxiety. Extend to your boss the kind of understanding you would hope to receive in similar circumstances.

If the problem seems to be yours exclusively, you should discuss it with her in a calm manner, removed from the normal work environment. You might consider taking her to lunch and confronting the issue head on: "Ms. Meyers, I'm uneasy about the way we've been failing to communicate lately. I'm aware of nothing I might have done to alter our working relationship. Has anything happened to cause you to change your attitude toward me? It's important to me to be able to communicate effectively with you. I like my job, and I want to be of maximum value to you and to the company. What can we do to get back in tune?"

I have put into practice many of your ideas, and they have worked well. Perhaps too well. My relationship with my boss has gotten so good that my colleagues are jealous. I don't want to alienate them.

C.H. Successful people are often envied, even resented. Are you willing to risk being disliked for the sake of satisfying work, material success, and a good working relationship with your boss?

But you may not have to make that choice at all. While you are improving your own lot, you can be making things better for your co-workers. None of the strategies in this book work *against* anyone—not your boss, not your company, not your peers. You might use some of the ideas to help your boss improve the performance and satisfaction of others. Reverse staff meetings are but one example of how you can share the benefits of your new awareness.

Further, you can use your good standing to broaden and strengthen your allegiances, and then use your impact to create working conditions that will make work work for everyone. Use your informal associations to spread the ideas that worked for you. Most information in organizations is transmitted during coffee breaks, lunch, commuting, and other informal settings. Let your colleagues know what has worked for you and why: "Things have really changed between me and the boss since I got him to clarify goals and measure results. This is what I did. You may want to try it." At the same time that you communicate your strategies, you can also act as a role model for the others. Lead by your example.

There is no reason whatsoever for you to fear the consequences of sharing these strategies. Always remember that cooperation works to everyone's advantage. It is highly unlikely that an individual's personal desires can truly be fulfilled unless the people around him or her are also fulfilled. It is in everyone's best interest for all the members of a group to be individually competitive and highly cooperative simultaneously. Use your power to "develop profits through developing people." The payoff for everyone and most especially you will be purpose, prosperity, and success.

"And Finally a Look Ahead"

Change—resist it, and you will certainly be different; accept it, and you will remain the same. Let me see if I can make sense out of this paradoxical statement. By resisting change, you will be required to change, often with pain. Continue always to hold on to the way you have done things, and your life may be turned upside down and inside out. However, look at new ways to do things that work better, and you will always remain the same.

That is, you will be a creative, competent person, even though your daily activities may not be the same as they were in the past.

While the future is beyond our ability to see, it is not beyond our ability and responsibility to create. In *Future Without Shock* (Norton, 1974), Louis B. Lundborg accurately states that we have choices about where our future will take us and that we can have a future without one shock after another.

One area we have dealt with in this book is the need to continuously expand your awareness by learning new skills. The new requirements to learn and apply information seem overwhelming. Researchers have made the following predictions: (1) A person entering our work force today will have to absorb and use twenty-four times as much information as a person who entered our work force a generation ago. (2) By 1985, 60 percent of an executive's time will be spent learning, which will allow only 40 percent for the execution of the person's responsibilities. (3) To excel from this point forward, an executive will have to be totally reeducated every five years.

Yet another survey indicates that we are each required to absorb more input in a calendar month than in an entire lifetime one hundred years ago. In a recent report made to the American Management Association, a psychologist studying job stress claimed that the single biggest factor in job stress was that managers at all levels were required to make decisions too quickly. They didn't have the time to grasp all the particulars and assimilate the information. They were required to act sooner than they were prepared to, thereby causing a tremendous level of stress.

Challenging? Indeed.

And yet there's a lot on the opposite side of the ledger. For example, there are new accelerated learning techniques being used whereby the average executive can increase his learning capacity more than 500 percent. Accelerated learning processes use deep relaxation training, which in itself is very valuable because in addition to increasing a person's ability to learn, it also causes the person to handle stress better and function more creatively at all levels.

Additionally, an M.D. colleague of mine has developed a new biofeedback process with which in a single one-and-a-half-hour session he has been able to release subconscious blocks that have caused people serious problems. The fear of failure, the fear of success, and anxiety about the future have all been issues that have been corrected in a single session.

There are many challenges ahead and there are just as many answers for the creative, competent person who is eagerly devoted to spending his or her life in pursuit of results. The question is not whether you can equip yourself to capitalize on the changes and be successful; the issue is whether you will. Will you?

Afterword

My first seminar workbook on this subject was written in 1974. At that time, I was unaware of any other sources of information about the topic of upward influence or managing upward. In the 1970s my program "Managing Your Boss" was perceived as radical and provocative.

However, in the 1980s the topic has been gaining popularity. Trade, technical, and professional journals, as well as the popular media, have all given attention to this new field. The work done by doctoral students, researchers, and academics is shedding new light on these topics (as well as confirming the validity of the principles expounded in this book).

One of the newer generation of experts to become distinguished in this field is a former college professor turned professional speaker, Dr. Bob Mezoff, president of the Amherst, Massachusetts–based management consulting firm ODT Associates. Mezoff regularly conducts programs for well-managed hi-tech firms. For example, he is currently conducting speeches and seminars for seven IBM divisions in North America.

In Bob Mezoff's and my experience, training people to manage their bosses is a very profitable venture (in terms of the return for each dollar invested in training) in those organizations that are already well managed downward. In other words, the upward-management approach works best in firms where downward management and communication exist at a highly effective level.

I predict the "Managing Your Boss" field will become

highly specialized and differentiated in the next ten years. Just as we incorporated a chapter for women in this book, other minorities will also have applications peculiar to their unique situation. You will also see, I believe, Managing Your Boss books targeted to specific industries (e.g. health care or, even more specifically, nursing). While the generic model taught now is extremely valuable, there will be a greater need to tailor the material for the unique circumstances that exist.

Prior to the management writings of Weber, Fayol, and Taylor at the turn of the century, few managers gave much thought to the structure and process of managing downward. The revolutionary concepts and practices of the early 1900s are old hat today. I look forward to the possibility of living in a society where the strategies of upward influence are similarly in widespread use and taken for granted. When that day arrives, our organizations will be more profitable and we will be living more happily, harmoniously, and productively.

* * *

At the turn of the century, William James said, "The greatest discovery of my generation is that human beings may alter their lives by altering their attitudes of mind." And here we are approaching the turn of another century, waiting again for another change of attitude.

Index

About the Author

Christopher Hegarty is an international award-winning public speaker. He is President of an executive training firm that has conducted seminars for numerous organizations, including more than 400 of the Fortune 500 companies.

The programs offered by his firm include:

THE FUTURE BELONGS TO THE COMPETENT
THE CORPORATE ENTREPRENEUR
HOW TO MANAGE YOUR BOSS
PEAK PERFORMANCE FOR EXECUTIVES AND PROFESSIONALS
HOW TO DEVELOP EXCEPTIONAL MANAGERS
SUCCESSFUL STRESS STRATAGIES

For more information contact:

Christopher J. Hegarty & Co.
P.O. Box 1152
Novato, CA. 94948 USA
(415) 892-2858